GLADSTONE

Some Gladstonian Attitudes: Sketches in the House of Commons.
Cartoon by Reginald Cleaver.
Top (left to right): Finishing Touches; Facts and Figures; An Apology.
Middle (left to right): For the Benefit of His Own Supporters; The Peroration; A Little Rhetoric; Light Refreshments.
Bottom (left to right): A Nasty One for the Opposition; Previous Authorities; The Right Hon. Gentleman Resumed his Seat amidst Prolonged Cheering.

Gladstone

Edited by

Peter J. Jagger

THE HAMBLEDON PRESS

LONDON AND RIO GRANDE

Published by The Hambledon Press 1998

102 Gloucester Avenue, London NW1 8HX (UK)
PO Box 162, Rio Grande, Ohio 45674 (USA)

1 85285 173 2

A description of this book is available from the
British Library and from the Library of Congress

Typeset by Wyvern 21 Ltd., Bristol
Printed on acid-free paper and bound in Great Britain
by Cambridge University Press

Contents

Contents

Text Illustrations

Plates

Between Pages 46 and 47

Introduction

Peter J. Jagger

This book commemorates the life and work of William Ewart Gladstone (1809–1898). He was a Victorian colossus: a man of boundless
energy and varied and great gifts. Gladstone's private diary, kept from
1825 to 1896, reveals to posterity endless detail about his character
and the nature and implications of his attempts to fulfil what he
believed to be God's will for his life. Work on the editing and publication of the Gladstone diaries began in the mid 1960s and was completed in 1994. The fourteen published volumes provide a remarkable
record not only of Gladstone but also of nineteenth-century British
history. *The Gladstone Diaries* provide researchers, writers, politicians,
and all who are interested in the nineteenth century, with a unique
and extensive collection of prime source material.

The contributions which make up this volume, most of which
originated as Founder's Day Lectures at St Deiniol's Library, clearly
indicate the continuing appeal of Gladstone a hundred years after
his death. (The year 1998 also marks the centenary of the foundation of St Deiniol's Library.) In them we read of the nature of
many of his political ideals and objectives during his sixty-three
years in politics. These essays offer studies of the nature and
evolution of his thoughts and actions as a Christian statesman, in
the rapidly changing and expanding society of nineteenth-century
Britain. Gladstone was also an international statesman. Some of
the disputes in which he was involved still remain unresolved,
including Ireland and the Balkans; other issues reemerge such as
the Anglo-American alliance, Welsh devolution and the British railway system. The essays in this collection provide many new insights
into a wide range of nineteenty-century topics, events, controversies
and personalities.

A later Prime Minister, Harold Wilson, who studied at St Deiniol's Library as an Oxford student in 1916, study which resulted in his winning of that year's Gladstone Memorial Prize, returned to Hawarden in 1986 to deliver a lecture on Gladstone, in which he stated:

> If Gladstone failed to solve the Irish Problem – though he did a good deal to cool it – no politician of my time is in a position to criticise him . . . He devoted a great deal of time and effort to much-needed institutions – for example opening the Civil Service to competition in place of patronage: abolishing the system of purchasing Army commissions . . . The judicial system, at his instance, was dramatically reformed; entrance to our great universities on the basis of university religious tests was ended; he masterminded the great advance in national education with Forster's Education Act – for the first time making elementary education compulsory, though it did not become free until 1891 . . . He was outraged by Disraeli's Eastern policy – and the Midlothian Campaign, perhaps the greatest series of political speeches in our history, not only transfixed audience after audience, but created a new approach to the problem of the rights of emergent nationalities – it is arguable that no previous or subsequent Prime Minister ever achieved so much in international terms.

By any standard, Gladstone's political achievements were great. He was a man of tremendous drive and extraordinary ability, But it must be remembered that, amid all the demands of his complex political career, Gladstone was extremely active in numerous other spheres. The two great concerns underpinning his life were religion and reading. For him the Christian faith was the foundation of every aspect of his life. It is impossible to understand him or his political career without understanding his position as a churchman. A contemporary wrote 'few persons in the world . . . will refuse to acknowledge him as the most illustrious of living Englishmen, his career belongs to history. . .'

Acknowledgements

The essays in this volume, with the exception of D. George Boyce, 'Gladstone and Ireland', and Peter J. Jagger, 'Galdstone and his Library', were given as Founder's Day Lectures at St Deiniol's Library, Hawarden. They all appear for the first time except Lord Blake's essay, which appeared, as 'Disraeli and Gladstone', in *Gladstone, Politics and Religion*, edited by Peter J. Jagger (Macmillan, 1985); and H.C.G. Matthew's essay which appeared, as 'Gladstone, Political Rhetoric and Public Opinion in Britain since 1860', in *Politics and Social Change in Modern Britain*, edited by P. J. Waller (Harvester, 1987). The lectures were given in the following years: Lord Blake (1967); H. C. G. Matthew (1984); Kenneth O. Morgan (1985); John Prest (1987); Peter J. Parish (1989); Derek Beales (1990); Michael Wheeler (1991); Lord Briggs (1992); John Vincent (1993); Glynne Wickham (1995); and David Bebbington (1996).

On behalf of the Trustees of St Deiniol's Library, Hawarden, who invited me to the edit of this volume, I wish to express their gratitude to the contributors, for agreeing to the publication of their essays. On behalf of the contributors, I would like to thank all those individuals and institutions who have allowed access to manuscripts and photographs, and have given permission to reproduce material for which they hold copyright. My personal thanks are due to Sir William Gladstone Bt, for his help and support.

I am grateful to the following for permission to reproduce illustrations: Lord Briggs (plate I); Flintshire Record Office (plates II, V, VI, VII and VIII; p. 78); C. A. Gladstone (plate III); St Deiniol's Library (plate II, bottom right; p. 35); University College London Manuscripts Room (plate IV). Rowland Williams, the Flintshire County Archivist, helped in identifying and reproducing appropriate material. Susan

Varah typed the original draft of most of the manuscript and Rene
Mycock typed additional material and implemented editorial altera-
tions, corrections and improvements on the whole manuscript. Eric
Kelly provided expertise in transferring material to computer. To
Patsy Williams, the Librarian at St Deiniol's Library and a former
colleague, I owe a debt of gratitude for her help and assistance in
many areas. Finally my sincere thanks are offered to Martin Sheppard
of Hambledon Press for his professionalism in seeing the manuscript
through to publication.

Chronology

1809   Born 29 December in Liverpool

1821   Attends Eton College (to 1827)

1825   Begins keeping a diary

1828   Attends Christ Church, Oxford (to 1831)

1829   Death of his sister Anne Gladstone

1830   Elected President of the Oxford Union

1832   His Continental Journey (February–July)
       Great Reform Act
       December, Elected Member of Parliament for Newark
       George Grote entered Parliament

1833   June, Maiden speech on slavery

1834   Junior Lord of the Treasury

1835   Under-Secretary for War and the Colonies
       April, Out of Office

1837   April, Returned unopposed for Newark
       Accession of Queen Victoria

1838   Publishes *The State in its Relations with the Church*

1839   Marries Catherine Glynne

1840   Publishes *Church Principles Considered in Their Results*

1841   Vice-President of the Board of Trade

1843   President of the Board of Trade

1844   July, Railway Bill

1845   Resigns from Cabinet

1846   June, Out of Office

        Begins reading G. Grote, *A History of Greece*, 12 vols
        (1846–56)

1847   Elected Member of Parliament for Oxford University

1850   Gorham Controversy on Baptism

        Reads J. Ruskin, *The Seven Lamps of Architecture* (1849)

1851   Reads J. Ruskin, *The Stones of Venice*, 3 vols (1851–53)

1852   Speaks against Disraeli's Budget

        Chancellor of the Exchequer

1853   First Budget

1854   Outbreak of Crimean War

1858   Publishes *Studies in Homer and the Homeric Age*

1859   Chancellor of the Exchequer

1861   American Civil War (1861–65)

1862   Newcastle speech on American Civil War

1864   Garibaldi visits England

1865   Defeated at Oxford University

        Elected for South Lancashire

        Royal Commission on Railways established

1866   Reform Bill

1868   Prime Minister in his first administration (to 1874)

1869   Irish Church Disestablishment Bill

1870   First Vatican Council declares papal infallibility

        Irish Land Bill

        Elementary Education Bill

1873   Irish Universities Bill

        August, Chancellor of Exchequer as well as Prime Minister

        Railway and Canal Commission established

1874   Dissolves Parliament

        Resignation as Prime Minister and as Liberal Leader

        Disraeli's second administration (to 1880)

        Publishes *The Vatican Decrees in Their Bearing on Civil
        Allegiance*

1876   The massacres in Bulgaria
          Publishes *The Bulgarian Horrors and the Question of the East*
          Publishes *Homeric Synchronism*

1877   January–March, Speeches and articles on Eastern Question
          Visit to Ireland

1878   January, John Ruskin visits Hawarden Castle
          The Congress of Berlin
          Publishes *Primer of Homer* and 'Kin Beyond the Sea'

1879   Midlothian Campaign
          Publishes *Gleanings of Past Years, 1843–1879*, 7 vols

1880   Elected Member of Parliament for Midlothian
          Prime Minister and Chancellor of the Exchequer
          Second administration (to 1885)
          First Boer War begins

1881   Irish Land Bill
          Death of Disraeli

1882   Plans for retirement
          Occupation of Egypt

1884   Third Reform Bill

1885   Fall of Khartoum and death of Gordon
          June, Defeat of Government – Gladstone resigns

1886   January, Prime Minister in his third administration
          June, Resigns premiership
          July, First reference to St Deiniol's Library in a conversation
          with his son Stephen
          Introduces first Home Rule Bill – defeated in Commons

1887   June, Welsh tour; speech at Swansea

1888   Land Purchase (Ireland) Bill

1889   Golden Wedding
          Purchases three acres of land on which to build St Deiniol's
          Library
          Speech on Intermediate Education (Wales) Bill

1890   Publishes *The Impregnable Rock of Holy Scripture* and *Landmarks in Homeric Study*

Tenure of Land (Wales) Bill

Completes temporary building of St Deiniol's Library

1892 June, Midlothian Campaign – Elected for Midlothian

July, Begins writing autobiography

August, Prime Minister and Lord Privy Seal

Fourth administration (to 1894)

September, Speech from the foot of Mount Snowdon

1893 Introduces second Home Rule Bill

Established Church (Wales) Bill

1894 March, Final Cabinet and last Commons speech

Resigns premiership

1895 July, General Election: the Liberals defeated

October, *St Deiniol's Trust and its Purpose: Preliminary Paper*

December, 'Foundation Deed' for St Deiniol's Library

1896 Publishes *The Works of Bishop Butler*, 2 vols, and

Studies Subsidiary to the Work of Bishop Butler

September, Delivers last important public speech on the

massacre of the Armenians by the Turks

1897 Publishes *Later Gleanings*

1898 7 May, Duke of Westminster writes to Rev. Stephen

Gladstone proposing the building of a permanent library as

the national memorial to Gladstone

19 May, Dies at Hawarden Castle

26–27 May, Lies in state in Westminster Hall

28 May, Buried in Westminster Abbey

1899 Foundation stone of St Deiniol's Library laid

1900 Death of Catherine Gladstone; buried in Westminster Abbey

1902 Official opening of St Deiniol's Library as the National

Memorial to Gladstone

1903 John Morley's *Life of William Ewart Gladstone*, 3 vols

1906 St Deiniol's Library residential accommodation completed as

the family memorial to Mr Gladstone

1

Gladstone, Oratory and the Theatre

Glynne Wickham

In his introduction to the first two volumes of Gladstone's private diaries, Michael Foot wrote: 'Curiously, no one seems to have asked where or how he learned to speak'.[1] It thus seems reasonable to try to supply a more extended answer to this interesting observation. It is perhaps also appropriate to raise the question of why Gladstone should have been the first Prime Minister to have recommended the bestowing of a knighthood on an actor.

It will thus be my object to suggest to you that a common answer is to be found to both these questions in radical changes within the future of Victorian society which affected politicians, churchmen and actors alike; changes which were occasioned by the need to adapt the arts of oratory and rhetoric – or public speaking – to meet the demands of ever larger audiences of ever wider and more varied composition.

My starting point must thus be a prefatory word or two about the relationship between the reputation of the theatrical profession and public opinion throughout Europe at the beginning of the nineteenth century. Branded by the Early Christian Fathers during the closing years of the Roman Empire as infamous corrupters of the social order, actors had to labour under this stigma for the next thousand years: even when co-opted during the middle ages by the Roman Catholic Church as exponents of Christian doctrine to illiterate laymen, they continued to be denied the status of a recognised profession in this world and to be refused Christian burial when entering upon the next. Only in the sixteenth century, in the wake of the combined forces of the Reformation and the Renaissance, were they grudgingly allowed to ply their trade for financial reward, thanks largely to royal and ducal patronage, and then only under strict government licence.

Despite this, actors continued in Protestant countries to be branded as rogues, vagabonds and 'caterpillars of the Commonwealth' for living, like parasites, off the hard-earned savings of thrifty citizens. In England, the right to Christian burial was restored to them, but in France that was still denied to Molière in 1673, as it continued to be to Carolina Nueber, the foundress of the German theatre, in Catholic Bavaria in 1760. And as the eighteenth century passed into the nine-teenth there were still only two theatres licensed under royal patent in London and three in the provinces. Such was the theatrical world into which Gladstone was born in 1809.

Within this context, therefore, it is perhaps not surprising that, given his Scottish, Presbyterian upbringing, he should have recorded this entry in his diary on 19 December 1832.

> I have now familiarized myself with maxims sanctioning and encouraging a degree of intercourse with society, perhaps attended with much risk, nay, perhaps only rendered acceptable to my understanding by cowardice and carnal heart. Yet still I do think that mirth may be encouraged, provided it have a purpose higher than itself ... Nor do I now think myself war-ranted in withdrawing from the practices of my fellow men, except when they really *involve* the encouragement of sin: in which class I do certainly rank races and theatres.[2]

By the time he recorded this observation on the state of his own moral health in 1832 – it was his habit to do this on his birthday every year – he had already left both Eton and Oxford behind him, together with the Grand Tour, and was turning his mind to embarking upon the road to the hustings for his first parliamentary election. On the face of things, it thus seems highly improbable that it should be this same Gladstone who, some fifty years later, would take the unpreced-ented step of finally bestowing respectability on the art of acting by recommending Henry Irving to Queen Victoria for the offer of a knighthood in her Birthday Honours List in June 1883. But things are seldom what they seem on first acquaintance: it is my principal pur-pose to explain this.

It is my firm belief that in all cases where matters of principle and personal conviction are concerned, no such metamorphosis can be fully explained without the grounds for so singular a change of heart being already present as much within the individual himself as in any subsequent changes of external circumstances. There must also be some self-evident link or connection between the skills and interests of the parties principally concerned.

In the case of Gladstone and Irving, this connection is patently clear in the need which both men shared from their schooldays onwards to acquire mastery over the arts of oratory, or rhetoric, as a prerequisite for success in their respective professions. It is equally clear that in middle life both men had to learn to adapt their respective styles to meet the needs of rapidly expanding numbers of listeners and spectators in an increasingly urbanised society, both at the hustings and in much larger theatres. What is far less familiar, but possibly the most significant common factor, is that as young men both had been confidently expected by their respective families to prepare themselves for ordination and to seek preferment in the church. Let us now return to oratory and rhetoric as these words were understood in the early years of the nineteenth century. Sadly, both words have become so tarnished today (by being debased to terms of near abuse) as to have been stripped of all the mystery and magic power to attract and move huge audiences of listeners that they held throughout both Gladstone's and Irving's lifetimes. To understand the world into which Gladstone was born we must thus first banish television from our minds; then dismiss radio as a source of knowledge about the world around us; and then travel with Dr Who in the Tardis a further hundred years backwards through time to arrive in a society denied a daily newspaper, and where nearly three-quarters of the population could not have read it even if one had existed. Moreover, only about one-twentieth of the male population had a parliamentary vote and many elections were uncontested.

In such a world, the only means of advocating change or reform – alternatively of blocking both – was public speaking, *alias* oratorical direct address. Notwithstanding the French and American Revolutions, the Napoleonic Wars – and, closer to home, our own Industrial Revolution – the world which greeted William Gladstone's entry into it was therefore still fundamentally that of Edmund Burke, MP for Bristol and probably the greatest parliamentary orator the House of Commons had ever known; the world of John Wesley and his brother Charles, the most outstanding preachers to have sprung from the ranks of the English clergy since the Civil War; and the theatrical world of David Garrick, Sarah Siddons, John Philip Kemble and Edmund Kean. And what all these illustrious persons shared in common was their outstanding command of rhetoric as forged in classical antiquity and then systematically remodelled through the seventeenth and eighteenth centuries to fit the English tongue.

It mattered little when Gladstone went to Eton in 1825 whether the podium chosen to exercise these skills was a pulpit, the parliamentary benches, the electoral hustings or the stage: what mattered was that preacher, politician and actor alike could capture and command the attention of very large audiences, *without the aid of a microphone*, whether in an echoing cathedral, a market square or a theatre in which the auditorium was still as brightly lit as the stage. What counted was the speaker's ability to take a swift grip on the attention of his audience – both visually and aurally – and then hold it: and the surest way to do that was to arouse both their emotional and rational responses to his argument through a perfect marriage of declamation with posture and gesture. Only by such means could a speaker hope to convince an overwhelming majority of those present that what he had said was both true and worth translating into action. In that way the biblical miracle of turning five small loaves and two fishes into 5000 could be repeated within nineteenth-century society in terms of legislative changes affecting electoral reform, hygiene, housing, education and the cost of living.

In that sense, therefore, when young Gladstone was debating within his own mind and heart whether to prepare himself for ordination or for politics during his formative years at Eton and Oxford, it scarcely mattered which way the dice would fall, since either way a firm command of rhetoric was as imperative a requirement for success and personal advancement as it was for any actor. His own diaries bear this out in so far as entries respecting his attendance at, and opinions of, sermons outnumber those relating to speeches prepared for the debating societies at Eton and Oxford.

On arrival at Eton he took immediate steps to acquire proficiency in this art from anyone willing to help him. With that said, however, a mastery of oratory, like that of all other arts, is not something that can be simply acquired through industrious study and energetic application. Somewhere, within the genes at birth, must reside that spark of the true Promethean fire which sets the star performer apart from the supporting actor. In the case of rhetoric, that quality must be the voice: a commodity which in the British Isles is more readily found among those possessed of Celtic blood (whether Scots, Welsh or Irish) than in those without it. Gladstone is said to have retained his Liverpool accent throughout his life. This may be true; but that should not persuade us to ignore his ancestry and his Scottish home at Fasque: for it is to Fasque that the bundle of letters which I possess, sent as a schoolboy at Eton to his family, are all addressed.

More seriously, if I ask myself why it was that young Max Beerbohm

Fig. 1. St Peter, having his orders for some time, refuses admittance to Mr Gladstone. Mr Gladstone then commences to speak – 'It was a great effort, worthy of a great occasion', wrote the Reporting Angel. 'Never had the Old Man Eloquent spoken with more fire and force, nor employed his inexhaustible resources of dialectic to greater effect. The O.M.E. is here proving that Heaven was one of his birth-places. The simple ex-fisherman gradually falls under 'the wizard spell of of his eloquence' and, in order to avoid the peroration, unbars the gates of gold and pearl.

Fig. 2. The same evening Mr Gladstone addresses a mass-meeting of Angels. He pays an eloquent and graceful tribute to God. Cartoons by Max Behrbohm.

should have depicted him in 1899 as capable of persuading St Peter to admit him to Heaven, despite being expressly forbidden by God to do so, I am sure that what he pounced on as a cartoonist was this Scottish streak of the fiery Presbyterian minister received from John Knox and John Calvin, that lurked below the smooth anglicised surface of Gladstone's entire parliamentary careeer.[3] Here is Max's vision of the G.O.M. on arrival at the gates of Heaven; an angelic press-reporter, seated on a nearby cloud, takes notes of his pleading to St Peter (Fig. 1). Once admitted, he addresses the Angels (Fig. 2). These two caricatures serve to clinch the point I've been trying to make about the paramount importance of Gladstone's voice and the uses to which he turned it when harnessing it to the appropriate postures and gestures of an accomplished actor for political ends.

> Spoken with fire and force . . .
> inexhaustible resources of dialectic . . .
> the wizard spell of his eloquence . . .
> eloquent and graceful tribute . . .

Max Beerbohm's carefully chosen phrases offer us an objective, if mischievous, appraisal of a living legend – G.O.M. or O.M.E. – a public figure at least as notable as an exemplar of the art of rhetoric for the nineteenth century as Edmund Burke had been for the eighteenth, or even as pre-eminent in his own generation as either Cicero or Demosthenes had been in classical antiquity.

We possess a recording of his voice; but sadly a recording made on one of the first Edison Cylinder machines when Gladstone was in his eighties. Thus anyone told today that this was the voice of the O.M.E. must be forgiven for failing to recognise any of the qualities ascribed to it so succinctly and amusingly by Max Beerbohm; but as Max's testimony is so amply confirmed in the written records of so many of Gladstone's friends, colleagues and biographers, it's perhaps best to dismiss the Edison recording for what it is and rely instead on the written evidence. Here is one example: the evidence supplied by his long-time Parliamentary Private Secretary, Arthur Godley, later Lord Kilbracken. I quote here from his privately printed book, *Reminiscences*:

> It is true that he used often to repeat himself: some subject, some piece of news, some anecdote that he had heard, would from time to time, take possession of his mind and would appear and reappear in his conversation for days or weeks, or even longer. But I am sure that most of his hearers felt, as I did, that this mattered little.

And there we reach the heart of the matter, for Godley continues: 'It was invariably a pleasure to listen again to what one had heard before, thanks to the admirable delivery, his command of words, and his grand voice.'[4]

If, then, we are obliged to ignore the Edison Cylinder recording of that voice, where else are we to search for the source of these qualities? Max Beerbohm supplies us with two clues. His telling descriptive phrases in his cartoon captions: 'the wizard spell of his eloquence'; and 'his inexhaustible resources of dialectic'. Neither of these rhetorical assets, any more than the 'admirable delivery' and 'command of words' remarked upon by Arthur Godley, can be attributed simply to inspiration or the gift of tongues. Rather did all of them have to be deliberately and painstakingly acquired through long hours of study and practice of the kind that makes a professional pianist or instrumentalist a master of scales and arpeggios. Michael Foot supplies a third clue which leads towards an authoritative answer. Replying to his own question in his introduction to the *Diaries* which I have already quoted about how and where Gladstone learned to speak in public, he says,

> The answer is clear: at Eton, and from Dr Keate – a little direct tuition from the headmaster; a careful reading of the *Lectures on Rhetoric* of Hugh Blair ... and a thorough soaking in Aristotle's *Rhetoric*. [The latter] he reread diligently at Oxford, preparing it as a set-book with one of his Christ Church tutors; and both at Eton and at Oxford he was an assiduous debater.

Nothing could be more direct or helpful. But, in that same introduction, Dr Foot commits himself to two other phrases which I regard as equally useful pointers to the directions in which we might profitably pursue our quest. The first is this: 'Everybody knows that Gladstone could be prolix; all great orators can. Yet he was also capable of an uncanny degree of compression.' Secondly, a general comment on all the diaries: 'Here is the daily record of the life of a man ... who trod the stage of history and directed the play in which he acted.'[5]

So, back to the classroom and Eton in the 1820s. In a long obituary printed as a special supplement to the *Graphic* in 1898, the writer, in a manner characteristic of journalists, told his readers that 'Eton owed more to Mr Gladstone than he ever did to the school and its masters'.[6] With hindsight, that snappy media verdict now has to be tempered by what we know today of the young Gladstone's relationships with his principal tutors: at Eton Mr Knapp (a great theatre-goer) and Dr

Keate; at Oxford with messrs Anstice, Briscoe and Cardwell. Under
their guidance, he was directed to Hugh Blair's *Lectures on Rhetoric* and
to those many ancient Greek and Roman orators Blair had relied on
when fashioning his own lectures on the composition and delivery of
a speech in English. They also introduced him to John Walker's *The
Elements of Gesture*.[7]

Blair was born in Edinburgh in 1718. He delivered his lectures in
the university during the 1730s, and published them in 1783 when
Burke, Wesley and Garrick were regarded as the outstanding living
practitioners of parliamentary, ecclesiastical and theatrical oratorical
style respectively. So eagerly were copies of Blair's *Lectures* sought after
that they swiftly went through ten editions and were then translated
into French. Thus they became the standard work on English style
both for literary composition and oratorical use for nineteenth-century
readers.[8]

Blair was very careful to preserve a sharp distinction between a
man's vocation and the style considered to be appropriate to that vocation. Thus any cleric rash enough to employ a vocabulary or gestures
in the pulpit considered to be acceptable in the theatre, whether the
play be comic or tragic, could expect to be severely censured if not
ridiculed by his congregation. The politician, likewise, had to discover
a *via media* between these two extremes, as did the university professor
and the barrister.

Young Gladstone's reading of Blair's *Lectures* began on 1 March
1826, shortly after his sixteenth birthday, and continued daily
throughout that term.[9] By June, he felt ready to try out in public what
he had studied in private: and on the 24th of that month he recorded
in his diary his participation in a debate on 'the morality of a man
who rebels against a usurper – traitor or patriot?' I quote from the
entry on 24 June. 'Spoke for his being a patriot – for the first time (I
think) extempore almost entirely. Debate good. I in majority.'[10] Blair
had devoted the first twenty-four of his *Lectures on Rhetoric* to a critical
analysis of language and literary composition, since a command of
grammar and vocabulary were not only the prime requirements of any
good writing, but also the essential foundation stones for the acquisition of mastery over what he described as 'Eloquence, or Public
Speaking' to which topic he devoted his next ten lectures. He concluded with three lectures devoted to dramatic poetry: two on tragedy
(Greek, French and English) and one on comedy (Roman, French and
English).

In this context, it is worth noting that young William Gladstone had been required, by the time he left Eton, to construe *in the original language*, most of Molière's plays; virtually all of Racine's; together with most of Ben Jonson's, Massinger's, Fletcher's, Ford's and some of those by Shakespeare and Otway. Selected set-speeches had to be learned by heart for declamation in class.

His study of Greek and Roman plays was no less thorough, spanning his years both at Eton and at Oxford. In January 1827 he was required to study John Walker's *Elements of Gesture*, to which I will return. The theatrical elements of public speaking were thus being forcibly fed to him while still in his late teens: and on leaving Eton, on 3 December 1827, he went to London and spent that evening at Covent Garden watching Kemble as Falstaff in *Henry IV Part I*.[11]

Four years later, however, when he was in his final year at Oxford and within a month of taking his final examinations, it becomes abundantly clear from the evidence of the diaries that his mind was firmly set, not upon a theatrical or a clerical career, but on a political one. Between 3 September and the 8 September of that year he played truant from Christ Church to attend a debate on the Reform Bill in the House of Lords. I quote from the diary: 'Present at five nights debate of infinite interest in the House of Lords.' An exceptionally long entry summarises the impressions made on him by the speeches:

> Lord Brougham's was a speech most wonderful – Lord Grey's most beautiful – Lord Goodrich's and Lord Lansdowne's extremely good, and in these was comprehended nearly all the oratorical merit of the debate.
>
> The reasoning, or the attempt to reason, independently of the success in such attempt, certainly seemed to me to rest with the opposition. Their best speeches, I thought, were those of Lords Harrowby, Caernarvon . . . and seven others, including the Duke of Wellington.

The government won the debate by 199 votes to 129, and riots broke out immediately throughout the country.[12] Here we may see, on the evidence of his own diary, young Gladstone, applying what he had devoted so many hours to studying in Blair's *Rhetoric*, Walker's *Elements of Gesture*, Aristotle's *Rhetoric*, and countless classical orations, to the real-life issues of contemporary politics.

Few can doubt, given this abnormally extended and contemplative diary entry, that he was already fully aware that success in legislative affairs depended directly upon the skills of seasoned orators in persuading their listeners to accept their side of the argument. It was, after all, the 'most wonderful', the 'most beautiful' and the 'extremely good' speeches which had won the debate for the Tories and for the cause which he himself supported so passionately. It is equally obvious from the distinction so clearly drawn here between the virtues of strictly rational, if dispassionate, argument, and those of mere oratorical merit – however passionately and eloquently delivered – that his own mind was at work, perhaps for the first time, on analysing the skills required of the professional rhetorician for his own subsequent use. This lesson – acquired in conditions of acute personal discomfort (squeezed as a juvenile nonentity into the benches of the Visitors' Gallery in the House of Lords) – was *not* wasted.

The logic of the argument in favour of any cause – whether it be fiscal reform, Balkan emancipation or Home Rule for Ireland – was unlikely *of itself* to prove sufficient to win that case within a society that was still largely illiterate, unless it was communicated to large public audiences with a high degree of strictly technical oratorical skills – simplicity of vocabulary; short sentences; clarity of diction – reinforced by carefully modulated vocal delivery, and matching stance and gesture; and all of these qualities informed by passionate conviction and commitment. *Not* then for Gladstone were the parliamentary performances of today with collapsed shoulders, strangled diaphragms, mumbled utterance and eyes cast downwards on to typescripts which pass muster for a speech. Rather was it imperative for both a prospective MP at the hustings, and for anyone seeking advancement from the back to the front benches within the House of Commons itself, to be both *heard* and *seen* to be possessed of a dynamic and theatrical personality. In short, a public speech, to command respect, had to be just that: articulate, resonant and impassioned.

Within four years of his truancy from Eton to snatch a glimpse of the hurly-burly of life in the Palace of Westminster, young Gladstone had successfully put the lessons learned to the test of the hustings at Newark and had found himself in the House of Commons – more comfortably seated, this time – on the Treasury Bench.

There he found himself with three, singular advantages. The first was his voice, acquired through his genes; the second was his fluency in finding the right words to use while standing on his feet rather than sitting at his desk: a skill acquired from reading Blair's *Rhetoric* and then polished for personal use by writing letters to friends in Latin instead of English, or by translating Shakespeare into Greek. The third, a skill nowhere mentioned in Blair's *Lectures*, was one derived from his First Class Honours Degree in Mathematics, which allowed him to apply his phenomenally good memory for words with equal dexterity to facts and figures. Recalling this in his *Reminiscences*, Arthur Godley wrote:

> It may be interesting if I record here the recipe which Mr Gladstone gave me one day in conversation for a speech on financial matters. 'Get up your figures', he said, 'thoroughly and exhaustively, so as to have them absolutely at your fingers' ends, and then give them out as if the *whole* WORLD was interested in them' – with tremendous emphasis upon 'the *whole* WORLD'.[13]

Here, Godley succeeds in conveying to his readers the histrionic style of one of the great melodramatic actor-managers of his day adopted by Gladstone in his delivery of this advice by italicising the word 'whole' and capitalising the word 'world'.

I turn next, therefore, to his training during his Eton schooldays in the use of his voice when speaking in public and the matching of that to the visual dimensions of posture and gesture. As already remarked, young Gladstone was there required to study not only the major part of the entire repertory of French, English, Roman and Greek classical drama, but to take practical steps to master John Walker's precepts respecting *The Elements of Gesture*, with a view to learning major speeches from these plays by heart prior to reciting them in class to an audience of his fellow students.[14]

Walker begins his book by dismissing standard texts on 'the adaptation of the action to the word and the word to the action "to express the Passions" as they appear in the countenance and operate upon the body' on grounds that such a task is beyond the comprehension of schoolboys. Instead, he seeks to substitute a simplified system, arguing that for boys to stand motionless while they are pronouncing the most impassioned language is absurd and unnatural: 'that they should sprawl into awkward, ungainly and desultory action is still more disgusting and offensive. What then remains', he continues,

> but that such a general style of diction be adopted as shall be easily conceived and easily executed; which, though not expressive of any particular passion, shall not be inconsistent with the expression of any passion; which shall always keep the body in a graceful position, and shall so vary its motions at proper intervals, as to seem the subject operating upon the words, and not the speaker on the subject.

Fig. 3. John Walker, *The Elements of Gesture* (1801), plate I.

This brings him to plate I (4th edn, 1801) (Fig. 3). This, he says,

> represents the attitude in which a boy should always place himself when
> he begins to speak ... He should rest the whole weight of his body on the
> right leg; the other, just touching the ground at the distance at which it
> would naturally fall, if lifted up to show that the body does not bear upon
> it. The knee should be straight and braced; and the body, though perfectly
> straight, not perpendicular, but reclining as far to the right as a firm posi-
> tion on the right leg will permit.
>   The right arm must then be held out with palm open, the fingers
> straight and close, the thumb almost as distant from them as it will go;
> and the flat of the hand neither horizontal nor vertical, but exactly
> between them both.[15]

Fig. 4. Disraeli at the Buckinghamshire Election (1847).

And here, twenty years after young William Gladstone was first taught to adopt this posture, is Disraeli addressing the Buckingham electorate in 1847 (Fig. 4).

Having addressed himself to the manner of lowering the right arm, and then shifting the weight gracefully off the right foot and on to the left and raising that arm, Walker proceeds to explain how a schoolboy may add variety to stance and gesture, concluding with instructions on how to approach a climax.

This he illustrates (Fig. 5), explaining that, at the last moment, the wrist and forearm 'should, with a jerk, be suddenly straightened . . .

Fig. 5. John Walker, *The Elements of Gesture* (1801), plate III.

at the very moment the emphatic word is pronounced'. Walker goes on to claim that, 'This coincidence of the hand and the voice will greatly enforce the pronunciation; and if they keep time they will be in tune as it were to each other, and to force and energy add harmony and variety'.[16]

By happy chance a picture survives which not only illustrates the

Fig. 6. Young Gladstone reciting before the school on the Upper School Room at Eton College.

completion of this final moment, when body, arm and hand swing into conjunction with the voice to reach the climax of a recitation, but which depicts Gladstone himself while still at Eton as its exponent (Fig. 6).

After completing his description of his other five postures or stances, Walker begins his second section entitled 'On the Acting of Plays in Schools', pleading that 'the acting of a play is not so conducive to improvement in Elocution as the speaking of single speeches'. The rest of the book consists of 'A Selection of Parliamentary Debates, Orations, and Speeches (Many of Them from Plays) from the Best Writers Proper to be Read and Recited by Youth at School'.

This goes far to explain why Gladstone was required both at Eton and Oxford to devote so much time to mastering major plays by Molière and Racine, Jonson and Massinger, and those by Greek and Roman dramatists, and to see the finest classical actors of the day when occasion offered at Drury Lane and Covent Garden. It also serves to explain why the nearest he got himself to the smell of greasepaint in a dressing-room during those years appears to have been a visit to a dress-rehearsal of a pantomime, or burletta, in his Dame's house at Eton. On 3 February 1826, his diary records,

> Attended, after supper, the rehersal of a play ... all the fellows, save myself and the three above me, actors. They have provided themselves with swords and shields – have tin helmets and some Breastplates – dresses principally made by themselves – scenes of paper, which they have made and painted.[17]

He also attended this production of *The Captive Princess* (an operetta by J.P. Kemble adapted for Hodgson's Juvenile Theatre as *Lodowska*) on its first night, five days later. Recording this event in his diary, he tells us that the cast consisted of eight actors, but supplies no comment on the play or the performers.

In vacations, he attended professional productions in Liverpool as well as in London; but in only one instance does his diary offer us any illuminating information about his attitude to them, or to this use of oratorical talent. That is the diary entry on 29 December 1832, that I have already quoted to you dismissing racemeetings and theatres as positive invitations to sin, seemingly for ever. Perhaps, in this context, we should recall that, in his Eton days, it can scarcely have escaped his acutely sensitive moral conscience when studying Racine's plays – more especially *Esther* and *Athalie* – that Racine himself not only refused to allow both of these plays to be performed by the King's own players, but renounced his own profession during the last years of his life as frivolous, subversive and sinful.[18] This was a view, we should remember, increasingly shared by all Methodists and members of other Nonconformist sects in England from the closing years of the eighteenth century onwards.

Just when his recantation respecting the theatre began remains uncertain – seemingly during the 1850s; but, since its consequences could never have been imagined by his contemporaries in the 1830s, this question is worth pursuing now. As H.C.G. Matthews has remarked in *Gladstone, 1875–98*, prior to the 1840s Britain was still largely a pre-industrial society: thereafter it was to change out of all recognition. The advent of railways, rotary printing presses and the rapid migration of artisans into towns and cities created to supply a work force to operate new machines saw to that. These were changes of so revolutionary an order that no one dependent for their careers on oratorical skills – whether as politician, churchman or actor – could afford to ignore them since they could only serve to reinforce the cry for 'Liberty, Fraternity, Equality' sparked off in the early decades of the century by the French Revolution. This, coupled with the industrialisation of city life, served to open up an abyss in theatrical life which theatre managers with eyes fixed on box-office receipts were the first to recognise. Eager to acquire new audiences, but frustrated by the laws restricting the number, size and repertoires of the legitimate patent theatres, they swiftly created new, if illegitimate, ones in music-rooms attached to taverns, circuses and pavilions erected in pleasure gardens specifically to meet the demand for entertainment from a large new labour force of illiterate labourers and artisans. In all of these venues they offered singing and dancing, or rousingly heroic and patriotic stories related in a pictorial rather than literary style. In short, the Age of Melodrama had dawned with representations of 'The Storming of the Bastille', 'The Burning of Moscow' and the adaptation of such notorious Romantic novels as Horace Walpole's *The Castle of Otranto*, Mrs Radcliffe's *The Mysteries of Udolfo* and Mary Shelley's *Frankenstein*. To the telling of these stories the theatre managers harnessed every device that the new industrial technology could offer to make them appear pictorially more realistic to ever large audiences. The casualty was the serious literary drama of earlier centuries. Sheridan had carried its flag into the first decade of the nineteenth century; but by the 1830s, with the single exception of Lord Byron, all poetic dramatists and novelists of distinction had come to despair of persuading the theatre managers to pay them enough for the script of a play for it to be worth their while to continue to write for the stage.

Fig. 7. Free Trade Meeting in Drury Lane Theatre, London (1844).

Fig. 8. Gladstone at Leeds: the banquet in the Old Cloth Hall.

By 1843, even the politicians – whether they liked Music Hall and melodrama or not (and Gladstone clearly did not) – had to acknowledge defeat when Parliament passed the Theatres Act, thereby greatly diminishing the Lord Chamberlain's powers over the stage while greatly extending the number and size of theatre buildings throughout the land. But as audiences grew ever larger in much bigger theatres equipped with controllable gas-lighting, so too actors had to adapt their rhetorical skills to ensure that they could still be heard and thus preserve their control over these audiences by enlargement or exaggeration of their acting style.

By the 1850s politicians, likewise, were finding it obligatory to adapt their style of oratorical address to new circumstances and for very similar reasons. The mass meetings organised by the Anti-Corn League during the 1840s had simply prefigured the political meetings of the 1850s which, by then, had been transformed into great theatrical events – staged in huge city halls, or in the open air, attracting audiences of thousands; and, as often as not, with 'Reform' as the battle-cry emblazoned on the banners and placards used as stage-settings. After 1867 audiences would grow larger still as ever more male, skilled artisans acquired a vote. Figs 7–10 (and Figs 23–25, below pp. 220–21) make it self-evident that politicians, like actors, had far more to contend with when seeking a hearing from very large middle- and working-class audiences than Hugh Blair could ever have contemplated when compiling his *Lectures on Rhetoric* as a training manual for young orators.[19]

The alternative to Blair that was then on offer had been pioneered, not by sophisticated academics, but by that same profession described by Gladstone in 1832 as 'sinful': in other words by those histrionic rhetoricians brought up in the populist, but tightly controlled, school of melodramatic theatrical techniques. Was it then this new style of oratorical delivery that reawakened Gladstone's interest in plays and their performers during the 1850s? No certain answer can be given to that question, but what is certain is that by then melodrama was concerning itself in its story-lines with many of the social evils of that time that were closest to his own conscience and convictions: single mothers turfed out from their humble homes into the snow by heartless bailiffs acting for the same caddish squires and landlords who had first put them into this pitiful condition and then abandoned them. Hence my inclusion of the picture of the Ladies Gallery at Manchester Fig. 11) and that of the St Pancras Workhouse (Fig. 12). Women may still have been denied a vote, but they were becoming evermore

Fig. 9. The South-West Lancashire Election (1868). The Nomination, in front of St George's Hall, Liverpool, with an audience of more than 20,000.

Fig. 10. Gladstone addressing the electors of Greenwich
at Blackheath (October 1871).

Fig. 11. Gladstone meeting in the Corn Exchange, Manchester (1868). The Ladies Gallery.

Fig. 12. Gladstone addressing the inmates of St Pancras Workhouse.

politically minded and motivated by the conditions governing their own lives.

Other melodramas displayed the glaring disparities between the public and the private morality of wealthy bankers and industrial tycoons as exemplified in their exploitation of their clients and employees. All these themes, moreover, and many others just as topical, were scripted within a strictly Christian (if necessarily oversimplified) ethical context. In short, by the 1850s, melodrama had come of age and become a force at least as potent as the novels of Charles Dickens in focusing the attention of mid-Victorian society on many of the political issues and causes that were to be espoused by Gladstone himself. For how much longer then could he describe theatres as 'sinful'? A picture supplies an answer (Fig. 13).

This is not the altar of some Nonconformist chapel, but the great room of St James's Hall. The figure standing on the right is Gladstone, then Chancellor of the Exchequer; that seated on the left is Charles Kean, the leading actor of his day. The date is 1862, and the elaborate array of table-ware includes silver candelabra, fruit dishes and a huge ewer, all of which were gifts from Old Etonian admirers to be presented by Gladstone to Kean and his wife at the end of his testimonial address as a mark of respect on their retirement from the stage.

What was it that induced him to accept this invitation to deputise for the Duke of Newcastle, who had been called to Windsor at the last moment? The fact that Kean was himself an old Etonian, and thus shared a common heritage with him in Blair's *Lectures*, Walker's *Elements of Gesture*, Aristotle's *Rhetoric* and an obligation to recite speeches from English, French, Roman and Greek classical drama, may have supplied an inducement.[20] Nor can the fact that the Queen and Prince Consort had so frequently commanded the Keans to bring their spectacular Shakespearean productions to Windsor have been lost on him.[21] It is within the main body of his speech, however, that he supplies us with the principal reason motivating the recantation of his earlier attitude to theatres and actors expressed in the diary entry of 29 December 1832. Referring directly to the Keans' services towards the revival of Shakespeare's plays, he told his audience also 'to look to the Keans [as] the ones who had laboured in the noble and holy cause of endeavouring to dissociate the elements of the drama from all moral and social contamination'. Our leopard had thus not wholly changed his spots; but he was already clearly capable of moving forward on this particular road to Damascus, as he indicates in his peroration. Claiming that 'that was the work to which Mr Kean had given

Fig. 13. Gladstone presenting a Testimonial to Charles Kean on his retirement from the stage, St James's Great Hall, Windsor, 1862.

many anxious years and all the best energies of his mind', he concluded by expressing the hope that 'others would follow [Kean] in endeavouring to improve the tone and elevate the character of the English stage'. And as we know, an Elisha was already in the wings awaiting the moment when the mantle of Kean's Elijah should drop onto his shoulders – the young Henry Irving.

Like the young Gladstone, Irving was expected by his family to prepare himself for ordination. Instead, where Gladstone had opted for politics, Irving was to opt for the stage. As a result he was disowned by his mother (a confirmed Cornish Methodist) leaving him shocked and with a lasting sense of guilt which he was thereafter determined to repudiate by forcing Victorian society to accept the theatre as one of the primary forces binding all classes into a common sense of their own heritage and identity. This he achieved, not only by his outstandingly innovative approach to the virtues of marrying the best of dramatic literature with strikingly realistic pictorial spectacle, but by his frequent excursions into the publication of essays, and into the acceptance of invitations to deliver lectures and addresses both in this country and in America. This was not only a marked advance on anything Charles Kean had achieved to restore respectability to the British stage, but a development which could not escape Gladstone's attention. Nothing could have proved more convincing in this respect than his patient and unwavering efforts to promote Tennyson's plays.[22]

Through the 1860s and 1870s Gladstone's recantation proceeded apace, extending not only to opera and to plays presented in London by French, German and American companies, but even to West End comedies and Music Hall, and a family visit to the Théâtre Français when in Paris in 1879. Yet more surprisingly, in an open letter to the *Theatre*, published on 13 March 1878, he advocated the creation of a National Theatre, thereby becoming the focal point of a movement taken up by Bernard Shaw and others, but destined to linger in the 'pending' tray for another eighty years before reaching fulfilment: but here he is, seated in Irving's private box at the Lyceum theatre watching Irving's *Hamlet* on the night of 12 December, 1878 (Fig. 14).[23]

My principal informant from now on is someone so improbable that I must forgive, or at least excuse, incredulity or flat disbelief when I provide you with his name: for it is none other than the author of *Dracula*, Bram Stoker. To recover your trust and belief I must remind you, therefore, that Stoker was an Irish novelist who became Irving's business manager and, after Irving's death, published his own reminiscences in two volumes in 1906.[24] From these we learn that Gladstone was a frequent visitor to the Lyceum, seeing Irving's *Hamlet* no less than five times, as well as his *Othello, Richard III, Much Ado, Henry VIII* and *Merchant of Venice*.[25]

Stoker tells us that, in December 1880, Irving was informed that Gladstone proposed to attend the first night of Tennyson's *The Cup*, which was to be presented, as a double bill, with a revival of that famous melodrama *The Corsican Brothers*, on 3 January 1881. Irving responded by arranging for him to occupy his own private box for that night. This, as depicted in Alfred Bryan's drawing (Fig. 14) was adjacent to the proscenium arch at stage level and equipped with a pass-door onto the stage.

Following the performance of *The Cup*, Gladstone sent a message to Stoker saying that 'he wished to come on stage [to] tell Irving and Ellen Terry how delighted he was with the performance'. Irving replied by giving him the key to the pass door and, 'fixed, as the most convenient time, the scene of the masked-ball [in *The Corsican Brothers*]'. What followed is so extraordinary, and so unprecedented before or since, that I will quote Stoker's account in full.

> Mr Gladstone was exceedingly interested in everything and went all round the vast scene. Seeing, during the progress of the scene that people in costume were going in and out of queer little alcoves at the back of the scene, he asked Irving what these were. [Irving] explained that they were the private boxes of the imitation theatre [represented in this scene]; and added that if the Premier would care to sit in one he could see the movement of the scene at close hand, and if he was careful to keep behind the little silk curtain he could not be seen.
>
> The statesman took his seat and seemed for a while to enjoy the life and movement going on in front of him. He could hear now and again the applause of the audience ... At last, in the excitement of the scene, he forgot his situation and, hearing a more than usually vigorous burst of applause, leaned out to get a better view of the audience.
>
> The instant he did so, he was recognized – there was no mistaking that eagle face – and then came a quick and sudden roar that seemed to shake the building. We could hear the 'Bravo Gladstone!' coming through the detonation of hand claps.[26]

This vivid description of a Prime Minister able to transform himself into an actor, and upstage Irving himself in his own theatre, brings me to the logical conclusion to this essay. But there is a sequel to this which is of sufficient substance in itself and so directly relevant to my subject as to warrant inclusion.

From this time forward, according to Stoker, whenever Gladstone visited the Lyceum, 'he always managed to visit Irving either on the stage, or in his dressing room, or both'.[27] In 1882 Gladstone returned the compliment by inviting Irving to one of his Downing Street 'Breakfasts', and followed that up within a year by persuading the Queen to take the unprecedented step of offering a knighthood to an actor in her Birthday Honours List.[28]

Surprisingly, Irving declined this offer on the grounds that he felt it to be improper 'for an actor, while still actively pursuing his profession, to accept it'.[29] Was it, I am prompted to wonder, just coincidence that the Roman actor Roscius had given the same reply to the Emperor when offered translation to patrician status on Cicero's initiative some 1900 years earlier? But let that pass. Only when approached again some twelve years later, this time by Lord Rosebery, did he change his mind. In doing so, he rescued the theatrical profession from the stigma of *sin* under which it had laboured ever since the Reformation – that of an under class of 'rogues and vagabonds'; mere 'caterpillars of the commonwealth', *alias* parasites on the hard-won earnings of sober, thrifty and thus virtuous citizens. It is to Gladstone, however, that credit must be given for effecting this dramatic reversal in the status of a much-maligned profession in twentieth-century society.

The sincerity of Gladstone's conversion is proved for me by what I heard from my father and my aunts who, along with their many Gladstone cousins, participated as actors in representations of Racine's *Esther* and *Athalie* in the drawing room at Hawarden Castle in the 1890s. And that swings the wheel back through its whole circle, from Gladstone's intimate friendship with Irving during the 1880s and 1890s as theatrical actor-manager, to his Eton days and his introduction there to the plays of Racine and Walker's *Elements of Gesture*.

If then we seek to penetrate to the centre of this connection we must, I think, focus our attention upon nature's gift to these two men: the gift of voices of quite exceptional resonance and modular flexibility, both of which were then fine-tuned by assiduous training and practical experience in the arts of oratory to meet the requirements demanded of them by very large public audiences throughout the latter half of the nineteenth century. The quality of Gladstone's voice, matched with a sustained vigour and rotundity of delivery was, as I

Fig. 14. Henry Irving's *Hamlet* at the Lyceum Theatre, London (1878). Gladstone is seated in Irving's private box immediately below the Royal Box. For a list of the other spectators present at his performance, see n. 23, p. 257.

have illustrated, a common theme among all of Gladstone's closest friends and biographers – even by Max Beerbohm: and the same was said of Irving's.

Esme Wingfield-Stratford, in a book of reminiscences, *Before the Lamps Went Out*, says this of Irving's voice:

> I never saw him in any of his famous parts, but one of the most unforgettable experiences of my whole life was to watch him, as Robespierre, give an exhibition of sheer, abject terror in a scene that with anyone else would have been simply funny, of the ghosts of Robespierre's victims appearing to him in prison. But there was nothing funny in the death-rattle gasp in which Irving [identified] each fresh apparition – 'Danton! . . . The Queen! . . .', all of which was only the build-up to an effect such as no one but he could have contrived, when the tyrant's voice suddenly changed to a little child's whimper 'I'm fright-ened!' I can hear it now, as plainly as when I was sitting in the Lyceum upper-circle; and having heard it, I could never think of any other actor as entering into the remotest comparison with Irving.[30]

Irving and Gladstone died within six years of each other; and with their deaths the curtain came down on an era in which a command of the arts of rhetoric was an essential prerequisite for anyone seeking promotion to the House of Fame in any walk of public life.

Bram Stoker says that Irving enjoyed Disraeli's company, if not his friendship, but then adds, 'It was, I think, the Actor that was in the man that appealed to him'.[31] He likewise chose to index his description of Gladstone's visit to Irving's production of *The Corsican Brothers*, which I've quoted, under 'Gladstone as actor'. Robert Cleaver's marvellously vivid sequence of sketches depicting Mr Gladstone in full oratorical flood when addressing the House of Commons during his last ministry (Frontispiece) will I think convince you that Irving came close to the mark in this assessment of his friend. And that, I think, explains the quite extraordinary response that Gladstone was to receive from the stage-hands at the Lyceum in answer to his request in 1890 to sit in the wings to watch Irving at work instead of in the auditorium. Stoker records it as follows:

> When it [became] known on the stage that Mr Gladstone was coming that night to sit behind the scene [the play was an adaptation of Scott's *Ravenswood*] the men [i.e. stage-hands and technicians] seemed determined to make it a gala occasion. They had prepared the corner where he was to sit as though it were for Royalty. They had not only swept and dusted, but

had scrubbed the floor; and they had rigged up a sort of canopy of crimson velvet so that neither dust nor draught should come to the old man. His chair was nicely padded and made comfortable. The stage-men were all, as though by chance, on the stage and in their Sunday clothes. As the Premier came in all hats went off. I showed Mr Gladstone his nook and told him, to his immense gratification, how the men had prepared it on their own initiative ... From then on, whenever he visited the Lyceum, that was where he sat, and that was how he was received. This throne became known as 'Mr Gladstone's seat'.[33]

This splendidly vivid, eye-witness description invites the question 'who was honouring whom?' Was it 'The Grand Old Man' who was honouring these simple and poorly paid stage-hands with his presence among them? Or were they honouring 'The People's William'? Or was it Irving himself killing the fatted calf to celebrate the return of the political prodigal son – Old Man Eloquent himself – to his rightful home? An actor who, in Michael Foot's words, had 'trod the stage of history and directed the play in which he acted'.

Fig. 15. Gladstone at the Despatch Box in the House of Commons.

2

Victorian Images of Gladstone

Asa Briggs

My interest in Gladstone goes back to my undergraduate days at Cambridge although I never wrote an essay about him then. Indeed, although I have written many words about the Victorians since, I wrote no essay at Cambridge on British political history after 1832. That, as we all know, was a year when Gladstone was telling the Duke of Newcastle that 'we seem to be approaching a period in which one expects events so awful that the tongue fears to utter them'. That the nineteenth century in Britain was to prove such a different a period from that which he then gloomily forecast owes much to Gladstone himself and to the first Prime Minister under whom he served, Sir Robert Peel.

The origins of this essay do not go back to my Cambridge days, but to my own subsequent development as a historian in Oxford, Leeds and elsewhere. When I started my professional career as historian and became the first Reader in Recent Social and Economic History in Oxford in 1950 Gladstone was not then at the centre of my interest. Indeed, it was Joseph Chamberlain and the city with which he was so closely associated, Birmingham, that then fascinated me. But already by then I was developing another line of interest which leads up to the choice of the subject matter of my essay. I had begun to be interested in broadcasting and through broadcasting in what came to be called 'the media', and this interest made me look at politics and politicians in a different way from the then fashionable political biographers. When I wrote the Centenary Programme for the Repeal of the Corn Laws in 1946, Cobden and Bright – and not Gladstone – were the popular heroes upon whom I focused, trying to explore the whole culture of the Anti-Corn Law League. I even managed to have a brass band taken into the studio in Leeds where the programme was made. I knew then, of course, that Gladstone at the time of the founding of the League had a very low opinion of it and that at the time of the general election of 1841 he even described it as a great political fraud. Of course, he was to change his mind about Cobden and Bright later on, and was to become a great popular campaigner himself.

As I myself moved after 1946 into mid nineteenth-century territory, much of it unexplored by professional historians, in *Victorian People* (1954), I began to take Gladstone very seriously and was particularly drawn to the question of how Gladstone, the Peelite, became Gladstone, 'the People's William'. To answer the question seemed to me to require an examination of non-verbal as well as verbal evidence. In my own home there was an image of Gladstone which I had inherited from my grandfather, which reminded me of Gladstone whenever I went in and out of it, a very familiar image which many of us have still in our homes – his image, a Gladstone plate. This provided a clue. My grandfather had seen Gladstone and heard him speak in Leeds and London, and he had bought that particular plate because he admired him long before Gladstone plates became collectable Victorian objects. It was a very different Gladstone who figured on that plate from the Gladstone who had been so critical of Cobden and Bright in 1841 and who had had such forebodings about the nineteenth century in 1832. It was a Gladstone, however, who had passed through his transformation into the People's William and had now become 'The Grand Old Man'.

Through the ephemera which were associated with him Gladstone has passed down to posterity in large numbers of homes, like mine, in a quite different way from the way in which he has passed down in books written by professional historians, but it was as a professional historian that, from the 1950s onwards, I began to be interested in collecting Victorian things, and which I was to write about in detail years later. The very first piece of Staffordshire that I ever bought was a beautiful figure of Cobden. I now have a large collection, and like to interpret history through them.

Victorian Staffordshires constitute a genre of popular art, very different from the china that Gladstone himself collected. Most of this popular art was not designed to last, much of it was very specifically for the moment. Yet, curiously enough, these objects have acquired a sense of permanence, perhaps not surprising, given that the people who made them in the Potteries themselves had a sense of permanence which in large measure derived from their religious rather than

Fig. 16. Gladstone plate.
(*St Deiniol's Library*)

their political views. There were not many books in the early 1950s about Staffordshire figures when I began to collect them. Now there are many, but few of them strong on the historical side. There was one book on nineteenth-century pottery and porcelain which began with the motto, a Staffordshire motto, 'We make our pots of what we potters are'.

Unfortunately in that book there was no reference to Gladstone, and very little reference either to the other political figures they recorded. The political preferences of the potters were Liberal, closely associated with the largely Nonconformist religion which most of them practised, but they were shrewd enough businessmen to produce objects of a totally different kind for foreign markets, including the Italian market, so that their religion was stretched at the edges in various directions, just as Gladstone's political imagination was stretched by Italy. Garibaldi was one of their favourites, and he was as popular in England as in Italy. I shall have more to say of Staffordshires later. As far as Gladstone was concerned, in a pre-television age they carried his image into the home. Surprisingly, one political figure who did not interest the potters was Palmerston, under whose Prime Ministership Gladstone's role as a political figure began to be transformed. There are many figures (and other images), however, directly related to Peel, who was celebrated after his tragic death in 1850 in parks and statues as well as in words. There were even more of the Duke of Wellington, many of whose images turned naturally into caricatures, the subject of a fascinating Victoria and Albert Museum exhibition in 1965.

Given this background, I would like to begin not with an image but with a book – Sir Thomas Wemyss Reid's *The Life of William Ewart Gladstone*, published in 1899, the year after Gladstone's death. Reid, a journalist, who edited the *Leeds Mercury* from 1870 to 1887, was the editor of this volume and not its sole author. He was offered his knighthood in 1894 on the recommendation of Gladstone's successor as Prime Minister, Lord Rosebery. The political chapters in Reid's book were written by Francis Hirst, a twentieth-century editor of *The Economist* who did much to keep the memory of Cobden and Bright alive. A devoted Gladstonian, he did more than that, however. He married Cobden's great-niece and when I had the pleasure of meeting him as a young Oxford don, he was living in Cobden's old house, Dunford House, in Sussex. Gladstone was one of the people we talked most about.

I have chosen to start with Wemyss Reid's book partly because I believe that biographies written immediately after the death of a public figure often reveal aspects of his life and influence subsequently forgotten and partly because it is a well-illustrated book which begins with images. Curiously, the first image on the first page is an engraving of the statue in Westminster Abbey not of Gladstone but of Disraeli, which, Reid points out, bears apart from Disraeli's name only the words 'twice Prime Minister of England'. 'None can doubt', Reid adds, 'that in this fact lies an irresistible claim to a place in the great central shrine of the British race.' And now he introduces Gladstone. 'The man whose life we are about to record possesses still higher claim than that of his old rival to the reverence and admiration of his fellow-countrymen'.

> The more generally he became known to his fellow-countrymen the more widely his influence spread, until at last it was rather his magnetic power over the masses of the people than his ascendancy in the councils of the elect few that seemed to be the most prominent feature of his career. Certainly no political leader of the century succeeded in evoking from the great body of the nation the passionate enthusiasm which he was able to draw forth.

Opposite this last passage there is an illustration of Gladstone presenting prizes after a band competition at Hawarden in 1896.

For the social historian all things connect, including brass bands, and having brought in Leeds *via* my grandfather and Reid, I should add that Daniel Fearon, author of an excellent Shire album publication, *Victorian Souvenir Medals*, notes that, while Gladstone's achievements do not seem to have been the subject of many souvenir medals, a visit of his to Leeds merited one. He depicts it – it is not a very good likeness – above a medal commemorating Disraeli's death in 1881 which bears the words 'One of England's Greatest Statesmen' and the motto 'Nothing is difficult to the brave'.

The pairing of words and images is almost as interesting as the pairing of Gladstone and Disraeli in Staffordshires and other objects, including plates. Thus on a statuette of Gladstone you read the magisterial words: 'The great social forces which move onwards in their might and majesty are marshalled on our side.' The combination of images and captions, reflected in the display of Gladstone on one Staffordshire (a pair to Disraeli) with a speech in his hand (another shows his hand resting on books), is central to my argument here, and the particular combination on the statuette was distinctively Gladstonian.

Speeches and objects go together as public utterances, and the rivalry between Gladstone and Disraeli, whose style of speaking differed as much as the content of their speeches, was expressed in images as well as in words, not to speak of music making, in W.S. Gilbert's words, for the sense of 'Nature's contrivance'

> That every boy and every gal,
> That's born into the world alive,
> Is either a little Liberal,
> Or else a little Conservative.

In the *Oxford Book of Quotations* only three characters separate Gilbert from Gladstone, but the former has 183 quotations to Gladstone's ten.

As far as Staffordshires are concerned, the notion of pairing added power to salesmanship, and there were three sets of Gladstone pairs. Besides the obvious pairing of Gladstone and Disraeli, there is also a pairing of Gladstone and Parnell, something which caused a good deal of anxiety towards the end of that relationship; and also, of course, there are pairings of Gladstone and Mrs Gladstone, which, however politically interesting – and they are – have been described as amongst the most deplorable aesthetically of the cast figures that were produced during the 1890s. By then Staffordshires were in their decline as aesthetic objects. The early Gladstone and Disraeli ones are far more interesting to look at. They were about $11\frac{1}{2}$ inches high, and they made Gladstone and Disraeli the same size. For a very long time I thought that the Gladstone and Disraeli pieces had come out of the same moulds. Now I am not sure. There is also one big Gladstone and a bigger Disraeli – 16 inches for Gladstone and, for some reason, $16\frac{1}{2}$ inches for Disraeli, an inversion of their natural heights.

It is difficult to know whether Gladstone and Disraeli were bought as pairs or whether they were bought just for the single images. The Staffordshires do not look much like either Gladstone or Disraeli, although I think that Gladstone comes out better than Disraeli in terms of likeness. Very frequently the *Illustrated London News* was used as a source of images in the Potteries, as techniques developed in the 1850s, for applying chromolithography to prints, pottery and porcelain making the transfers of the same image from one kind of medium to another. We know that as techniques improved they got rather better likenesses, and the likeness of Gladstone on the plate is a good one.

Referring back to the plates, they could be circular or octagonal, and some had words and captions, often full ones, on them and some not. There is a matching plate of Mrs Gladstone, just as there is a matching pair of Staffordshire figures. There is also curiously enough

Fig. 17. Gladstone reading the lesson in Hawarden Church.

a matching plate with Stafford Northcote, which is interesting in that for a time (after Disraeli and before Salisbury) he was the one Conservative figure to be depicted on a plate and that he had had his own close connection with Gladstone earlier. Some of the plates were funeral plates which were produced commemoratively, like funeral medals, after the person had died. But in the case of Gladstone they are plates dealing with the living politician.

One of the most interesting Staffordshire images of Gladstone, a Toby jug in his likeness, was not one of a pair. It was made by Sampson Smith in the 1860s, possibly in 1863 when Gladstone visited Burslem to lay the foundation stone of the Wedgwood Institute, an event in his private life as a collector as well as in his public life – more probably, after the formation of Gladstone's first ministry in 1868. It shows a woodsman's axe between his knees. I shall return to the axe later. There were other related objects too, among them a well-known but rather rare Gladstone tea-pot stand. There are also pot lids of various kinds, so that collectors of pot lids, a specialised group, are very familiar with Gladstone faces. The two living political figures who figure most clearly on pot lids, another popular medium, are another extraordinary pair – Gladstone and Lord Salisbury – one does not expect that particular combination. They also figure in terracotta.

To round off my own collection, which is not specialised in terms of genre, I turned to images of Gladstone in Parian ware and silk. There is a very good Parian ware Gladstone, which I think is beautifully done. The Disraeli too is of high quality. The image of Gladstone on silk, in a Stevengraph, shows the same Gladstone you find on some of the plates. He is shown in one of them, however, with a spray of thistles (post-Midlothian) and roses beside him. Of five catalogued Stevengraphs one bears the words 'the late Rt Hon. W.E. Gladstone'. It was another memorial piece.

I have read very little about this range of presentation of Gladstone in any book written about him – most books copy others – and it was with him and with other political figures in mind that I decided – long ago – to follow up my two books on *Victorian People* and *Victorian Cities* with a book on *Victorian Things*: a historian's and not a collector's book on artefacts as witnesses – with an emphasis on the great variety of Victorian things, old and new things, with more new things on offer than there had ever been in human history before, and on the strong sense of plenitude and in late-Victorian years of 'poverty in the midst of plenty'. Gladstone had figured quite prominently in *Victorian People*, and he figured quite prominently also in *Victorian Cities* where I took him to Middlesbrough, the Victorian new town, where he made one of his most remarkable tributes to nineteenth-century business enterprise in 1862. I might have taken him too to Newcastle in the same year, where he made a memorable visit, when he was given a tumultuous popular reception before he went on to Middlesbrough. He himself said of his visit to Newcastle that 'the spectacle was really one for Turner, no one else'.

It is interesting that Gladstone turned to a painter to catch the wholeness of the scene. He also mentioned, however, a Newcastle photographer who 'laid hands on me'. There is a reproduction of a studio photograph of him there, for technical reasons not well reproduced, in the Reid volume, along with photographs of Gladstone at different stages in his long life, the earliest that taken at Newcastle, the last one of 1892. It is particularly interesting to compare Gladstone photographs of 1868 with those of 1873, when Disraeli was accusing the members of his government of turning into 'exhausted volcanoes'.

The camera was a new Victorian thing, catching change, including change of experience, yet it took time for perceptions of politicians to be influenced by it, the first stage in a long historical process that was to culminate in television. At no stage in Gladstone's life did newspapers include photographs of him. You had to rely therefore, even in papers like the *Illustrated London News*, on engravings. Some of them are very beautifully produced. One of them, the well-known and frequently reproduced Spy cartoon – the People's William – appeared in 1879 in *Vanity Fair* only one year after Disraeli's apparent national triumph after returning from the congress of Berlin. The caption of the Spy cartoon read 'Mr Gladstone is still the most popular man in England'. That was the verbal accompaniment of the Spy image. The Spy image also incorporated Gladstone's collar, which was to be employed in cartoons throughout a very substantial part of Gladstone's later life.

Photographs could no more ignore Gladstone's high collar than cartoonists, who were equally fascinated by his axe. Nor could those in close contact with him. Thus, one of his secretaries, Algernon West, in recalling his first meeting with Gladstone in 1868, eleven years before the Spy cartoon, described him as

'sitting' . . . at his writing table, wearing a dark frock-coat with a flower in his button-hole [photographs often left this out]; a pair of brown trousers with a dark stripe down them, after a fashion of twenty years earlier; a somewhat disordered neckcloth and a large collar, the never-ending subject of so much merriment in contemporaneous caricature.

West drew attention too to 'the black finger-stall' which he invariably adjusted over the amputated finger on his left hand before he began to write.

Reid includes the Spy cartoon in his illustrations, along with a number of other cartoons, including some drawing attention to the axe, like a remarkable cartoon of 1874 showing Gladstone 'with his axe slung over his shoulder'. A Liverpool reporter had described him 'busy' felling trees two hours before a meeting at Hawarden. He went to work 'in true woodsman fashion, with his braces thrown off behind him and his shirt collar [*the* collar] unfastened'. 'After completing his task, he walked home with his axe slung over his shoulder, and two hours afterwards was at the meeting, looking not tired and weary, but quite refreshed.'

The reporter was inspired by what he saw: some years later Lord Randolph Churchill was amused by what he heard about, and in the House of Commons, as sacred a place for Gladstone as his own library, he mocked at the Grand Old Man's woodmanship. There was no mockery, however, in a *Punch* cartoon of 26 May 1877 during the Eastern crisis, when Disraeli was about to claim that he had brought back peace with honour from the Congress of Berlin. In the cartoon, as Gladstone wields his axe in front of a dying tree called 'Turkish Rule', a shocked Disraeli calls out 'Woodman, Spare that Tree, I love its every Bough'. It should be added that admirers presented Gladstone not only with illuminated certificates and with congenial books (there is a whole library of both) but with axes, and that at late-twentieth century Hawarden there is a bucket of solid wood chips brought into the house after Gladstone's tree-felling. I was proud to be given one of them. I recalled lines about the chips in *The Times* of 1877: 'The very splinters which fell from this axe were picked up and treasured as relics.'

Such sentiments revealed how firmly not only Gladstone and his axe captured the popular imagination but how Hawarden, house and estate, were placed on the Victorian map, with Gladstone at the centre of it. Rightly was it called a centre of pilgrimage to which railways ran special trains to carry there parties, sometimes of several hundred people. One pilgrim in a Lancashire group of 1400 people wrote to Gladstone on his return how he had decorated the largest wood chip which he had taken back with him and 'put it under a glass shade'. 'Scores of people' had subsequently come to his home to see it, 'both Liberals and Tories'. He intended to keep it as 'an heirloom during my life time' and hoped that his children would do the same.

Gladstone would have liked to be the family heir to inherit Fasque in Scotland, where his older brother Sir Thomas, a Tory Evangelical and a successful businessman, lived from 1851 to 1889. They were not on good terms until there was a family reconciliation a few years before Thomas's death. Thereafter Gladstone became a regular visitor. Today it is, like Hawarden, a place of twentieth-century pilgrimage, and there is an exhibition there of Gladstone's possessions, including large numbers of illuminated addresses which merit a lecture on their own. Above the fireplace is a copy of the Gladstone portrait that hangs in 10 Downing Street.

At Hawarden, there is a Gladstone memorial in the parish church. It shows the ship of life bearing Gladstone and his wife 'in eternal peaceful movement on through eternal ages'. The prows are winged as in the winged ships described by Homer, the most ancient figure in Gladstone's own version of ancient and modern. Reid devoted a whole chapter to 'Mr Gladstone as a Scholar'. It includes an engraving of him sitting in the British Museum. Tenniel produced a *Punch* cartoon of him and Robert Lowe, his Chancellor of the Exchequer in his 1868 government, discussing Homer. It is called 'A Deplorable Sceptic'.

The guide to twentieth-century Hawarden reprints the most famous of all Gladstone engravings, 'The Summons from Queen Victoria', which was sold in considerable quantities and appeared in many places. It shows Gladstone receiving a telegram from Windsor Castle where he was summoned to take office as Prime Minister in 1868. It is the telegram, not the axe, which Gladstone is holding, that gives this illustration special interest within the context of my concern with new nineteenth-century things. If I were dealing with another great nineteenth-century political figure, Bismarck, whom Gladstone never understood, I would have to take a telegram from his life too. We have one interesting recollection of the Hawarden event of 1868 by Evelyn Ashley, which puts the story in words.

One afternoon of November 1868 in the park at Hawarden I was standing by Mr Gladstone holding his coat on my arm while he in his shirt sleeves was wielding an axe to cut down a tree. Up came a Telegraph Messenger, he took the telegram and read it and then handed it to me speaking only two words namely, 'Very significant', and at once resumed his work. The message merely stated that General Grey would arrive that evening from Windsor. This of course implied that a Mandate was coming from the Queen charging Mr Gladstone with the formation of his first Government. I said nothing, but waited while the well directed blows resounded in regular cadence. After a few moments the blows ceased and Mr Gladstone resting on the handle of his axe looked up and with deep earnestness in his face exclaimed, 'My mission is to pacify Ireland'.

He then resumed his task and never said another word until the tree was down. There is one very popular and still fascinating image of Gladstone in the nineteenth century, and the presence in this story of the axe and telegram conveys a sense of ancient and modern. The hymn book with this title appeared in the same decade. When I think not of the axe but of the telegram my mind moves laterally across to Ruskin's first visit to Hawarden in 1878 when he was so worried about what would happen during the visit that he arrived armed with a telegram which would recall him at once if he found that the visit was intolerable; and, of course, to the famous unciphered telegram which was sent by the Queen to Gladstone after Gordon's disappearance in the Sudan. Telegrams as a part of the new technology of the nineteenth century came into the Gladstone story more than once, as once does the phonograph. Gladstone recorded a message on it for posterity. We have a record of his voice, therefore, with no parallel record of Disraeli, who died too soon.

Both men were recorded for posterity by cartoonists and one of the most brilliant of Gladstone's cartoonists, Henry Furniss, spans old and new. Several of his best Gladstone cartoons are reproduced in Reid's book. Furniss was chosen as a regular cartoonist by Sir Henry Lucy, 'Toby MP', who took over *Punch's* 'Essence of Parliament' in 1881. The Gladstone cartoons focus on the 'Grand Old Man', not always flatteringly. One shows him in 1886 with his hand to his ear – he was by then deaf – trying to listen to a parliamentary speech. Another, 'Interrupted', shows him disturbed and annoyed when he was interrupted while making a parliamentary speech. A third shows him 'At the Table'.

Furniss, who is an important figure in the landscape of communication covered in this essay, did not die until 1925. In 1912, at the age of fifty-eight, he was to take up the new art of the moving picture, working for Edison in New York, and later London, as writer and producer. In 1901 he had published *Confessions of a Caricaturist*. In 1914 he published *Our Lady Cinema*. He died at Hastings where J.L. Baird had already carried out some of his first experiments with television.

To see the nineteenth and twentieth centuries in perspective it is necessary to consider the eighteenth century also. This means comparing photographs – and cartoons – with portraits. Gladstone was a favourite subject for portrait painters, including Millais, whose portrait, now in Christ Church College, Oxford, is the chosen frontispiece to Reid's book. It was also turned into a popular mezzotint. The duplication and multiplication of images was much hailed by Victorians interested in access and diffusion. None of the portraits seems to me as revealing as the magnificent photograph of 1894 taken by John C. Murdoch. It is reproduced in Sir Philip Magnus's *Gladstone*, published in 1954: on the back of its dust wrapper are reproductions of more than thirty *Punch* cartoons of the face of Gladstone, taken from M.H. Spielmann's *History of Punch*, a few of them female, one wearing a mortar board. It is disappointing that Magnus does not explain how and when they came to be drawn and what was their significance. In fact, they bring out many facets of Gladstone, who had not one image but many. Neither the 'People's William' nor the 'Grand Old Man' image adequately represented him. In this respect G.K. Chesterton compared Gladstone with another eminent Victorian, the painter G.F. Watts, who did two portraits of Gladstone, the first of them in 1859. For Chesterton 'there is an eternal kinship between solemnity and high spirits, and almost the very name of it is Gladstone'. He was writing in 1904, when an anti-Victorian reaction was already setting in.

Gladstone himself had a strong visual sense, and one of the cartoons in Reid's book shows him looking at a picture in the Royal Academy. It is called 'A Sketch from Life'. He was, of course, a collector not of Staffordshires or Stevengraphs but of china, although after his defeat at the general election of 1874 and before the start of the Near Eastern crisis which propelled him back into power he sold at Christie's his collection of Wedgwood ware, Meissen, Sèvres and Capodimonte porcelain, and a Doccia group of the Deposition from a model of Massimiliano Soldani-Benzi. In his *Talks with Gladstone* (1898) Lionel Tollmache, whose revealing book I have edited and republished with the title *Gladstone's Boswell*, quotes an anonymous friend of Gladstone as saying of him – and it is the one remark about Gladstone's collecting which most historians have noted: 'He will talk about a piece of old china as if he was standing before the judgement-seat of God'. Some later biographers of Gladstone – but fortunately not all of them – have adopted that posture.

Presumably the staff of *Punch* did not; and late in his life Lucy invited Gladstone to a *Punch* dinner where he met *Punch* staff together. There were present some of the people who had been associated with the way in which his image had been and was being presented at different times, including Sir John Tenniel, whom Gladstone had once invited to 10 Downing Street. An early twentieth-century historian of *Punch* refers to the members of its staff having rendered Gladstone steady support for nearly half a century. In his speech on this unique occasion Gladstone paid his particular tribute to them:

> In my early days an artist was engaged to produce political satires and he nearly always descended to gross personal caricature and sometimes to indecency [whereas] today in the humorous press, particularly *Punch*, there is a total absence of vulgarity along with a far fairer treatment which has made this department of warfare always pleasing.

This was an observation that was not entirely true.

Gladstone had recognised more than once what *Punch* had done for him. When Mark Lemon died in 1870 he awarded a pension of £100 from the Civil List to Mrs Lemon, and he was also responsible for recommending Tenniel's knighthood. Yet there had been many cartoons in *Punch* of which Gladstone could not have approved. The notorious Mrs Gummidge one of 1885 showing Gladstone as a weary Mrs Gummidge, thinking of 'the old un', Disraeli, must have disturbed him, and Tenniel was very frightened indeed of meeting Gladstone after he had produced it. Tenniel claimed that he had no political opinions of his own, or at least none that he expressed in *Punch*, but it is interesting that Disraeli sometimes comes out surprisingly well in *Punch* cartoons. The best way to describe the situation was that *Punch* paired Gladstone and Disraeli in the same way as the Stafford-shires, as in a famous 'Doctors Differ' cartoon of June 1878 where you see John Bull with one doctor on each side of him, each given his caption. Dr William Gladstone says, 'I warn you Mr Bull your constitution is being seriously impaired by that person's treatment'. Mr Benjamin Disraeli remarks, 'My dear Mr Bull your constitution is perfectly safe in my hands'.

On at least three issues *Punch* and Gladstone were not in agreement with each other. *Punch* was plainly anti-Irish throughout the nineteenth century, and a terrifying cartoon pairing Gladstone and Parnell

I. Disraeli and Gladstone: pottery figures. Disraeli (Beaconsfield) (*top left*); Gladstone (*top right*); Gladstone, with bag (*bottom left*); Disraeli (*bottom right*). (*Lord Briggs*)

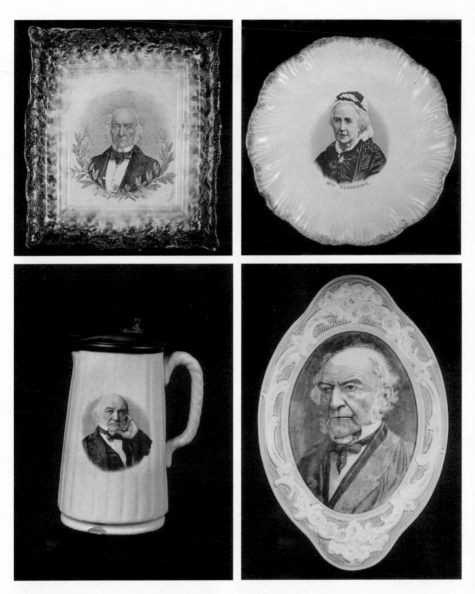

II. Gladstone, rectangular dish with blue lattice work (mid 1880s) (*top left*); Mrs Gladstone, cream plate with sepia portrait (mid 1880s) (*top right*); Gladstone jug (mid 1880s) (*bottom left*); Gladstone, rectangular plaque, B. & L. Middleport (mid 1880s) (*bottom right*). (*Flintshire Record Office; bottom right St Deiniol's Library*)

III. William Ewart Gladstone, the Young Politician, portrait by W. Bradley (1839).
(*C. A. Gladstone*)

IV. George Grote (1833). (*University College London, Manuscripts Room*)

V. Gladstone as Prime Minister (early 1870s). (*Flintshire Record Office*)

VI. Gladstone reading. (*Flintshire Record Office*)

Shelving his books in the original St Deiniol's Library (1890s).

In his study, 'The Temple of Peace'. Hawarden Castle (late 1880s).

VII. Gladstone and his books. (*Flintshire Record Office*)

VIII. Gladstone tree felling (1877). (*Flintshire Record Office*)

Fig. 18. Gladstone reciting.

called 'Gladstone Committing Treason', appeared at the time of the Kilmainham Treaty. *Punch's* stereotype images of Irish men and women, depicting them as lazy and dirty, are the least attractive features in a major medium of communication. (By contrast recall that it was Reid's *Leeds Mercury* that flew the Hawarden Kite.) *Punch* was imperialist in attitudes also, while Gladstone was not.

In my view historians have over-used *Punch* cartoons and not looked carefully enough at other people's cartoons of Gladstone, including an anti-Gladstone collection of cartoons which appeared in booklet form in the 1880s and which shows what Conservatives were making of Gladstone at that time when the Liberal Party he had created was disintegrating. Alongside the Furniss cartoons of a later period we should set those of Phil May, many of the most interesting of them showing Gladstone in the course of speaking, his favourite occupation. He loved reciting, too, although few of his loyal supporters had the opportunity of hearing him do so. That was reserved for private society.

This brings me to my point which is a plea for finding a place in Gladstone studies for what at present may seem to be communications – or popular culture – studies beyond the fringe. In concentrating on the public I am aware how important and, indeed, how profound are studies of the private Gladstone which have acquired a new depth as a result of the scholarly long-term enterprise of editing Gladstone's diaries which my colleague Colin Matthew has completed. It is always necessary to look behind the public persona, however it was devised – and my essay serves as a lead-in to this subject – to the Gladstone of the diaries.

Some key passages in them relate the public and the private, as Gladstone himself thought that they were related. Thus, for example, on the first Sunday after Christmas in December 1879, he wrote revealingly – and perhaps very quickly – in a style very different from his public speeches:

For the past $3\frac{1}{2}$ years I have been passing through a political experience which is I believe without example in our Parliamentary history. I profess ... to believe it has been an occasion, when the battle to be fought was a battle of justice humanity freedom law, all in their first elements from the very root, and all on a gigantic scale. The word spoken was a word for millions, and for millions who themselves cannot speak. If I really believe this [an eloquent *if*] then I should regard my having been morally forced into this work as a great and high election of God. And certainly I cannot but believe that He has given me special gifts of strength . . . But alas the poor little garden of my own soul remains uncultivated, unweeded and defaced. So then while I am bound to accept this election for the time, may I not be permitted to pray that the time shall be short.

His time was not to be short, and in meditating on himself he was to spend at least as much time addressing the millions.

Such key passages, some of considerable length, stand out prominently in the diaries, but many of the other entries are short and do little more than record activities and events. As far as the Gladstone of this essay is concerned, I am awaiting eagerly the publication of Matthew's index volume to the diaries. It will be an invaluable work of reference telling me, I hope, just how many photographs and portraits and busts and statues of Gladstone there really are. The cartoons will be legion. Some of the other artefacts will be difficult to index. There is scope, therefore, for continuing research.

One set of bridge studies, linking the studies of the private and the public Gladstone, is the study of the Gladstone family, initiated by another colleague of mine, S.G. Checkland, who, like me, was interested in Birmingham before he turned to Hawarden. His book *The Gladstones: A Family Biography* (1971) sadly ended in 1851. Reid included one relevant chapter in his large volume on 'Mr Gladstone's Home Life'. It started in his 'Temple of Peace' at Hawarden. I have referred at some length in this essay to photographs of Gladstone. Those he particularly prized included a family group, taken by a Chester photographer in 1884. Disraeli could never have paired that.

3

Gladstone and Disraeli

Robert Blake

The general election of April 1880 resulted in a crushing defeat for Disraeli and his party. On 24 April, just after Gladstone had returned in triumph to office, Lord Granville wrote to Queen Victoria, who was deeply distressed. He wished to calm her down with regard to the strong language which Gladstone had used against the late Prime Minister during the election campaign.

> Lord Beaconsfield and Mr Gladstone are men of extraordinary ability; they dislike each other more than is usual among public men. Of no other politician Lord Beaconsfield would have said in public, that his conduct was worse than those who had committed the Bulgarian atrocities. He has the power of saying in two words that which drives a person of Mr Gladstone's peculiar temperament into a state of great excitement.

Granville had always been on good terms with Disraeli; he was a guest at Disraeli's first and, as it turned out, last dinner party at his new house in Curzon Street on 10 March 1881. He was also, perhaps more than any other Liberal Minister, on really intimate terms with Gladstone himself. He actually persuaded him on one occasion to attend the Derby. So his verdict is not to be lightly set aside.

There is no point in pretending that the two old statesmen did not detest each other. They did. Gladstone, it is true, denied that he actually hated Disraeli, and said that he did not believe Disraeli hated him. It is to the credit of Gladstone's heart, rather than his head, that he should have been under this delusion. Lord Acton, who knew Gladstone very well, implored him after Disraeli's death not to propose a public monument to a man whom, he said, Gladstone regarded as 'the worst and most immoral Minister since Castlereagh'. If Gladstone did not in his own interpretation actually hate Disraeli, he certainly regarded him as essentially a force for evil in public life. 'In past times', he wrote at the end of his life, long after Disraeli's death, 'the Tory party had principles by which it would and did stand for bad and for good. All this Dizzy destroyed'. And when Disraeli died, having given instructions in his will to be buried quietly at Hughenden beside his wife, Gladstone, who had offered Westminster Abbey to the executors, wrote in his diary: 'As he lived, so he died – all display without reality or genuineness'. He could not believe that this was anything but a last theatrical gesture of fraudulent false modesty. It was for Gladstone, the most magnanimous of men, a quite exceptionally unmagnanimous remark.

But Gladstone's language about Disraeli was more moderate than Disraeli's about Gladstone. Just before his death Disraeli had been engaged on an unfinished novel designed to hold up his great rival to odium and ridicule. There is something wonderfully disreputable, undignified and yet engaging about this curious fragment. It is as if Sir Winston Churchill, instead of writing his memoirs in 1945, had started a latter-day version of *Savrola* in which he lampooned Lord Attlee. The hero, if that is the right word, is Joseph Toplady Falconet. The Christian names are not chosen accidentally: Joseph alludes to Joseph Surface, the immortal hypocrite in the *School for Scandal*, and Toplady was an intolerantly vituperative divine who detested Wesley and – more to the point – wrote 'Rock of Ages' which Gladstone in 1839 had translated into Latin.

Joseph Toplady Falconet, son of Mr Wilberforce Falconet, a wealthy evangelical merchant, is 'arrogant and peremptory'; as a boy 'scarcely ever known to smile ... with a complete deficiency in the sense of humour'; a prodigy of Eton and Oxford where he was 'the unrivalled orator of its mimic parliament'; 'his chief peculiarity was his disputatious temper and the flow of language which even as a child was ever at his command to express his arguments'. He was essentially a prig and among prigs there is a freemasonry which never fails. All the prigs spoke of him as the coming man. Disraeli's opinion of Gladstone earlier had been even worse. Perhaps the nadir of their personal relations was reached during the Eastern Crisis of 1876–78. In October 1876 he wrote to Lord Derby: 'Posterity will do justice to that unprincipled maniac Gladstone – extraordinary mixture of envy, vindictiveness, hypocrisy and superstition; and with one commanding characteristic – whether Prime Minister, or Leader of the Opposition, whether preaching, praying, speechifying or scribbling – never a gentleman'.

Fig. 19. 'Critics', cartoon by Tenniel, *Punch* (14 May 1870). Mr G-D-S-T-N-E, 'Hm! Flippant!' Mr D-I-R-Li 'Ha! Prosy!'

Disraeli oscillated between Queen Victoria's view that Gladstone was insane and the more common Tory theory that he was a monstrous hypocrite. On the whole he plumped for the latter – 'a ceaseless Tartuffe from the beginning', as he wrote to Lady Bradford, and in his letters Mrs Gladstone not infrequently figures as 'Mrs T' for short.

Too often biographers of these two extraordinary men have felt it their duty to see their hero's enemy through their hero's eyes, and to denigrate or at least sneer at the opponent almost as if the battle was still raging when they wrote. This is absurd over a century after Gladstone's death, and he after all outlived Disraeli by seventeen years. Sir Philip Magnus in his excellent life of Gladstone was one of the first to break this custom. He is indeed generous to Disraeli. We can, surely, today give up archaic partisanship and consider instead the origins and nature of their conflict, and its consequences on the political scene.

Their youthful years could scarcely have been in sharper contrast. Disraeli, unlike Gladstone, did not keep a diary, except for a short period in the early 1800s. But *Vivian Grey* is avowedly and sufficiently autobiographical for our purpose. To Vivian at eighteen, surveying the possibilities of his career, 'The idea of Oxford was an insult'.

> ... THE BAR – pooh! law and bad jokes till we are forty; and then with the most brilliant success the prospect of gout and a coronet ... THE SERVICES in war time are fit only for desperadoes (and that truly am I); but in peace are fit only for fools. THE CHURCH is more rational ... I should certainly like to act Wolsey; but the thousand and one chances against me! ...

What Vivian Grey decided to do is irrelevant. What Disraeli did, as we all know, was to entangle himself in a self-woven web of financial, journalistic and speculative intrigue which left him with a heavy load of debt and ill repute while he was still twenty-one, but in no way diminished that restless ambition, that determination to get to the top of the greasy pole, which dominated all his dreams. Gladstone for the whole of his life thought about the church, though scarcely in the spirit of Disraeli's fictitious hero. At Oxford he was convinced that to take Holy Orders was his real career. He was dissuaded partly by his father, partly by the opportune offer of a pocket borough by the Duke of Newcastle, whose son was one of his closest Christ Church friends. To the end of his days he regarded politics as subordinate to religion. No purely political biography of him, however valuable it may be as history, can ever adequately portray him as a man.

Gladstone's diary is a most remarkable document which provides the material for a reassessment of his entire career. Those for 1825–39, admirably edited by Professor Michael Foot, are in themselves enough to convince anyone of his extraordinary character: the deep obsession with his own sinfulness; the agonising self-examination; the determination to render account to God for every moment of his life; the guilty consciousness of worldly – or as he put it 'carnal' – backsliding. One of the most revealing passages about his time at Oxford is the entry written on 24 March 1830. The day before, he noted, he 'had to go to Veysie [one of the Censors, i.e. disciplinary officers of Christ Church] about a most disgraceful disturbance in Chapel last night'. Evidently the disturbers took umbrage and what followed made Gladstone abandon the normal telegraphese in which he wrote.

> Last night between twelve and one I was beaten by a party of men in my rooms. Here I have great reason to be thankful to that God whose mercies fail not. And this for two reasons.
>
> 1. Because this incident must tend to the mortification of my pride by God's grace; if at least any occurrence which does not border on the miraculous can ... I hardly know what to think of my own conduct myself. It is no disgrace to be beaten, for Christ was buffeted and smitten – but though calm reasoning assures me of this my habit of mind, my vicious corrupt nature asserts the contrary – may it be defeated.
> 2. Because here I have to some extent an opportunity of exercising the duty of forgiveness. So long a time has elapsed since anyone has in any way injured me that I have feared, in repeating the words 'forgive us our trespasses as we forgive them that trespass against us' that I really had no practical knowledge of the nature and spirit of the words I was uttering.

What was it that convinced Gladstone that he was, in his own words on his twentieth birthday, 'the chief of sinners'? We shall probably never know. It may have been connected, as Professor Foot suggests, with the impossibly high ideals which he absorbed from his much older sister Anne who died when he was nineteen. It may have been what he called, in an entry written on his twenty-second birthday, 'the blackness of my natural (and vigorous) tendencies'. There are many possibilities. What is certain is that self-mortification, the consciousness of sin, the desire to make amends by bringing the highest moral principles into the political career which he always regarded as second best to the church were among his principal springs of action. It is an easy step from the particular to the general. If Gladstone more than most statesmen was ready to see the sin of pride in his fellow countrymen, to regard a certain degree of self-mortification as being good for them too, we need not be surprised that he was the very opposite to a jingo, that he found himself ill at ease in a Cabinet headed by Palmerston, and that Disraeli's 'alien patriotism' aroused his deepest disapproval.

Disraeli from his youth onwards was a much less complicated character than Gladstone. His life, his affairs, his manoeuvres were of course highly complicated, but his objective was simple, his reactions predictable. His aim was above all to *be* someone, to get to the top. What he did when he was there would be settled by circumstances, pressures, events. If one is to seek the causes of his driving ambition, it is possible to suggest two, though it is impossible to be completely certain of either. One was his sense of being an outsider, an alien, a person who did not belong. He never said this, but no one can read the autobiographical passages of his novels, particularly *Contarini Fleming*, without a strong conviction that he felt it and that he was determined to conquer the great world partly because he knew that he could never belong to it. The other is his unhappy relationship with his mother, who regarded him as 'a clever boy but no genius' and who never gave him the devotion which his intensely egotistical nature craved. Again and again, through Disraeli's sophistication, his poses, his play-acting, one sees the little boy crying out 'look at me' to an unreceptive sceptical mamma 'troubled about many things', not unkind or hostile, but not prepared to adore.

Let us trace the way the careers of the two men entwined with one another. Disraeli, as everyone knows, began his many unsuccessful efforts to storm his way into Parliament as a Radical. Gladstone did not have to storm at all. Macaulay later dubbed him 'the rising hope of those stern and unbending Tories'. Gladstone was five years younger than Disraeli and got into Parliament five years earlier – in 1832 when he was just under twenty-three. Their ways did not cross much in those days for they dwelt in totally different worlds: Disraeli moved in the raffish salons of aristocratic Bohemia and his time was spent in avoiding his creditors and conducting a prolonged liaison with a married woman, varied at intervals by attempts to get into the House and by the production of literary works which at best never quite came off and at worst were disastrous (his good ones nearly all belong to a later date); Gladstone was deeply involved in theological reading, improving his debating power and searching, though not with immediate success, for a suitable wife. Sir Philip Magnus quotes two symbolic extracts from their diaries. On 1 September 1833 Disraeli wrote: 'I have spent the whole of this year in uninterrupted lounging and pleasure'. On 29 December 1832 Gladstone wrote: 'I have now familiarised myself with maxims encouraging a degree of intercourse with society, perhaps attended with much risk, nay perhaps only rendered acceptable to my understanding by cowardice and a carnal heart'.

The first recorded occasion on which they actually met was at a dinner party given by Lord Lyndhurst, the Tory Lord Chancellor, on 17 January 1835. Gladstone was a junior Lord of the Treasury in Peel's government. Disraeli had given up Radicalism and was a sort of private secretary to Lyndhurst – one of the oddest and least reputable figures to have been keeper of the king's conscience. Disraeli was still without a seat. Gladstone made no note of Disraeli's presence in his diary, though years later he declared that he recalled with amazement the foppery of his clothes. Disraeli noted in a letter to his sister that 'young Gladstone' was present. The dinner, he continued, was 'rather dull but we had a swan very white and tender and stuffed with truffles, the best company there'. Two years later he got into the House. Whether Gladstone was present at the fiasco of his maiden speech we do not know. When the Conservatives returned to power in 1841 Gladstone was naturally given office, and soon afterwards entered the Cabinet. Disraeli, not surprisingly, and despite his own importunacy, was left out. He never forgave Peel but there is nothing to show that he and Gladstone had any particular relationship, hostile or otherwise, at this time. Disraeli did express in a letter to his sister after Gladstone's resignation speech over the Maynooth Grant early in 1845 his belief that Gladstone had no future in politics. But many others also found Gladstone's behaviour incomprehensible on this occasion. So far there had been no conflict between the two men.

Yet by summer 1852, seven years later, it is clear that Gladstone had come to entertain a profound personal mistrust for Disraeli. Much had happened in politics by then. Gladstone would still have called himself a Conservative but he belonged to the minority of the party who had followed Peel over the repeal of the Corn Laws, and his group was more hostile to the majority of the Conservatives under Derby and Disraeli than to the Whigs. Moreover, Disraeli was Chancellor of the Exchequer, and Gladstone, ever since his pupillage at the Board of Trade when Peel was Prime Minister, had regarded himself as in a peculiar degree the guardian of Peelite fiscal orthodoxy. On 30 July we learn that he regards every speech of Disraeli that summer on finance as being 'more quackish in its flavour than its predecessor'.

And for the first time we find that he is entertaining personal feelings of hostility not explicable simply by differences in political outlook. He complains on 5 August to Lord Aberdeen of the government's 'shifting and shuffling' on the Catholic question due, he says, 'partly to the (surely not unexpected) unscrupulousness and second motives of Disraeli, at once the necessity of Lord Derby and his curse'.

Clearly by then Gladstone had a strong personal mistrust of Disraeli's character. There is nothing to show that it was as yet reciprocated. Rather the contrary. As late as September Disraeli was commending his protégé, Lord Henry Lennox, for using his vote in favour of Gladstone at the Oxford University election earlier that year. But he can have had no doubt where he stood with Gladstone two months later. For in December there was a confrontation – and a dramatic one. Disraeli had made the winding-up speech, or so he supposed, in defence of his highly vulnerable budget. He had engaged in personal remarks against his opponents and, although he had much provocation, he had gone beyond the normal limits tolerated by the House. Gladstone had not been personally attacked but he was indignant for those who had been. When Disraeli sat down most members expected a division. But Gladstone, amidst catcalls, hoots and screams – the House of Commons has not changed! – leapt to his feet, and, first delivering a grave personal rebuke to Disraeli, proceeded to cut the budget to pieces. When the division was taken the government was defeated, and Disraeli was to be in Opposition for the next five years.

Of course many people mistrusted Disraeli. There was something highly provocative about him, a brazenness, a sarcastic turn of phrase, an insolence, a readiness to discard inconvenient pledges, and a refusal to cover up that process with the normal politician's linguistic cotton wool; all of these enraged his opponents beyond measure – and no wonder. Then there was a particular resentment felt by the followers of Peel. Although Peel really was open to the charge of betrayal – perhaps just because he was – his friends particularly resented the onslaughts upon him; and no one delivered these more tellingly than Disraeli and no one was more loyal to Peel than Gladstone.

But in Gladstone's case there may have been another cause for hostility to Disraeli. Like many great statesmen and almost all successful politicians, Gladstone was a master of oratory, only really at home when clothing his thoughts in the spoken word. As Lytton Strachey puts it, 'Speech was the fibre of his being'. Yet at a crucial moment in his own career and in the affairs of the nation this was just what was denied to him. For, although he returned to the Cabinet in 1845 and was Colonial Secretary for six months during the great Corn Law crisis, he failed to get himself reelected to Parliament. So he could not intervene in debate and come to the aid of his beloved chief. He had to sit in the Strangers' Gallery and listen in silence to Disraeli's brilliant, cruel and very funny attacks upon Peel. The situation was the more galling because Peel was no good at answering back himself. For whatever reason he simply could not cope with this sort of thing. Years later, after Disraeli's death, Morley asked Gladstone whether Disraeli's famous philippics were really as effective as people said. 'Mr G', he recorded, 'said Disraeli's performances against Peel were quite as wonderful as report makes them. Peel altogether helpless in reply. Dealt with them with a kind of "righteous dullness".' Is it possible that Gladstone's real hostility to Disraeli first stemmed from a sense of frustration at his own forced inability to answer on behalf of a chief to whom he was devoted?

However that may be, there is no doubt about the animosity felt on both sides after the budget of 1852. It was not made any less by the fact that Gladstone succeeded Disraeli as Chancellor of the Exchequer. Almost at once they had a row about two things: first, about the Chancellor's robe, which Disraeli, believing it to have been Pitt's, was determined to keep; secondly, about the payment for the furniture at 11 Downing Street. It is enough to say that on the robe Disraeli was in the wrong though he got away with it – literally (it is on exhibit at Hughenden to this day), while on the furniture he seems to have been in the right. The correspondence, which is entertaining, has been published in full. Its tone can be gauged by Disraeli's last letter, which was written in the third person and ended: 'As Mr Gladstone seems to be in some perplexity on the subject, Mr Disraeli recommends him to consult Sir Charles Wood who is a man of the world'. (Wood was Disraeli's predecessor as Chancellor.)

This last expression, 'man of the world', brings me to a point about their relations which has sometimes been overlooked. Disraeli consciously prided himself on being a man of the world, sophisticated, unshockable, moving easily in society. In some respects he was a Romantic in politics, but in ideas rather than behaviour. For example, he adopted Lord Chesterfield's advice to his wretched son and scarcely ever laughed in public. It was part of the Byronic pose to be both Romantic and cynical at the same time. A man's heart could seethe with poetry, drama, rhetoric, but his manners could be cool and urbane, his tone at a dinner party witty and sardonic, his general air that of a somewhat bored man of fashion. This was very much Disraeli's style, and a great deal of his effectiveness in the House of Commons was that of a sensible cool-headed man of affairs, not fussing too much about high moral issues which were a matter for the middle classes, but putting a reasonable case to other reasonable men of affairs. Disraeli and Gladstone both came in one sense from the middle class, though Gladstone was far richer and had a typical upper-class education at Eton and Christ Church, whereas Disraeli went to obscure schools and no university at all. On the face of things, with his marriage into the Whig aristocracy Gladstone ought to have been socially above Disraeli. True, he always spoke, even as Peel had, with a provincial accent, whereas Disraeli talked in the Queen's English (although in a rather curious way: for example he always said 'par-l-i-ament', 'bus-i-ness', etc). But the social nuances of a bygone era are not easy to distinguish. The fourteenth Earl of Derby, the Prime Minister, spoke impeccable English. His son, the fifteenth Earl and Foreign Secretary, spoke, if Disraeli is to be believed, 'in a sort of Lancashire patois'.

In fact Disraeli thought of himself as an aristocrat. He persuaded himself that the Jews were the most 'aristocratic of races' – whatever that expression means; and that he belonged to its most aristocratic branch. His facts were very dubious but this does not affect the genuineness of his belief. Hence some of those curious Disraeliana – or curious as from the son of a middle-class Jewish littérateur. 'What can one expect', he wrote once when in opposition, 'with a government that does not move in Society?' Or his comment on his Home Secretary, Sir Richard Cross, who had explained to the House that the Prime Minister was absent 'on account of the *state of his health*!!! What language. This comes of giving high office to a middle class man'. Thus then we have Disraeli, a self-promoted member of the upper class, friend of the Queen, repository of her family secrets, consulted on royal marriages, mediator in the great row between Lord Randolph Churchill and the Prince of Wales, and from 1874 to 1880 at the apex of society as well as politics. The social world may have thought him odd but it accepted him.

Now Gladstone for all his background was never 'a man of the world' in Disraeli's sense. And his marriage actually enhanced this unworldliness, for Mrs Gladstone was in some ways socially naive, though not of course to anything like the degree of Mrs Disraeli. Gladstone's attitude should not be misunderstood. He was not in the least a prig, despite Falconet. He had for himself a standard of the highest moral rectitude, but he did not expect others to conform to it, and he was tolerant of human failings. I often think that some people at the height of the Profumo scandal might with advantage have remembered Gladstone's words to Morley at the height of the Parnell scandal. He refused all pleas to issue a public moral condemnation. 'What!' he cried, 'because a man is what is called leader to a party, does that constitute him a censor and a judge of faith and morals? I will not accept it. It would make life intolerable!'

The notion that he was an austere, bleak figure – a sort of Sir Stafford Cripps of the Victorian era – is quite untrue. I once asked, in a miniature and highly superficial Opinion Poll of my pupils, whether they thought Gladstone was an abstainer. The great majority did. Quite incorrectly. There is an interesting note in the minutes of Grillions – a very old and still flourishing parliamentary-cum-literary dining club to which both Gladstone and Disraeli belonged, one of the few places where they sometimes met socially. On one occasion Gladstone was the only member present: the minutes record that a bottle of champagne was consumed. As a young man Gladstone was fond of shooting, cards and wine parties. He took wine with his meals all his life and almost to the end of his days abhorred a teetotal dinner.

Nor was he a severe *paterfamilias*. His family life was gay and happy. His children adored him. He in return was kind and tolerant to them. He used to try to catch them out. Guests at the family table were astonished when after some deliberately false dictum of their host a childish treble – 'a lie, a lie!' – would be heard from the other end, treated with urbane amusement by the GOM himself.

There was nevertheless something about him which to Disraeli and a great many other Tories was repugnant, and even to many Liberals disconcerting. Gladstone had an intensity, a fervour, a conviction of absolute right and wrong, which astonished and disturbed the aristocratic world that to the end of his life continued to dominate politics. It was the secret of his appeal to the Nonconformist conscience, and it was, more often than not, directed against things which most of us now agree to have been either outrageous, like the Bulgarian atrocities and the Armenian massacres, or in the end indefensible – the Irish Church and the rule of Dublin Castle. But there was something about Gladstone's (metaphorical) tone of voice which enraged the sophisticated, the 'man of the world', in both parties. It enraged no one more than it enraged Disraeli who, just as he overplayed most of his parts, overplayed that of the slightly cynical man of sense. At times one feels that Disraeli's antipathy to Gladstone – and Gladstone's to Disraeli –

was not simply caused by the differences of their political outlook on concrete issues, important though these were, but rather by their whole approach to politics, their way of thinking, their political style. What Disraeli disliked was the bringing of morality and religion into politics – to him an essentially practical business. By the same token Gladstone deplored the cynical amorality of his old enemy.

The two nations that fought each other during much of the nineteenth century were not Disraeli's 'THE RICH AND THE POOR' but divergent groups among the rich – or moderately rich. As Dr Kitson Clark put it: 'There were . . . in Britain two nations struggling in the bosom of one land – an old nation based upon the old nobility, upon the squires and upon the Established Church, and a new nation based on commerce and industry, and in religion mainly dissenting'.

It was not a straightforward conflict. There were many crosscurrents. Yet at the risk of oversimplification it is fair to see in Peel and his disciple Gladstone symbols and standard bearers of the new nation. Of course they were not dissenters or commercial men; they had an upper-class education, they belonged to upper-class clubs, they possessed, or controlled, or believed in, landed property. None the less they stood not only for compromise with, but also for sympathy with the new nation. They were at least in part converts to its values and ideals. Gladstone in particular had all its earnestness, its belief in hard work, its attachment to the ideal of godliness and good learning.

Disraeli was a complete contrast. However much later circumstances obliged him to take a Peelite line, despite having led the attack on Peel in 1846, he had no sympathy whatever with the new nation. He might, like every statesman of the age, have to compromise with it, but he was never a convert. His personal values were those of the early nineteenth-century aristocracy. One paid one's debts of honour but tradesmen had to take their chance – and in Disraeli's case it was a pretty thin chance too. As for religion, one conformed outwardly, perhaps even inwardly, but did not make a public display of it. If one was insulted, the response was a challenge to a duel. One was not necessarily promiscuous in matters of sex, but one certainly did not worry unduly about the seventh commandment. Politics was a matter of practical management of particular problems, with the underlying purpose of keeping things much as they were at home – upholding 'the aristocratic settlement of this country', as Disraeli wrote to Derby – and preserving the honour and grandeur of England abroad.

Gladstone was not, at least in one sense of the phrase, hostile to the aristocratic settlement. He may have disapproved of the 'Upper Ten Thousand' but he never envisaged a social order in which the landed aristocracy would not be in the governing class, and he regarded with horror anything that would tend towards the confiscation of landed property. But he believed profoundly in the need for that class to be imbued with the earnestness, the moral purity, the readiness for hard work which, in his eyes, characterised the best elements of the Nonconformist middle class and, as the years went by, the best elements of the Nonconformist working class too. Above all, the aristocracy should govern morally and impartially in the public interest, not in any narrow class interest. It was Gladstone's tone of voice more than his actual policies which appealed to the world outside the magic circle. This explains the seeming paradox of the Old Etonian, Puseyite landowner becoming the hero of the dissenting shopkeeper and the chapel-going artisan.

Not that Gladstone had no influence on the upper class. On all counts Lord Rosebery, who seemed almost a caricature of a Young England aristocrat, ought to have been a Disraelian. Yet, fascinated though he was by Disraeli, he joined Gladstone. And on a more frivolous level there is the sad story of Monckton-Milnes, Lord Houghton, the possessor of a pornographic library which was said to be unrivalled in Europe. He once dreamed that he was being pursued by Gladstone in a hansom cab. In his effort to escape he fell out of bed and broke his collar bone.

The position which the two men held in relation to particular social classes partly answers the question often asked: why has there never again been another Disraeli and Gladstone at the head of the right and left respectively? The reason is partly of course the accident of personality: they were unique figures. Apart from that, one cannot easily envisage quite such an adventurer again climbing to the top of the Tory Party or quite such an Old Testament prophet being swept to the summit of the Liberal or Labour Parties. The old aristocracy was never a caste. It was raffish, gay, tolerant of new men as long as they were amusing and justified their keep. But even in Disraeli's lifetime a change was occurring. The aristocracy and the wealthy middle class began to merge. Each accepted something of the other's values. Respectability now became essential. 'I was never respectable', Disraeli truly told one of the Fourth Party. And so the pirates and the buccaneers could no longer get away with it. Lord Salisbury defeats Lord Randolph Churchill. Only the convulsions of war can bring F.E. Smith to the Lord Chancellorship, Lord Beaverbrook to the

Cabinet, Winston Churchill to the premiership itself. Otherwise it is the Baldwins and the Chamberlains who win the day. Would the young Disraeli get the nomination today for even a shaky Conservative seat? I doubt it.

A change also took place on the other side of the political divide. Bread and butter issues replaced the great moral questions on which Gladstone thrived. The Bulgarian atrocities had rallied the Liberal Party and created a convulsion in the nation. Twenty years later the Armenian massacres, in comparison, created scarcely a stir; and by then the Irish Question – another great moral question – far from rallying the Liberal Party had divided it as damagingly as ever Peel's policy had divided the Tories. There was no longer a place for the religious crusade appealing to the higher moral sentiments. Campbell-Bannerman, Asquith, Lloyd George were the men of the Liberal future.

It is very rare that two political opponents polarise the political sentiments of their day to quite the extent that these two did. Balfour and Campbell-Bannerman, Bonar Law and Asquith, Baldwin and Mac-Donald, Churchill and Attlee were at times divided politically almost as deeply and were certainly dissimilar characters. But somehow the battle never became quite the same sort of personal combat. So strong an impression has this made on posterity that we tend to see the direct confrontation between Gladstone and Disraeli as lasting for a large part of the Victorian era. In fact it was not for so very long. They faced each other as respective leaders of their parties in the House of Commons for little over eight years. Nevertheless, posterity is basically right. Their conflict did affect political attitudes for longer than that, and well beyond Disraeli's death: for example, the bitter suspicion with which the Conservatives treated Gladstone's espousal of Home Rule in 1886 is at least partly explained by their resentment at his attacks on Disraeli during the Eastern Crisis and the Midlothian campaigns nearly ten years earlier.

When they actually did confront each other in the House of Commons it was like one of those curious conflicts between incongruously armed opponents, beloved in the circus of ancient Rome – Retiarius against Secutor, Thracians against Mirmillones. Disraeli never tried to meet Gladstone on his own ground. On the contrary, he would listen with half-closed eyes, his hat forward over his head, to the torrential eloquence of his great enemy. But he never missed a trick. Once when Gladstone paused a moment, seeming to lose the thread of his oration, Disraeli leant forward as if to help and said in a voice audible all over the House 'Your last word was re-vo-lut-i-on'. But Gladstone sometimes got his own back. On another occasion Disraeli's manner of speech suggested that he had consumed rather more wine than was prudent. Gladstone in reply said: 'The Rt Hon. Gentleman speaking under the influence . . ', – and he paused – 'of great excitement', and the House roared with laughter.

One could probably say of them as parliamentarians that honours were even. As Ministers, no. The most ardent admirer of Disraeli must concede that Gladstone was more thorough, more knowledgeable, more energetic, better briefed. One has only to contrast the slapdash nature of Disraeli's first budget (1852), in which he muddled up all the income tax schedules, with the immensely competent and carefully planned first budget of Gladstone the following year. And Gladstone, who was of course in office far more than Disraeli, showed his superiority in the field of legislation again and again. The contrast in the length of their official experience is worth mentioning. Down to Disraeli's death in April 1881, Gladstone had been in office for nineteen and a half years, Disraeli only eleven. More strikingly perhaps, Gladstone had had thirteen years of official experience before he became Prime Minister, Disraeli less than four: figures which of course reflect the fact that for half a century or more after 1832 the Liberals were the normal majority party. In common they had their apprenticeship at the Exchequer. Disraeli held no other post before he reached the top. Gladstone held it for nine years all told. It is partly because of them that the Chancellorship became so important. Hitherto the second man in the government had usually been at the Foreign or Home Office. The Foreign Office remained an important stepping-stone, but the Home Office was replaced by the Exchequer.

But statistics and institutions are dry-as-dust affairs; let us return to personalities. What were they like? Two points are to my mind commonly misconstrued. Most people, basing themselves on his novels and other dicta, would regard Disraeli as the more cosmopolitan and cultivated of the two. In fact it was Gladstone. He travelled much more than Disraeli. In addition to a first-class knowledge of the classics, he was at home in French, Italian and German. He was very widely read, probably more so than any Prime Minister before or since, and he conducted a vast correspondence with theologians and scholars all over Europe.

Disraeli, apart from his famous grand tour of the Mediterranean and Near East in 1830–31, which left an indelible impression on his mind, went abroad very little and when he did it was for the most part to rather conventional places, Paris or the Rhine Valley. His classical knowledge had very shaky foundations, though he could put up a good show and managed to pull the wool over the eyes of Sir Stafford Northcote. His command of modern languages was negligible, his French being notoriously atrocious. For example, he pronounced the last three letters of the French for grocer – *épicier*, as if it rhymed with 'beer'. When he made his famous breach with diplomatic protocol and addressed the Congress of Berlin in English instead of French, the customary international language, it was not, as was believed at the time, because he wished to make a John Bullish assertion of English prestige but because he was incapable of speaking in any other.

Disraeli, at any rate after he had sowed his wild oats, led a rather parochial life compared with Gladstone. Apart from visits to grand houses – no more nor grander than corresponding visits by Gladstone – he divided most of his time between London and the country. Here the two men did have something in common. Disraeli was as devoted to Hughenden as Gladstone was to Hawarden, and both received the same sort of mental and physical refreshment from their country houses and estates.

My second point is that most people who are asked whether Disraeli or Gladstone was the better company at luncheon or dinner or an evening party would unhesitatingly opt for Disraeli. I doubt whether they would be right. Gladstone was more conversational and easier to talk to – perhaps something of a monologuist but not a person to relapse into embarrassing silence. There was nothing of a stick about him. Rather, he was like quicksilver.

Disraeli's conversational gifts were, at their best, brilliant. But his best was rare. Much depended on the company. He was never good with men only. This was the defect of his education. Leaving an obscure school at sixteen, conscious even then of being in a sense an 'alien', missing Oxford contrary to his father's hopes, Disraeli never made those friendships with boys and men of his own age which were made by Gladstone and by most of Disraeli's political contemporaries. He had patrons like Lord Lyndhurst in his youth, disciples like Smythe and John Manners when he grew older. Equals were rare: Bulwer Lytton perhaps; and James Clay, a forgotten figure and his partner in the dissipations of the Orient. It is hard to think of others. Whatever the reason, Disraeli was on the defensive with men, disliked masculine dinners, and at mixed parties hated the moment when the ladies left and the port circulated amidst bawdy anecdotage and gossip about pheasants. He was far less gregarious than Gladstone. He was apt to shoot some barbed witticism into the air and leave his listeners vaguely uneasy and unsure how to reply. Even Queen Victoria must have been disconcerted when he said to her apropos of nothing in particular: 'I am the blank page between the Old Testament and the New'.

But in the company of women of all ages he blossomed marvellously. There he was at his most agreeable, amusing and entertaining. However strange some of them must have thought him, they rarely failed to be entranced. Disraeli maintained that his whole career depended upon women. It was an absurd exaggeration, but he certainly had a career in which the opposite sex played a bigger part than in that of his great rival. Yet they had one great thing in common: both made happy, indeed ideally happy, marriages, curiously enough in the same year, summer 1839; Disraeli after more than one dubious amour; Gladstone after two unsuccessful proposals to others. Their marriages were very different. Gladstone, who was thirty, married Miss Glynne, twenty-seven, a member of the Whig aristocracy – and married for love. Disraeli, who was thirty-four, married a childless middle-class widow, Mary Anne Wyndham-Lewis – twelve years older – and he married for money. The Gladstones were blessed with a large family. The Disraelis had no children, but although Disraeli married for money, it is true, as Mary Anne herself said, that 'Dizzy would have married me again for love'. Even Gladstone could find nothing to censure in Disraeli's conduct towards his wife, with whom indeed Gladstone personally got on quite well. His letter to Disraeli on her death is eloquently sympathetic, and Disraeli made a touching reply. There is something engaging too in the fact that the wives of the two great Victorian statesmen could at times make them in the privacy of their homes abandon their habitual grave deportment. Mr and Mrs Gladstone, we are told, in moments of exhilaration could stand on the hearthrug with arms round each other's waists singing the chorus

> A ragamuffin husband and a rantipoling wife,
> We'll fiddle it and scrape it through the ups and downs of life.

On at least one occasion Mr and Mrs Disraeli relaxed in a similar fashion. This was after one of Disraeli's rare visits to Scotland, a country which owing to its inveterate Liberalism he normally regarded with disfavour. 'The Scotch shall have no favours from me', he once wrote, 'until they return more Tory members to the H. of C.'. But in

November 1867 he successfully addressed a great Conservative banquet at Edinburgh, and the University conferred an honorary degree upon him.

> I fancied, indeed, till last night that north of the border I was not loved [he told Sir John Skelton], but last night made amends for much. We were so delighted with our reception, Mrs Disraeli and I, that after we got home we actually danced a jig (or was it a hornpipe?), in our bedroom.

However happy they made their husbands in domestic life, it has to be recorded that neither Mrs Gladstone nor Mrs Disraeli were assets in the social and political world. Mrs Disraeli's gaffes were and are famous, and Disraeli's iron restraint while he listened to them aroused general respect. Less well known is Mrs Gladstone's indifference to the social *convenances*. She was courteous and kind, like Gladstone, but she was casual and bad at returning calls, and did little to counteract her husband's worst political defects, his inability to remember names and faces, his reluctance to conciliate those neutral or wavering figures whose support was sometimes vital to him. Neither of the two ladies kept lavish tables, but Mrs Gladstone's was better than that of Mrs Disraeli, whose reputation among the gourmets could not have been lower.

The subject of the women in the two men's lives leads one inevitably to the Queen. The traditional notion that Gladstone treated her like – I will not say a public meeting – but like the embodiment of an institution, whereas Disraeli treated her like a woman, is broadly true. Gladstone certainly lacked tact. His wife saw what was needed. She wrote to him in 1863 before he visited Windsor: 'Now contrary to your ways, do *pet* the Queen, and for once believe you can, you dear old thing'. But, alas, Gladstone could no more have brought himself to pet the Queen than to pet a crocodile. In contrast Disraeli's skill at managing her, whether you call it tact or oriental flattery, is one of the commonplaces of history. Did he seek to consolidate his position, as some members of Gladstone's family came to believe, by making malicious innuendos about Gladstone's rescue work among the London prostitutes? There is no evidence for this in his papers or in the Royal Archives, but negative evidence cannot be conclusive. Much of their most private correspondence was destroyed by Edward VII, and in any case there are things one does not commit to paper.

Nevertheless, I like to think that he did not stoop to this, and on the whole it seems unlikely that he did. For it was unnecessary. The Queen disliked, indeed dreaded, Gladstone, not because he was tactless or because she suspected his morals, but above all because she deeply disapproved of his policies. Her language about him in private was indeed violent, for example, 'This half mad firebrand who would ruin everything and be a dictator'. But when Rosebery, whom she personally liked, replaced him, her language was scarcely less extreme. 'Lord Rosebery has made a speech so radical as to be almost communistic', she implausibly wrote on one occasion. The truth was that in the last thirty years of her enormous reign the Queen, however much she called herself 'a true Liberal', was in fact a Conservative Imperialist, and deeply opposed to almost every feature of Gladstonian Liberalism. No amount of 'tact' on Gladstone's part could have overcome this difficulty.

This brings me to a final question. How different were the actual policies of the two men, as opposed to their political styles and public images? The perspective of history tends to diminish political differences. We can see now that their basic views on the monarchy, the rights of property, the importance of landed estates, the enlargement of the electorate did not differ so very greatly. Both would have repudiated the levelling trends of the twentieth century. Gladstone declared that he was 'an out and out inequalitarian'. So was Disraeli. Both were opposed to the extension of the sphere of government, and both would have been horrified by its features today.

Yet, when that is said, important divergencies remain. Gladstone believed intensely in nationalism, in the virtues of 'nations struggling rightly to be free'. He sensed the 'wind of change' in Ireland long before anyone else of his calibre and status. He combined this with a deep conviction that political action should be a moral crusade, and that the great issues were essentially moral issues transcending particular British interests. He believed in the comity of nations, the concert of Europe, obedience to international law, the acceptance of arbitration. His attitude, with its idealism, its contradictions, its dilemmas, has coloured the parties of the left to some extent ever since.

Disraeli repudiated all this. The only nationalism with which he sympathised was English nationalism. This was in no way incompatible with being singularly unEnglish himself. All other nationalisms he suspected or ignored. Politics to him was not a question of high morality or crusading zeal. It was a matter of practical problems to be solved by common sense and a proper assertion of English interests. He believed in *Realpolitik* and the use of power. This was why he got on so well with Bismarck. His language may have been high flown, extravagant, fantastic, but it clothed a Palmerstonian attitude of straight English patriotism, no nonsense with foreigners, and preservation of the Empire. His attitude, with its dilemmas and difficulties, has to some extent coloured that of the right ever since.

It is largely this contrast which makes study of the two men so fascinating. And we need not today be partisan. Gladstone was not necessarily a superior statesman to Disraeli, though he was morally and intellectually superior, and in courage not inferior. But he was much more a creature of his own period. His language lacks the wit, freshness, the originality of his great rival who is a much more timeless figure. Disraeli could have lived either today or in the era of Gibbon and Lord North. This is not true of Gladstone. Although he was in no sense a typical Victorian, one feels nevertheless that he could only have flourished in the Victorian era.

That is perhaps why Disraeli has fascinated posterity more than Gladstone. But the interest of posterity is not necessarily an index of a person's worth, and precisely because the Victorian era is becoming a matter of such interest today to historians and to the educated public, interest in Gladstone's character and achievement is beginning to revive. Perhaps we should not try to make comparisons between them at all. Perhaps we should end as we began, with Lord Granville – 'Lord Beaconsfield and Mr Gladstone are men of extraordinary ability' – and leave it at that.

4

Gladstone and the Working Man

Simon Peaple and John Vincent

In the taproom of the Waggon and Horses, somewhere in the south
midlands, some time in the 1880s, all voices used to join in singing:

> God bless the People's William,
> Long may he lead the van,
> Of liberty and freedom,
> God bless the Grand Old Man.'

So Flora Thompson recalled in her magical *Lark Rise to Candleford*,[1] and
surely no other Prime Minister has so roused labouring men to song.
It was not a question of Gladstone being uniquely popular.
Palmerston, and the Duke before him, had been figures of legend.
Palmerston, not Gladstone, invented the media premiership. It was
more than mere renown that elevated Gladstone in taproom song. It
was the sense that he was the first Prime Minister to have the best
interests of the working man at heart.

Religion, Finance, Ireland, Peace: those are the four great Gladstonian themes. By comparison, Gladstone and the working man might
appear a topic of lesser concern, yet it has certainly endured longer.
We shall not see Gladstonian finance again. We see Ireland a foreign
republic, not, as Gladstone hoped, autonomous within a united British
Isles. Peace we may hope for, but it will not be a *Pax Britannica*. As for
church and state, they eye each other warily from an ever-increasing
distance. It is only the great Gladstonian intangible, social cohesion,
which has endured; and here the Victorian working man is at the
heart of the matter.

As always, there are two sides to any relationship. On the one hand,
there is what Gladstone thought the Victorian working man should
do and be.[2] On the other, there is the adulation offered by Victorian

working men to Gladstone. In both respects, there is new evidence to consider. Besides these two planks in our platform, there is the question of the broader historical context. Here it is a question of correcting a false, but still all too common, stereotype: that of the old man who had lost touch, the Gladstone who failed to adjust to the mass politics of the future, the Gladstone who, as it were, failed to be Clement Attlee.

At first sight Gladstone seems strangely silent about the working man. The condition of England question never received his concentrated attention. Hospitals and housing were not among his topics; about education he was strangely passive; there are no clusters of speeches, memoranda or articles. To fill the apparent void, one has to turn from the political to the non-political Gladstone, and look for clues in the little known Hawarden homilies, as they might be called: short exhortatory addresses given almost annually between 1875 (when Gladstone succeeded as squire) and 1897, on village occasions, usually in August, and usually but not always at the Flower Show. Speaking to village audiences, Gladstone could not but touch on the theme of how the working man might best live and thrive; and since, though speaking on a local occasion, the Press reported every word, Gladstone came to recognise that 'he had become an expositor to the nation at large'.[3]

His ideas were definite and altered little over the decades. His emphasis was more on what life demanded of the working man than on what the working man should demand from life. Thriving, to Gladstone, meant exertion. He wished the working man to improve his mind, to improve his income and to improve his skills, in roughly equal degree. He wished them to do this, without ceasing to be working men. He did not wish Adam Bede, George Eliot's noble carpenter, to become Bob Cratchit, Mr Scrooge's wretched clerk. Upward social mobility, into the overstocked ranks of the office worker, was not a plausible option. He thought rather that the working man should rise in the world by diversifying his sources of income and enriching his mind. The way forward lay in the labourer becoming an artisan, the artisan becoming in Ruskin's sense an artist, and in both becoming penny capitalists and in both reading the greatest products of the human mind.

This rural vision for an urban country contained elements of Samuel Smiles's mid-Victorian gospel of Self-Help,[4] laced with Ruskin's evangelical fervour about manual labour and combined with a foretaste of Chestertonian Christian distributism.[5] Gladstone's examples, however, were purely his own, and they were naturally those of a country landowner, spending half the year in the country, representing a farming constituency, and speaking to a village audience. The city poor, of whom Gladstone knew all too much, and Mrs Gladstone a good deal more,[6] did not connect, in his mind, with the world of the manly, responsible working man. The first, the world of outright deprivation,[7] was a field for charitable endeavour; the second, the world of the decent manual worker, admirable because charity did not come into it. This was no harsh judgement between deserving and undeserving poor, but simply how the respectable working man of the day himself saw matters and expected others to see them.

Year after year, Gladstone boldly stated three ideals: the value of cottage gardens – gardens, that is, as distinct from allotments;[8] the importance of fruit growing; the necessity of being like the Scotch. These of course, though important enough in their own right, were also symbols: symbols of the vigour and wit needed to keep the traditional rural social order intact in the face of the agricultural depression of 1879 and later.[9]

'Be like Scotland' was a recurrent theme. Scottish superiority in everyday living was extolled in 1875, 1877, 1879, 1882 and 1890. Just as when Gladstone spoke of Ireland he hardly had Dublin or Belfast in mind, so with Gladstone's Scotland: it did not mean Glasgow or even Edinburgh. What it brought to mind was Aberdeenshire, time and again, than which 'there was no more flourishing county in the whole island'. After all, only accidents of family history had prevented Gladstone's becoming a remote Scottish laird in the first place.

This Scottish theme supported his general case. Pioneers in fruit growing, pioneers in jam making, the Scotch were also much ahead in general culture: might there not be a connection? Warning the miners of Buckley, Flintshire, against the temptations of mental indolence, he urged them 'to go straight to the very heart of the Temple of Literature', seeking 'the greatest and best works which your country has ever produced', adding a reminder that the Scotch labouring classes, far from begrudging paying for education as in England, had always made it their rule to make parental sacrifices to pay school fees. Converting England to the sturdy way of life of eastern Scotland was no small part of Gladstone's agenda for the working man.

Cottage industry, or small culture (*petite culture*) as he called it, fascinated Gladstone, as much for moral and social as for economic reasons. Well it might, for it reconciled the two faces of Gladstonian liberalism: one, based on a stable moral order, founded on an alliance between the great landed estates and the church, and the other, the free and energetic initiative of free men in an almost stateless society. Spade cultivation, he held, was 'of enormous national importance':[10] he denounced the mid-Victorian fashion for consolidation of farms, pointing out that by common consent small farms had stood up to depression much better than large ones.

Cottage industry strengthened home and family, as allotments did not. Cottage industry used precious odd moments, where allotments involved time wasted on journeys; the produce was more secure; children were put to useful work. Cottage industry gave tenancy both independence and a capital value, yet with the landlord furnishing most of the capital. Cottage gardens, with supporting arguments carefully marshalled as if for a vote, represented landlordism at its best. Politically, they had the merit of not being part of the stock in trade of Joseph Chamberlain, with his 'Three Acres and a Cow' and its divisive overtones.

Distributist ideas normally turn on ownership of small property, with all its drawbacks. Gladstone, untypically, wanted to restore Naboth to his vineyard, but as a tenant. Small property, if directly owned, ties up so much of a poor man's scant capital, to so little productive purpose. Gladstone hoped to see the day 'when there will be no such thing as a cottage without a garden', as he said in 1876. In 1878, the year Ruskin twice visited Hawarden, Gladstone put the case of what he called 'art labour', such as embroidery, enjoining his hearers, or their wives, to work 'in the spirit of an artist' producing articles 'as full of beauty as they can make it'. (Embroidery, he remarked, was 'very well paid indeed'.)

In the dismal sodden summer of 1879, Gladstone preached the importance of gardening, for farmers as well as cottagers, as a remedy against distress. Flowers, vegetables, fruit could all become lucrative, as the long-headed Aberdonians had found. An acre of strawberries alone might fetch £200 or three men's annual incomes. Were not £2,200,000 fruit and nuts, all capable of being grown here, imported annually? With vegetables, the position was even worse, with some £3,000,000 per annum imported from abroad. As for apples, the picture was still blacker: where in 1839 71,000 bushels were imported, in 1888 3,800,000 bushels came from abroad. The great Free Trader, at heart, preferred national self-sufficiency, based on the adoption of various forms of market gardening which were immune to competition from cheap foreign producers.

If anyone had still not got a garden, he added, he would do his best to give them one. He had always sought to promote cottage gardening, and had tried to give everyone a garden when the village Horticultural Society was founded. Gardening, unlike modern industry, he added, was beautiful: it 'cultivated the sense of beauty in the people'.

Though teased, and aware of being teased, especially about the strawberries (which became a national byword), Gladstone was far from being deterred, becoming more not less zealous in his annual address with each passing year. By 1884 he could express pleasure that his advice was being taken. As so often, he had history on his side: the acreage under fruit rose from 90,000 acres in 1839 to 214,000 acres by 1889; with 60,000 heads of families, or so he claimed, employed in that glorious late Victorian innovation, the jam industry. As he put it: 'Though Free Trade was a fine thing, it was better to grow food ourselves.' There was 'a great commercial void to be filled'; in fact, several voids. There were tomatoes, a positive gold mine at 4d. a pound in 1888; there were hens, which he saw as earning 1d. per hen per week; and by 1887 honey, knitting, sewing, butter, and milk at 1d. a quart had all entered the picture. In 1890 he devoted his speech to the merits of Major Moran's *Profitable Rabbit Farming*, price 1s., to much rustic mirth.

Gladstone's remedies for agricultural depression were essentially opportunist and perhaps only half right: but better sympathetic concern and half a remedy than none at all. But philosophically his hints and indications go far beyond the immediate question of agricultural depression. They point towards a more equitable society, towards more varied sources of happiness, towards pride in work, towards a manly independence, towards escape from the narrow rut called division of labour, towards the family as a shared endeavour, towards the creation of a body of Christian social thought whose underdevelopment remains a strange feature of English cultural history.

Gladstone moved slowly, and far from deliberately, towards popular politics; he was in his fifties when the *Daily Telegraph*, the greatest Liberal newspaper, crowned him the 'People's William'. True, his first constituency, Newark, though a rotten borough controlled by the Duke of Newcastle, was also by an electoral freak a predominantly working-class seat. In that narrow respect, he was flung in at the deep end. In his thirties, at the Board of Trade as one of Peel's bright young men, he passed socially conscious legislation. The parliamentary train, immortalised by Gilbert and Sullivan, was his work, as was a law forbidding, with reason, the payment of dockers' wages in public houses. In this respect Gladstone was the first public figure to concern himself with the miseries of the East End. But, and this is the point, Gladstone's involvement was that of a Christian paternalist, believing no doubt in what he called 'the Christian superiority of the poor', but also rejoicing 'that feudalism, thank God, is still common among us'. It was not the involvement of the popular politician, but of the exponent of applied Evangelicalism.

In his forties, far from moving nearer to popular politics, Gladstone became more of a technocrat. But for the accidents of faction he might have ended his days as the austerely ecclesiastical M.P. for the University of Oxford, with its invisible electorate of non-resident Tory country parsons. As it was, he found himself catapulted, at the ripe age of fifty, into an alien Cabinet, still more Whig than Liberal, and face to face with the foremost personality of the age, Lord Palmerston, the very embodiment of those bellicose and spendthrift ways which were anathema to good Peelites. To hold his own, Gladstone had to appeal to those outside Parliament. Within four years, a politician who had never been openly and freely elected had become the working men's hope.

The working man had himself changed. He had become trustworthy. As staunch members of the Volunteer movement, they had drilled to save their country from invasion. Never before had a government armed the urban worker. Financially, as depositors in Gladstone's Post Office Savings Bank, they displayed the middle-class virtues. And, as Gladstone later put it, 'the noble and heroic conduct of the Lancashire cotton operatives during the cotton famine' evinced their sterling worth.

Gladstone's rise to popular hero had several aspects. First, he reduced income tax from ten pence to four pence, an act which though not directly affecting working men won him a good press. Secondly, he began engaging in provincial speaking tours it is not quite clear why and electrified working-class audiences – again, it is not clear why. Perhaps with monarchy in abeyance, and professional sport not yet in sight, urban humanity lacked a hero. Thirdly, Gladstone turned his mind to parliamentary reform, setting the Thames on fire by saying, in 1864, and with obscure qualifications, that 'every man . . . is morally entitled to come within the pale of the constitution'.

In 1868, it was said if a candidate lost the thread of his argument he only had to utter the word Gladstone to bring the house down. Heady stuff, such crowd psychology, capable in other hands of misuse; but, even in bad times, Gladstone educated his audiences, speaking up to them. The great case was his speech at Blackheath (Figs 10, 23–

25). It was raining; the audience, of 6000, included dockyard workers just sacked; 'loud and angry murmurs ominous of storm' came from the crowd. Before long, he had them laughing at the quackery of social reform, as recently proposed in the (Tory inspired) New Social Movement, and retired amidst hurricanes of earnest applause. As in the Midlothian campaigns of 1879–80, when he typically concentrated on such abstruse themes as the retrocession of Bessarabia, the Berlin memorandum and press freedom in India, he had the happy knack of speaking above his audiences' heads, and thus enfolding them in the great processes of state.

Gladstone's immediate relations with the wider public had many aspects. To the pottery industry, for example, and even to the glassmakers, the trade in his commemorative plates and busts was a boon indeed. More startling still was the growth of Hawarden as a tourist attraction. Even at church, ardent Liberals stood on the benches to catch a glimpse of their hero. Huge numbers descended on the park, often travelling surprising distances.[11] To give various examples culled from the press: 500 Lancashire Liberals arrived in 1876; 5200, in three doses, in 1877, 1500 in 1888; and 10,000 in a single day in 1890. In 1881, 800 Liberals from distant Batley, in the West Riding, descended without warning. In 1892, the Flower Show (with fête and bazaar) attracted 20,000 visitors in two days, presumably not to see village produce. In the same year, some 26,000 paid to see the Gladstones' golden wedding present, the proceeds going to the Hawarden working-men's reading room. One's sympathies are with the park.[12]

Gladstone is said, by his son, never to have made a speech on these occasions, beyond a few inescapable appropriate words of greeting. His supposed involvement in such junketings raised many a cultured eyebrow; moreover, it generated its own impression of approachability, which in turn led to floods of unsolicited letters from entire strangers. Gladstonians liked their leader to be a grave and earnest statesman, but they were happy too to think of him as 'a bit of a card'.

His fan mail of the more unqualified kind was kept, by whoever sorted his mail, secretaries or family, as a category apart. Of these letters over a thousand survive, enough to give a flavour of popular attitudes. We find a seven-year-old writing: 'I shall always pray for you and say God bless you before I go to bed at night. From your little friend.'[13] An unknown visitor, writing from 2 Gladstone Place, Farnworth, near Bolton, wrote: 'On Saturday we had the pleasure of passing a few hours inside your grand and noble Park, along with about 1400 other persons from the town of Bolton.' The writer and his wife 'were pleased to see Mrs Gladstone and your son also accompanying you to that tall ash tree', adding: 'It pleased us to see a man in your capacity strip off his clothes down to the waist and your son also.' The writer took home the largest chip from the tree-felling, put it under a glass cover, and now, he concludes: 'Scores of people come to my house, to look at it, both Liberals and Tories.'[14]

From other correspondents came innocent gifts; a working man sent a paper knife he had made;[15] a Durham miner's wife sent him some mittens;[16] one admirer, 'a little boy who is very fond of you', sent a birthday present;[17] a little girl sent some pressed flowers, saying that she had dared to write as she had heard how good he was to children.[18] A working man sent a telegram, as Gladstone's train was about to pass through his town: 'Look out window facing right side north on leaving Darlington desire to welcome you – wish you God speed and success.'[19] Here surely we pass beyond the letters from cranks which all public personages sometimes receive and see a folk myth in the making.[20]

Then there were the gifts of axes. Gladstone's family explain his tree cutting, more or less plausibly, as a result of shooting becoming increasingly closed to him after losing a finger in a shooting accident. He last went out shooting in 1870. Opponents had their own views: 'The forest laments that Mr Gladstone may perspire.' But, to *vox populi*, wood cutting eminently brought out the heroic aspect of their hero: indomitable to the end, he last went out felling trees in 1895, aged eighty-five. By 1898, his collection of axes, 'once large', was down to thirty or forty. The Princess of Wales sent him a silver pencil, shaped as an axe. Outside his study, in a rack, were fifty or sixty walking sticks: going a little beyond ordinary needs, one can but guess that they, and the axes, were offerings to the cult.

In 1864, still more in 1874, and in fair degree in 1884, Gladstone was happy to be behind the times; certainly as a stern opponent of secular radicalism, an upholder of old traditions in church and state against modern rootlessness, a rather too self-conscious *laudator temporis acti*.[21] Socially, he did not adapt easily to the middle class, and it is often hard to tell whether his dislike for radical company was political or social – for the generation gap did not stand in the way of friendly relations with young sprigs of the upper class. John Morley, an atheist, was a curious exception; but then he was a fellow bookworm.

Yet by 1894 Gladstone was rather ahead of the times, in action at least, if often not in words: but few of us have the stamina to reach 1894, so Gladstone's latter days are rarely given full weight. The idea

Fig. 20. Gladstone's Life. (*Flintshire Record Office*)

of his being out of touch with working-class opinion – of his being behind the times; of his not inventing the Welfare State; of his driving the working men away from Liberalism – would have sorely perplexed the tremendous array of working-class mourners at his funeral. In scholarly terms, it is comprehensively refuted in Michael Barker's splendid *Gladstone and Radicalism: The Reconstruction of Liberal Policy in Britain, 1885–1894*. The idea that Gladstone sundered the Liberals from the working class has nevertheless come to be widely believed; and indeed, in the conventional terms of 1998, to be against the state and against collectivism, as Gladstone was to the last, is to oppose the wellbeing of the poor and of the working class. If the dominant view of the twentieth century is right, then Gladstone is wrong. But to apply such ideas to Gladstone and his audience would be wildly anachronistic. Gladstone's last decade in politics should be seen, at least in social terms, not as miserable epilogue but as a happy and fruitful apotheosis, indeed a liberation. In 1879 he might say, unyieldingly, 'blessed are the poor who accept with cheerfulness the limited circumstances and conditions in which they have to pass those few fleeting years', but by 1894 his government was readily replacing market or 'starvation' wages with trade union rates of pay. The more Ireland dominated, the more relaxed Gladstone became on working-class issues; and the less he was threatened by radicals the more room he found for radicalism.

Gladstone could not have enforced a Welfare State even had he wished. The facts of the situation forbade it. In his time, organised labour was hardly yet organised. Big unionism had not begun. Big business was not yet big. The state was as small as it had ever been. The Welfare State was but a gleam in Sidney Webb's eye. Local government barely existed. It did not fall to Gladstone to deal with the twentieth-century eternal triangle of big unionism, big business and big state.

Even in the great Liberal landslide of 1906 social reform was low on the agenda, only 10 per cent of Liberal MPs holding the new collectivist creed, and Campbell-Bannerman's mandate was to spend less, not more. Until 1914 Liberal politics was dominated by the political issues of Gladstone's time, not least its constitutional, financial and religious agenda. If individualist Liberalism remained robust in 1906, how much more so must it have been in Gladstone's day. The dominant view of our century, that support for collectivism and support for the working man are indivisible, was late to surface: to Gladstone, individualism and the best interests of the working man were indissolubly linked. As he wrote when quitting office in 1894: 'Of one thing I am, and always have been, convinced – it is not by the State that man can be regenerated and the terrible woes of this darkened world effectually dealt with.'

As Dr Pelling put it, nobody wanted social reform except for a few farsighted millionaires like Rowntree. Consider this: in 1898, the year of Gladstone's death, the issue that stirred the mob to riot was not pensions, poor law or social reform, but the supposed misdeeds of Ritualist parsons. Second as a cause of popular turbulence came Anti-Vaccinationism – localised censures by the mob upon the very ideas of science and progress.

What Gladstone had to combat, indeed, in later life was not a drift towards socialism, but a strong pull to the Right. On the one hand, the propertied wing of Liberalism had long, since about 1870, sought repose in the bosom of suburban Toryism; on the other, the great unwashed felt the lure of a not very creditable rowdyism of the Right, centring on Empire and Khaki, Beer and Bible, taxing the foreigner and exporting unemployment, and demonstrating Christian unity against Jewish immigration. To give examples, Stepney, Rotherhithe, Limehouse, Brixton and Poplar, names evocative of hardship, were strongly Tory; much of Manchester, most of Liverpool, and all of Birmingham were anti-Gladstonian; nearer home, so were Ashton-under-Lyme, Birkenhead, Blackburn, Bootle, St Helens and Widnes, for all their smoke and industry. Faced with the alliance of genteel Toryism and popular Toryism, symbolised perhaps by Mafeking, the eternal laws of electoral combat compelled Gladstone to look almost entirely to safeguarding his Right, rather than to propitiating his exiguous Left. The electoral sociology used by Gladstone in 1866–67, in which 'Rochdale' had symbolised the 'great social forces' of the age, could no longer be taken for granted.

Gladstone made England a tax-free country for the working man and, moreover, kept it that way. This needs some explanation. It was a tax-free country in the sense of being one where the working man did not pay direct taxation. Exemption from income tax applied to all incomes of £100 or below, specially in order to exclude 'the territory of labour'. Certainly there would have been a fringe of skilled workers and supervisors or foremen above this borderline, but the great mass of working people would have been outside tax.

They could, and did, pay voluntary taxes: by taxation related to liquor they paid half the national revenue. That, it might be said, was their affair: for a teetotal workman might, depending on the date, be conceived who was a total abstainer from taxation. Gladstonian finance was based on an unholy alliance of rich and poor, the middle-class income tax payers probably getting off too lightly, the working man paying nothing at all into the pot unless he wanted to, and the system resting firmly on the twin pillars of Customs and Excise, which between them met around two-thirds of the budget. The contrast with the twentieth century could not be greater. Indeed the chief consequence of the modern Welfare State and modern democracy has been the taxation of the great mass of manual workers, including those on far below average incomes, for the first time. To Gladstone this would have seemed too atrocious to contemplate, an outrage upon social justice; though he firmly believed in taxing lower middle-class incomes of between £100 and £150.

At a more personal level, Gladstone liked or at least broadly approved of the new Labour or Lib-Lab MPs for a number of reasons. He liked them because they liked him (always a good reason) and were probably the least fractious section of his fractious crew. He went out of his way, socially, both to butter them up and to make sure that word of his high regard for them was spread around. On labour representation, perhaps the most important issue in working-class politics before 1900, he waxed strong on a number of occasions. Having working men in Parliament, he asserted, had 'done immense good'. To have more such was 'not only desirable, but in the highest degree urgent': not only must their election expenses be paid from public funds, but their claim to a regular salary was 'irresistible'. Indeed, in a rash moment, Gladstone let fall the idea that a Labour Party was to be desired, to prod official Liberalism into action. These were not mere words: Gladstone gave £500 to support Labour candidates in 1886, and his family gave regular support thereafter. 'We have not had one single person returned by the labourers', Gladstone declared, 'to represent the labourers except such men as are both high in intelligence and thoroughly sound and trustworthy in character.' In their earnestness, in their religion (normally Nonconformist) trade union men like Thomas Burt, MP, the miners' leader, were the very embodiment of what Gladstone had been trying to teach all his life.

It is not surprising, therefore, that, when Keir Hardie was first elected as a Labour MP, his election address pledged him to support Gladstone, or that in Keir Hardie's two-member seat of Merthyr the working-class voter regarded Hardie and the local millionaire Liberal coalowner as almost equally worthy of support. Being Labour and being Gladstonian were not seen as incompatible or divergent courses.

No display of affection and respect has ever been more majestic (until 1997, at least) as Kenneth Morgan points out, than that offered by the endless procession of working-men's organisations at Gladstone's funeral.

In a sense Gladstone achieved nothing permanent, for each generation has to strive anew for the preservation of what he called 'the great human tradition', the inheritance of the mind, for a clean public life; for the interweaving of Christianity with the life of the nation. The question he set before us, a question not yet answered, is how to make an all-conquering capitalism moral without hypertrophy of the state and paralysis of individual energy.

In one sentence, Gladstone's greatest achievement was to bring the working man within the pale of the constitution. This move from aristocracy to 'democracy', from a constitution which excludes to one which includes, with scarcely a pause or a jolt in between, was in one sense a radical venture into new ground, but in another it was profoundly conservative, a continuation of what was good in aristocracy by other means. No other country has made such a transition at so low a price.

Others had a hand in the matter, Disraeli and Baldwin not least. We have been fortunate in our Prime Ministers, a fact too little recognised in a hypercritical age. But making the working man feel that he belonged was Gladstone's own special and greatest work. The labourers in the Waggon and Horses were not too wide of the mark.

5

Gladstone and America

Peter J. Parish

The theme of this essay links one of the truly great men of the nineteenth century with one of the truly great world events of the same
era. Why should a domestic dispute among the Americans at this relatively early stage of their history be regarded as an event of world
importance? It is not simply that this was the greatest war anywhere
in the western world between 1815 and 1914. One only needs to contemplate for a moment the consequences if the outcome of the
struggle had been different, and the Southern Confederacy had gained
its independence – an outcome, incidentally, generally predicted in
Britain at the time, not least by Mr Gladstone himself. A permanent
division of what we take for granted as the *United* States would have
altered the whole shape and course of twentieth century world history.

But the international significance of the conflict extended far
beyond its impact on the balance of power and the pattern of subsequent rivalries and alignments among the great powers. The American Civil War was a contest over great issues: of majority rule versus
minority rights, nationalism and localism, centralisation and state
rights, liberty and equality, democracy and privilege, slavery and freedom, racial justice and injustice. These issues conveyed no single,
simple message across the Atlantic to Britain and Europe; the different strands interweaved, criss-crossed and formed themselves into
tangled knots of European controversy.[1]

Here are two short lists of names of the great and the good (and
the not so good) of the mid nineteenth century. On the one hand, we
have Karl Marx, Tsar Alexander II, John Bright, Bismarck, Victor
Hugo, Robert Browning and John Stuart Mill. On the other hand, we
have Napoleon III, King Leopold of the Belgians, Lord Robert Cecil
(later Prime Minister as Lord Salisbury), Sir John A. Macdonald (later

Prime Minister of Canada), John Ruskin, Lord Acton and William Ewart Gladstone. It would be hard to concoct two more disparate or incongruous collections of names. What could each group possibly have in common, and what differentiated one group from the other? The answer is simply that the first group consists of men who supported, or were regarded as supporters of, the Northern cause in the American Civil War, while the second group lists men who supported, or were thought to support, the Southern cause.

The Civil War was pregnant with meaning for Britain and the Atlantic world generally, but clearly it provided no simple, reliable litmus-paper test for separating the forces of progress and reaction, liberalism and conservatism. Its message was confusing, and full of ironies and paradoxes, but it was none the less important, happening as it did at the very time when, in Britain, the great age of Gladstonian liberalism was in the making. As an introduction and a context for an examination of Gladstone's own very individual, not to say idiosyncratic, attitude towards the American conflict, some brief explanation of the more general British reaction, especially on the side of more liberal and progressive opinion may be useful.

From the vantage-point of the late twentieth century, one might take it for granted that those in mid-Victorian Britain of a liberal disposition, or concerned for the advance and defence of liberty, would have favoured the Northern side, the cause of the Union, for two over-riding reasons. First, the United States was the standard-bearer in the mid nineteenth century of free institutions and representative government, and was admired as such by liberal and radical opinion in Europe, and feared for the same reason by the forces of privilege and reaction. Now the great American experiment was threatened with disintegration as a result of a challenge mounted by a group of Southern states to the perfectly legitimate result of an election which had placed in the White House Abraham Lincoln, the candidate of a Northern antislavery party. Lincoln himself saw the Civil War as a test of the viability of a system of representative government – specifically of its ability to withstand what he called an 'appeal from ballots to bullets'.[2] Secondly, this rebellious challenge to the integrity of the Union had been made by a group of Southern states whose social and political system was based on Negro slavery. Surely Britain's own strong antislavery tradition would place all men of good heart and right mind unequivocally on the Northern side.

The choice seemed clear, or so one might have thought. To support the South was to support the subversion of free institutions and to embrace the cause of racial slavery. That was the view not only of radicals like John Bright and Richard Cobden, the two great champions of the Northern cause in Britain, but also of someone like W.E. Forster, later to be a distinguished member of Gladstone's first great ministry, and even the Duke of Argyll, who was a colleague of Gladstone's in the Palmerston Cabinet during the Civil War. All four of these men were dismayed by Gladstone's attitude towards the war, and adduced a variety of somewhat unflattering explanations of it. In face of all their arguments, he pursued a course which either was pro-Southern (a charge which he denied) or which was assumed to be pro-Southern by almost all his contemporaries.

Before any attempt is made to examine and explain Gladstone's views and actions during the war, it may be instructive to pause for a moment to see if one can construct a possible or hypothetical case which someone of moral sensibility, high intelligence and liberal disposition might have made in support of the Southern position.

One might begin with the argument that the South was conducting a struggle for local self-rule, that it was defending its own interests and freedoms, and its constitutional rights, against the tyranny of a Northern-dominated majority – and the tyranny of the majority was no more acceptable than any other kind of tyranny. The South could be portrayed as the victim of the forces of creeping centralisation and increasingly powerful, interventionist national government which was a threat to basic liberties. One might then add a further argument to the effect that the newly-created Southern Confederacy, with its massive cotton crop and its need for imported manufactured goods, favoured a policy of free trade, while the dominant Republican Party in the North espoused protectionism. This was an argument with a powerful appeal in mid nineteenth-century Britain. Even Cobden wavered briefly when the war first broke out, in the face of this free trade argument, before committing himself to the North. However, another passionate free trader and doughty champion of the North, William E. Forster asked the crucial and cruel question: who would say that 'freedom in goods must enter into competition with freedom of men?'[3]

This was the rub for liberal opinion in Britain. However persuasive the case for Southern rule and national independence, it came up against the stumbling-block of slavery. The best available response was to declare that the slavery issue, as raised by the North, was a piece of humbug. For their own domestic reasons, Lincoln and the United States Congress both insisted in 1861 that the war was simply a struggle to save the Union and not to free the slaves.[4] Critics were not slow to point out that Northern prejudice against black American was scarcely less virulent than Southern, and that the abolitionists had always been a tiny and hated minority in the North. Moreover, the bulk of British opinion shared in the conventional wisdom of the time that the black race was inherently inferior to the white. In other words, it was by no means out of the question to argue that slavery was not a central issue in the conflict – and thus to shift the debate back to political and consititutional issues. The American Civil War posed a series of questions which were variations on the theme of liberty.

Several other factors conspired either to complicate or to obscure the British view of the Civil War. The first was the massive ignorance about the United States which was, and for that matter still is, endemic in Britain. As far as politicians and diplomats were concerned, the United States was still only an occasional bit-player on the world stage. An international statesman of the generation of Palmerston was more at home with Italian unification or the Schleswig-Holstein question than with the internal wrangles of the Americans.

Ignorance often finds a natural partner in prejudice, and a broad undiscriminating anti-Americanism, embracing both North and South, was widespread among many sections of British society. At a very crude level, this found expression in an anonymous letter received by the American legation in London in 1863. Its message was simple:

> Dam the Federals. Dam the Confederates. Dam you both.
>
> Kill your damned selves for the next ten years if you like; so much the better for the world and for England. Thus thinks every Englishman with any brains.
>
> N.B. P.S. We'll cut your throats soon enough afterwards for you, if you ain't tired of blood, you devils.

The same kind of sentiment was expressed, much more elegantly if scarcely less brutally, by Thomas Carlyle, when he expressed his impatience with a people who were 'cutting each other's throats, because one half of them prefer hiring their servants for life, and the other by the hour'.[5]

In the kind of political and social circles in which Gladstone moved, malicious glee at the way in which those vulgar, boastful Americans had inflicted grievous bodily harm upon themselves often found expression in antipathy to the North and cheerful encouragement for the South in its efforts to create even greater mischief. The official representatives of the United States in London felt themselves beleaguered by this kind of pervasive, if not necessarily profound, feeling in favour of the Southern Confederacy. The American Minister himself, Charles Francis Adams, complained of the mixture of ignorance and prejudice which fed this kind of attitude. Rejoicing in the news of the Northern success at the battle of Antietam in 1862, he wrote that only 'hard blows' of this kind would produce any effect on British opinion. He hoped that the Northern generals

> will go on and plant a few more of the same kind in [their] opponents' eyes. I shall be [their] very humble servant, for it will raise us much in the estimation of all our friends. Mr Gladstone will cease to express so much admiration for Jefferson Davis, and all other things will begin to flow smoothly again.[6]

Another Northern emissary to London, John Murray Forbes, recalled many years later a dinner-table conversation where the expression of pro-Southern sympathies finally undermined his patience and his politeness:

> Among the guests was the Rev. James Martineau, who, with the rest, could see no good in prolonging the 'fratricidal contest.' The subject of the Chancellorsville defeat, the news of which had just been received, of course chiefly absorbed our attention, and led to many chilly remarks as to the folly of protracting the useless struggle to save the Union, all meant for my especial benefit, and having the effect of pouring very cold water upon a volcano covered with a thin layer of snow. I listened with the cold outside manners of good society to all the stuff, but simmering internally like the aforesaid Vesuvius, until my patience fairly gave way. In one of the pauses which all dinner parties experience, our host appealed to me for information as to the truth of the sad, heart-rending rumor that the hero, Stonewall Jackson, had been killed by his own soldiers on the evening of the rebel attack, and at the most critical period of the whole battle. With a hesitating voice, under the boiling feelings which had been aroused by the sentimental stuff which had been uttered, I replied, 'I don't know or care a brass farthing whether Jackson was killed by his own men or ours, so long as he is thoroughly killed, and stands no longer in the way of that success upon which the fate of everybody and everything I care for depends!' Had a naked Indian in war-paint, with tomahawk and scalping-knife, appeared at the dinner-table, the expression of horror and dismay at my barbarous utterance could hardly have been greater; but anyhow we

heard no more that evening about the wisdom of concession to the 'erring sisters', and their chivalrous heroes and lamented leaders.

Bright, Cobden, W.E. Forster, the Duke of Argyle, and a few others were with us heartily, and took bold ground in our cause; but, generally speaking, the aristocracy and the trading classes were solid against us. Gladstone, the magnificent old man of today, had not found out the merits of our cause.[7]

It is no coincidence, I think, that both Charles Francis Adams and John Murray Forbes expressed particular disappointment or resentment at Gladstone's attitude. They clearly felt that he ought to have been much more sympathetic to their cause, and they could not understand his apparent pro-Southern stance. This leads us to the central question (or puzzle) of the nature of his very personal view of the American conflict, and the principles and sentiments which lay behind that view.

I say 'principles and sentiments' and not interests, because his view was always that foreign policy should be guided by more than calculation of national interest. Indeed, he thought on balance that British *interests* would be best served by the preservation of the Union – unlike Palmerston who welcomed secession as a diminution of the power of a dangerous rival. For Gladstone, there were higher things at stake than interest.[8]

The phrase 'false prophecy and genuine humanitarianism' has been used to identify certain fundamentals in Gladstone's view of the war which sometimes pushed any question of sympathy or antipathy for one side or the other into second place.[9] By 'false prophecy' one means quite simply that, like innumerable other observers, Gladstone was wrong in his prediction of the outcome of the war. From a very early stage, he believed that the South was sure to win its independence and that the Union could not be restored by force; and he was slow to abandon that belief even when the fortunes of war turned inexorably against the South from 1863 onwards. He differed from others who held similar views mainly in the unequivocal and unqualified expression of his opinions. One can only stand in awe of the reckless courage with which he used all the words which modern politicians, advised by their cohorts of spin doctors are told to avoid at all costs: words like 'certain', 'inevitable', 'impossible', 'never' or 'must'. So confident was he in the summer of 1862 of Southern success that, in a conversation with Henry Hotze, the agent responsible for Confederate propaganda in London, he actually discussed where the boundary line between the truncated United States and the newly-independent Southern Confederacy should be drawn – he took the view that some states like Virginia and Tennessee would have to be divided.[10] It would have been small wonder if Northern opinion suspected that the wish was the father to such thoughts and such premature speculations in Gladstone's mind.

If a man is utterly convinced that one side in a conflict is bound to win, this belief is bound to colour his whole view, including his judgement of the appropriate response to the situation. In Gladstone's case, it inspired two main lines of thought: first, that, even if it *were* possible to restore the Union by force, the whole character and quality of the Union would be destroyed in the process; and, secondly, that if restoration of the Union was not possible, and would be achieved at unacceptable cost even if it were possible, the first priority was to bring the slaughter to a halt without delay.

The first of these propositions is an interesting and important one. Although there were others who expressed similar thoughts, it was a distinctively Gladstonian contribution to the debate on the meaning of the Civil War. Within a month of the outbreak of the war, he was writing to the Duchess of Sutherland as follows:

> I think the whole notion of twenty millions of republicans making war on ten other millions to compel them, irrespective of all differences of climate, interests, space and circumstances, to continue in free voluntary union with them, and again of a free community compelling a slaveholding community . . . to continue in political union . . . which taints and infects their very freedom, one of the most strange paradoxes, and one of the most lamentable pictures, that has lately been presented to the eye of humanity.

In a speech at Manchester a year later, he declared that 'we have no faith in the propagation of free institutions at the point of the sword . . . Freedom must be freely accepted, freely embraced. You cannot invade a nation in order to convert its institutions from bad ones into good ones'. The phrase 'invade a nation' is interesting; it seems to take for granted that the South was already a separate nation, whereas the whole Northern case rested on the claim that the Union was still intact and that the Southern states, though in rebellion, were still a part of it. However, Gladstone's essential point was that, if the heart of the South was set on separation, there was no point in trying to prevent it. Even if military conquest of the South were possible, it would lead to severe civil and political difficulties, and destroy the true nature of the Union. Writing to an American correspondent, Cyrus Field, in November 1862, Gladstone sought to define what he saw as the true destiny of the United States:

> Why have you not more faith in the future of a nation which should lead for ages to come the American continent, which in five or ten years will make up its ... first loss of strength and numbers, and which, with a career unencumbered by the terrible calamity and curse of slavery, will even from the first be liberated from a position morally and incurably false.[11]

In effect, Gladstone rejected Lincoln's arguments that any system of government must provide means for its own survival; and that to accept the right of secession was to descend into anarchy. He thought that the framers of the constitution had not laid down rules for such a situation, and that they had been wise not to do so. The powerful forces which had broken up the Union could not be controlled by 'paper conventions' – one of a number of indications that, at this time, his admiration for the notion of a written constitution was somewhat less than wholehearted. He also made the valid point that the vast expanse and regional diversity of the United States made political division a not unnatural destiny; it was 'difficult to insist permanently ... that nation and continent should always remain nearly coterminous'.[12]

If restoration of the Union was impossible, and self-defeating even if it were possible, it followed naturally that a man of Mr Gladstone's humanitarian instincts would seek an early end to the futile carnage and destruction. This was a key factor in his support during 1862 for the idea of some kind of European mediation in the conflict. In August, he wrote to the Duke of Argyll that Europe could not 'stand silent without limit of time, and witness these horrors and absurdities'. In December, after the appalling casualties suffered by the Union army in its defeat at Fredericksburg, he commented astringently that 'the Americans, poor things, had evidently a large stock of insanity on hand, and have spent it like gentlemen, but it must be nearly run out'.[13]

Whatever their motivation and intention, such pleas for an end to the fighting were inevitably interpreted as evidence of pro-Southern sympathies, for a negotiated settlement would only be possible on the basis of Southern separation. If he wished to dispel such notions, Gladstone made too little effort to clarify his position. On the other hand, it is noteworthy that Sir George Cornewall Lewis, his Cabinet colleague and sometime rival, who opposed the mediation plan, also took the view that a peaceful separation between North and South might be the best solution for all concerned. In 1861, he had described the war as 'the most singular action for the restoration of conjugal rights that the world ever heard of'.[14]

Although he later denied any bias towards the South, many of Gladstone's comments during the war point firmly in that direction. Undoubtedly, he saw much in common between the struggle for Southern independence and the process of Italian unification which he had warmly supported. When taxed by John Bright and others with inconsistency in supporting unification in the one case and division in the other, he retorted that local freedom was the principle common to both cases. It was perfectly possible for the goal of local self-rule to point to national consolidation in the one case, of Italy, and to separation in the other case of the United States. It is clear that Gladstone felt an instinctive warmth towards the cause of the Southern Confederacy as the cause of local freedom and the right to home rule, as against the claims to authority of the central government. Equally, he was inclined to see the Northern cause as the cause of centralisation, monopoly and protection, and he did not share Bright's enthusiasm for the North as the champion of democracy. On the contrary, he thought the North was perpetrating 'an immense mischief, not merely to democratic but to all liberal and popular principles whatever'. To destroy the Confederacy would be to destroy 'nothing but the constitution and liberties of a great nation'. (Again, one notes the use of the word nation, as if Southern national independence was already a fact.)[15]

There were other factors which entered into Gladstone's thinking about the Civil War, including concern for the security of Canada (coupled with determination that the Canadians should accept responsibility for their own defence); and, nearer to home, concern for the sufferings of the Lancashire cotton workers, put out of work by the cotton famine. A small number of those workers found relief at Hawarden; in a footnote, Morley informs us that one of the winding paths through the park was laid out by unemployed cotton operatives.[16]

The large question-mark hanging over Gladstone's apparent sympathy for the South, however, inevitably concerns not such matters as these but slavery. Was it really possible to support a Southern struggle for freedom, when one of the freedoms claimed was the freedom to enslave others? Many of Gladstone's liberal-minded contemporaries thought not. His own complex response to this delicate issue deserves close attention.

In the first place, he denied that the conflict between South and North was essentially a contest between slavery and freedom. Undoubtedly, during the first eighteen months of the war, he could have found ample evidence from Abraham Lincoln and others to support this view. In a letter written in the early days of the war, Gladstone emphasised that he found the principle behind Negro slavery 'detestable', but he went on to say that: 'No distinction can in my eyes be broader than the distinction between the question whether the Southern ideas of slavery are right, and the question whether they can justifiably be put down by war from the North.' Slavery was essentially a Southern problem of race relations, Gladstone argued, and the North could not impose a solution by military force. At one time he even suggested that separation of North and South might be in the interest of the slaves themselves. Slavery had been sheltered by the power and prestige of the Union, and would be more vulnerable if the South had to bear the responsibility alone. Britain, he argued in 1862, should not needlessly antagonise an important new nation in the making by giving excessive voice to strong feelings about slavery. Rather, a more friendly Britain would be able to use its moral influence on an independent Southern Confederacy to bring about the removal, or at least the mitigation, of slavery.[17]

With the advantage of hindsight, one might find all these arguments less than wholly convincing, but they cannot be lightly dismissed, and they must be seen in the mid nineteenth-century context. Gladstone backed them up by frequent expressions of scepticism about the attitudes of the Northern leadership and the Northern people on matters of slavery and race – and again, there was ample justification for such scepticism. He thought that, if the Northern states had the same sub-tropical climate as the South, they would soon resort to the use of slave labour and the same arguments to justify it as the South now employed. He saw the Northern abolitionists as a troublesome and disruptive minority, and took exception to Harriet Beecher Stowe's description of the antislavery movement as 'the Christian people of the Union'. He saw Lincoln's first Emancipation Proclamation of September 1862 as an act of hopelessness and recklessness. Professor Shannon describes Gladstone as being immune to what he himself called 'Negrophilist enthusiasm'. As late as 1864, he expressed astonishment at the eagerness of the 'Negrophilists' to

sacrifice three white lives in order to set free one black man:[18] a somewhat unworthy remark which, although Lincoln could not have known
of it, he answered devastatingly in his great Second Inaugural Address
in March 1865:

> Yet, if God wills that it [the war] continue, until all the wealth piled up
> by the bond-man's two hundred and fifty years of unrequited toil shall be
> sunk, and until every drop of blood drawn with the lash shall be paid by
> another drawn by the sword, as was said three thousand years ago, so
> still it must be said 'the judgments of the Lord are true and righteous
> altogether'.[19]

It is not the business of the historian to make excuses for Gladstone
on this difficult issue – and one or two of his remarks would be hard
to excuse. But he does need to be explained and understood, particularly in the context of his times. A few of his contemporaries, including
John Bright, ascribed his aberration on this matter to a kind of moral
blind spot or to the lingering influence of his family's West Indian
connections.[20] I do not find this argument convincing or even fair.
A better explanation may surely be found in Gladstone's confident
expectation that the South was going to win its independence and his
belief that the North was not waging the war as an antislavery crusade – and in any event war was not the appropriate route to emancipation. One might add two other somewhat speculative points. The
first is that his understanding of American affairs was inadequate and
sometimes misleading – a failing which he shared with almost all his
contemporaries. He did not appreciate that, although the abolitionists
did not enjoy wide popular support in the North, antislavery feeling
was widespread and genuine; and that opposition to the further extension of slavery into the west had carried Lincoln and his party to
power. Secondly, I suspect that, for Gladstone, or certainly for the
Gladstone of the early 1860s, a social injustice like slavery did not
command as high a place on the agenda for political action as the
kind of political, administrative and financial reforms which mainly
preoccupied him.

As a footnote to discussion of this particular problem, it is worth
noting that, in a letter written just after the end of the war, Gladstone
said: 'Had the Southerners detached their cause from its association
with slavery by actually or virtually abolishing it, my sympathies would
have been with them.'[21] The sad thing is that so many people at the
time assumed that his sympathies were with the South in any case –
and of course to express the wish, even with hindsight, that the South

might have detached itself from the peculiar institution which was the foundation of its society and its identity was to ask for the impossible.

So much for Gladstone's thoughts and feelings about the great American conflict. One also needs to consider his actual participation in events and his role in government policy towards America during the war – and in particular one famous or notorious episode. As Chancellor of the Exchequer, he was after all a major figure in the Palmerston ministry which was in power throughout the four years of the American Civil War. Whatever the sympathies or antipathies of members of the Cabinet, the government pursued fairly consistently a policy of neutrality and non-involvement in the American conflict – mainly for the good Palmerstonian reason that no major British interest would be served by becoming involved. In practice, such a policy of neutrality was bound to favour the North, for it was the South which desperately wanted European intervention.

The Confederates believed that, if only they could win diplomatic recognition from Britain and France, or perhaps bring about some kind of diplomatic intervention possibly in the form of mediation, then victory in the war and the achievement of independence would be assured. The irony of the situation was that only if military success had brought them to the brink of winning the war would the British government have considered recognition or intervention. In the late summer of 1862 it looked as if that moment had almost arrived; between August and November 1862, the members of the Palmerston government conducted their only serious debate about whether to make some kind of diplomatic intervention, preferably in concert with France and Russia.[22]

It was against this background that Gladstone delivered his Newcastle speech of 7 October 1862. When he had last been in touch with Palmerston and the Foreign Secretary, Earl Russell, they had seriously discussed a proposal for mediation, and Gladstone had supported the idea. But before Gladstone rose to speak at Newcastle, important events had taken place in America; the tide of Southern military success had been stemmed at the battle of Antietam, and Lincoln had seized the opportunity to issue his first Emancipation Proclamation, which, for all its limitations, altered the whole character of the war. Gladstone, however, went ahead with his speech, believing that he was reflecting government policy, though expressing it in forthright and undiplomatic language. The key passage in the Newcastle speech reads as follows:

We know quite well that the people of the Northern States have not yet drunk of the cup – they are still trying to hold it far from their lips – which all the rest of the world see they nevertheless must drink of. We may have our own opinions about slavery; we may be for or against the South; but there is no doubt that Jefferson Davis and other leaders of the South have made an army; they are making, it appears, a navy; and they have made, what is more than either, they have made a nation . . .[23]

This famous passage is noteworthy for several reasons. Clearly it is based on the firm Gladstonian assumption that Southern independence, though not yet a recognised fact, was a certainty – the cup which the people of the North *must* drink of. Again there is the reference to the Southern *nation*, which even Cabinet colleagues like Russell who agreed with his basic position regarded as going rather too far. Again, also, there is the relegation of the slavery question to a subordinate position.

The Newcastle speech created a major sensation and it needs to be placed in context. First, it was the result of no sudden impulse, no sudden rush of blood to the head on the part of Gladstone. A year earlier he had discussed privately the possibility of the British government offering its good offices to the contending parties. In July 1862, he sent a long memorandum to Palmerston urging some kind of mediation by the European powers. In September he wrote to the Duke of Argyll to say that 'it is our absolute duty to recognise . . . that Southern independence is established, i.e. that the South cannot be conquered'. It would be an act of charity for Europe to intervene to bring the war to an end. In another letter, he wrote of 'the wholesale slaughter' in America, and 'its thoroughly purposeless character'. It had long been clear that secession 'is virtually an established fact, and that Jeff Davis and his colleagues have made a nation' – the very phrase used publicly a few weeks later at Newcastle. He pressed for prompt action for a very Gladstonian combination of reasons. If intervention was delayed, the rapid progress of Southern arms and the growing fear of major unrest in the Lancashire cotton towns 'would prejudice the dignity and disinterestedness of the proffered mediation'. In Cabinet discussions, he actively encouraged Palmerston and Russell to move in the direction of diplomatic intervention.[24]

In his excellent essay on 'Gladstone and the Civil War', Cedric Collyer was surely right to suggest that the Newcastle speech was the product of a number of factors, including political principle, humanitarian feeling, policy considerations and the military situation in America.[25] Whatever its intentions, the Newcastle speech produced a powerful, if mixed, reaction.

John Bright denounced the speech in extravagant language and cast aspersions on Gladstone's mental stability as well as his motivation. Benjamin Moran, of the American Legation, thought the tone of the speech insulting, but noted that much of British opinion was applauding the speaker for his insults. 'But an insult in England is no insult at all', he continued, 'if directed against foreigners. They are the most thin-skinned people alive, and can't even bear to hear the truth of themselves from strangers; but they beslime other people without stint.'[26] (Incidentally accusations of hypersensitivity of this kind were commonly hurled both ways across the Atlantic. Anthony Trollope, who wrote a book about his travels in America in 1861, referred to his putative American readers as 'our thin-skinned friends'.)

The Newcastle speech excited the press and the politicians, and threw the cotton markets into confusion, because it was widely interpreted as a signal that the government was about to recognise the Confederacy. Palmerston put up Sir George Cornewall Lewis to make a speech refuting this suggestion. In the next few weeks, both Palmerston and Russell got cold feet about any proposal for intervention, and opted for a continuation of the policy of wait and see. When, in November, Napoleon III tried belatedly to revive the idea of a six months' armistice between the belligerents in America, the only senior figure in the British Cabinet to favour the idea was Gladstone. In a famous passage in his *Education*, Henry Adams who had served as his father's private secretary at the American legation throughout the war, described how, in his youthful innocence, he had supposed that Palmerston would have supported such a proposal, Russell would have opposed it and Gladstone would have violently denounced it. His subsequent political education had shown him to be completely wrong, and he concluded bitterly, 'the only resolute, vehement, conscientious champion of . . . Napoleon and Jefferson Davis was Gladstone'.[27]

The real explanation, in my view, is that Gladstone was so utterly, if erroneously, convinced that the South was bound to win its independence that he was interested in any means of bringing the carnage to a swift end. Certainly, from 1863 onwards, as the character of the war and the balance of advantage shifted, he became much more circumspect in his pronouncements on the subject. In July 1863, in his only House of Commons speech on the war, he performed a delicate

balancing act between admiration for the heroic resistance of the
South and the strong counter-current in his mind generated by the
Southern slavery connection.[28] But he still believed that restoration of
the Union by force was unattainable. As late as November 1863, in a
letter to Charles Sumner, the prominent Republican Senator from
Massachusetts, he still combined his two basic, if honourable and
understandable misjudgements, about the war. He voiced disapproval
of a war to end slavery but would be glad if slavery ended as a consequence of the war:

> I could go further and say it will please me much if by the war the Union
> shall be re-established. But it would be a shabby way of currying favour
> with you to state a proposition which though in its terms strictly true
> contemplates a contingency which as it seems to me is wholly unattainable.

One can only add that Gladstone was not alone in clinging to such
estimates of the outcome of the war. Even in May 1864 *The Times*
could still assess Confederate prospects as brighter than ever.[29]

There remains an important and fascinating tail-piece to the story
of the Newcastle speech. Over thirty years later, in 1896, Mr Gladstone wrote of 'an undoubted error, the most singular and palpable, I
may add the least excusable of them all, especially as it was committed
so late as the year 1862, when I had outlived half a century'. Whether
or not the sin had been great, the confession and repentance could
scarcely have been expressed more unreservedly. Gladstone still
insisted that he had not spoken in 1862 out of pro-Southern partisanship or hostility to the North. The fortunes of the South were at their
zenith, and he was simply seeking ways of avoiding further bloodshed
and greater calamity. He had 'weakly supposed' that suggestions of
this kind 'were required by a spirit of that friendship which, in so
many contingencies of life, has to offer sound recommendations with
a knowledge that they will not be popular'. He now understood why
this act of friendliness was not perceived as such in the North. He
continued:

> That my opinion was founded upon a false estimate of the facts was the
> very least part of my fault. I did not perceive the gross impropriety of such
> an utterance from a cabinet minister, of a power allied in blood and lan-
> guage, and bound to loyal neutrality ... My offence was indeed only a
> mistake, but one of incredible grossness, and with such consequences of
> offence and alarm attached to it, that my failing to perceive them exposed
> me to very severe blame. It illustrates vividly that incapacity which my
> mind so long retained, and perhaps still exhibits, an incapacity of viewing

subjects all round, in their extraneous as well as in their internal properties, and thereby of knowing when to be silent and when to speak.[30]

For a last word on this, as on so many other subjects, one may turn to Morley, who had a splendid capacity for schoolmasterly reproof of even the best and the greatest which late twentieth-century biographers would not dare to attempt. In the Newcastle speech, he said, 'the speaker was forgetful of a wholesome saying of his own, that "a man who speaks in public ought to know, besides his own meaning, the meaning which others will attach to his words."' More generally, Morley argued with great force that Gladstone, like so many in Britain at the time, failed to see that the American Civil War was not like superficial old world conflicts about boundaries, successions and dynastic preponderance. 'The significance of the American war was its relation to slavery' – and the economic, social and political consequences which flowed from it. Secession was undertaken, said Morley, 'for the purpose of erecting into an independent state a community whose whole structure was moulded on a system that held labour in contempt [and] and kept the labour in ignorance and cruel bondage'.[31]

Morley wrote with the advantage and the disadvantage of hindsight. He put his finger on the fundamental issue, but in doing so he also oversimplified it, and neglected the many other factors which complicated or obscured this basic truth at the actual time of the war. Gladstone had to react to the situation at the time. Surely he, like many others, made serious misjudgements, and his whole response to the war was shaped by what proved to be an unwarranted assumption about its inevitable outcome. His later protestations that his attitude was never pro-Southern were surely sincere, but do not entirely fit with what he said and did at the time – and certainly not with how his words and deeds were perceived. However, the later protestations are very important in themselves, because they are one reflection of the profound change which came over his view of America in the years after the war.

The story of Gladstone and America should end on a positive and constructive note. A few months after the conclusion of the war, he wrote somewhat ruefully to Charles Sumner: 'On the whole the history of your great war impresses me with no feeling so much as this; that it is, as I now learn, hazardous in the extreme for us to pronounce upon American questions of the future.' The courage and perseverance displayed on both sides revealed energies which 'surpassed our scale and measure'.[32] Even before the conflict ended, and certainly in the months that followed, he had already begun to rethink his position. As he took up the question of parliamentary reform, to the surprise of many of his colleagues, he acknowledged the lessons of the war in demonstrating the power and purpose of popular governments based on the national will – even if he remained concerned about the dangers of centralisation.

The year after the war, in a speech at Liverpool, he recalled that, a few years earlier, it had been the fashion to describe the American constitution as a failure – but the war had altered that, and even shown the virtues of 'extended franchises'. The fact, and even more the legend, of the stoic restraint and patience of the Lancashire mill workers during the cotton famine induced by the war pointed in the same direction. Very characteristically, Gladstone was particularly impressed by the prudence and self-denial with which a democratic republic was tackling the financial problems left over by the war. Having condemned the irresponsible issue of paper currency during the war, he now acknowledged the debt redemption measures undertaken by the Republican administration:

> Is it really possible that this extraordinary people . . . are going to cap their almost superhuman efforts in the war by teaching us in the Old World how to grapple with the problem of the National Debt?[33]

Nothing was more calculated to impress Gladstone with the virtues of democracy than such evidence of financial responsibility and probity.

In broader terms, the bold development of Gladstonian liberalism in the later 1860s owed something – among other and more direct influences, of course – to the lessons of the Civil War. Morley referred to the 'strange paradox' of the Civil War in helping to create 'as a great popular leader the very statesman who had failed to understand it'.[34] The American example was quoted by both sides in the debates over parliamentary reform, but with some of the enthusiasm of a penitent sinner, Gladstone used it as a positive argument for reform.

Over the twenty years or so after 1865, Gladstone indeed developed a new perspective on America, and on the nature of the Anglo-American relationship. He acknowledged retrospectively the victory of 'the commanding moral influence of the North' and the providential destruction of the 'hideous solecism' of slavery.[35] In the 1870s, he began to talk in terms of a natural Anglo-American community, and he is credited, somewhat dubiously, with being the first person to use the phrase 'the English-Speaking Peoples'. In the 1880s, he encour-

aged James Bryce to write *The American Commonwealth,* which remains
the greatest of all British commentaries on American institutions, politics and society.[36]

The most striking evidence of all is in the article entitled 'Kin
Beyond the Sea', which he contributed to the *North American Review* in
1878. It is a most eloquent, and often moving, essay, particularly in
the light of all that had gone before. The United States and Britain,
he says, were the two most powerful nations in the world, and he
happily conceded that the daughter was now bound to outstrip the
mother. He goes on to celebrate both the similarities and the diver-
gences of the political institutions and processes of the two countries.
Both shared a common tradition of self-government, and freedom of
speech and thought, but, because of their very different histories and
environments, each needed different institutions. Then follows the
famous passage, often quoted as a great tribute to the American constitution, but which is really a contrast between the British and American systems. The British constitution was the 'offspring of tendency
and indeterminate time', the American 'of choice and of an epoch'.
But, 'as the British constitution is the most subtle organism which has
proceeded from the womb and the long gestation of progressive history, so the American constitution is, so far as I can see, the most
wonderful work ever struck off at a given time by the brain and purpose of man'. The way in which that constitution had survived a century of trial proved 'the sagacity of the constructors, and the stubborn
strength of the fabric'. This represents a giant leap from what Gladstone had thought and said during the Civil War.[37]

As for slavery, America had 'purged away the blot with which we
brought it into the world' – and he compared the consequences of
emancipation in the American South very favourably with what had
happened in Jamaica. Again, the history of the United States since
1865 had dispelled fears that the huge military effort of the war years
would lead to military domination of postwar society. 'Cincinnatus, no
longer a unique example, became the commonplace of every day, the
type and mould of a nation.' Similarly, the financial responsibility displayed by 'the most unmitigated democracy known to the annals of
the world' once again earned his fulsome praise. Such conduct of
affairs not only did honour to the United States, but 'rendered a splendid service to the general cause of popular government throughout
the world'.[38] American politics and government in the so-called gilded
age may scarcely have deserved such a handsome tribute; but the

change in Gladstone's thinking about the United States, in the space of a decade and a half, is truly remarkable.

With all its many and complex variations on the theme of liberty, the American Civil War did not fit neatly into the Gladstonian view of the world. It raised too many awkward questions and difficult dilemmas. The absorption of the lessons of the war was a painful but profoundly important process for Gladstone, for British politics, and for the future of the Anglo-American relationship. Only a man of exceptional breadth of mind and largeness of heart could have recovered from his initial misreading of the situation to reach the heights of the essay on 'Kin Beyond the Sea'.

Abraham Lincoln is widely regarded as the supreme exemplar of the American political tradition. Lincoln and Gladstone were surely the two great spokesmen and leaders of the Anglo-American liberal tradition in the nineteenth century. In their backgrounds, education and public and private lives, the two men could scarcely have been more different. And yet, prompted first by the coincidence that they were born in the same year, one may begin to see other points of similarity. Both displayed an extraordinary capacity for growth and development, both combined high political skill with a grasp of fundamental principles, and both combined deeply conservative instincts with a readiness to face up to the need for bold and even radical reform. It was a tragedy that, at the point where their public lives intersected, during the four years of the Civil War, they found themselves at cross-purposes, and, at a distance of three thousand miles, failed to understand or appreciate one another. In the moment of victory, Lincoln's life was cut short by the assassin's bullet, while Gladstone lived on for three decades and more. It is comforting to find that the Gladstone of the post-Lincoln era carried on the work of building up the strength of that Anglo-American liberal democratic tradition to which both men had contributed so much.

6

Gladstone and Ireland

D. George Boyce

Gladstone and Ireland: the very words have a resonance denied to those of any other British political figure in his or her relationship with that country. For a generation of Irish historians (and, more significantly, non-historians) brought up on the idea that the only connection between British politicians and Ireland was one of at best benign neglect, at worst deliberate ignorance, Gladstone's name stands like a beacon. Here was a crusader for the cause of the redress of Irish grievances, whose career was inextricably entwined with the effort to ward off the day of reckoning that must otherwise come between Great Britain and that 'cloud in the west', that 'coming storm', a career, moreover, that came to a dramatic and even tragic climax, as Gladstone stood in the House of Commons in June 1886 to plead for the concession of a Home Rule Bill to the Irish Parliamentary Party, and thus end the conflict of centuries.[1]

Attention has been focused so closely on Gladstone and Home Rule that it is hard to believe that the question of the government of Ireland only occupied the end of a long political career. But it is harder still to imagine that career without the recurring problem of Ireland and Gladstone's response to it. This response – or rather responses – punctuated Gladstone's other preoccupations between his decision to disestablish the Church of Ireland in 1868 and the 1886 Home Rule Bill; and while modern historical research has stressed the complexity of Gladstone's Irish forays, it has hardly diminished the sense that indeed his Irish policies mark a turning point in the history of Ireland, and of its relationship with Great Britain.

It is this moral dimension that pervades Gladstone's connection with Ireland, one that some historians have sought to diminish, if not demolish altogether.[2] Other British politicians might grapple with

Ireland; one, Lloyd George, even earned one of A.J.P. Taylor's finest epitaphs: 'Ireland ruined Lloyd George, as it had ruined Peel and Gladstone before him. But at least he was ruined by success, they by failure.'[3] Somehow, it seems that Gladstone's failure is more worthy, more noble, certainly more ethical than Lloyd George's success in finding an Irish settlement that lasted in most important respects for fifty years.

The moral view is enshrined in two old, but none the less valuable, studies of Gladstone, both of which focused exclusively on his Irish experience. These are Lord Eversley's *Gladstone and Ireland* (1912) and J.L. Hammond's *Gladstone and the Irish Nation* (1938).[4] Both these books contain much important information; but both were written in the spirit of Gladstonian Liberalism, and especially of Gladstonian Irish Liberalism; underlying their texts was the assumption by the authors that Gladstone was the maker of the Irish solution that never was – the final settlement of the Irish Question that, in Eversley's day, remained unsettled; and in Hammond's had been resolved, or at least partially resolved, only after violence and partition. Eversley noted that 'the arguments to be drawn from these events in favour of conceding autonomy in domestic legislation to Ireland, are enormously strong, and whenever such a measure is accomplished it will be recognised that to Mr Gladstone it will have been mainly due'.[5] Hammond went further, arguing that 'we may perhaps describe Mr Gladstone's career by saying that he used the democratic forces created by the second and third Reform Bills to break down the prejudices that had governed England's treatment of Ireland during two thirds of the nineteenth century'. Gladstone differed from his contemporaries in that he thought of the Irish as a people, and he held that the ultimate test of a policy was whether or not it helped this people to satisfy its self-respect and to find dignity and happiness in its self-governing life. Gladstone 'and Gladstone alone among political leaders treated the Irish Question as the supreme problem'. He understood 'national sentiment'.[6]

These sentiments, while not wide of the mark, do not convey the complexity of Gladstone's approach to Ireland, though it is fair to say that Hammond, for his part, noted that nothing in Gladstone's career in the 1850s and 1860s suggested that he would make Ireland the main task of the last twenty years of his life.[7] Gladstone approached the problems of Ireland in the same way as did his British contemporaries: as essentially intrusive issues. But he believed that Ireland sought to remind England that she was answerable to a higher power for her misdeeds; and Ireland could certainly be construed as suffering from English misdeeds. Yet if the most ill-directed period in Anglo-Irish relations was the Great Famine of 1845–49, when even Conservative Irish politicians like Isaac Butt, founder of the Home Rule Party, and Conservative journals like the *Dublin University Magazine*, called in question a Union in which such a catastrophe could occur, then it must be admitted that this disaster found Gladstone wanting: or at least wanting in anything more than a propensity to wring his hands over the visitation that was symptomatic of the 'cruel, inveterate, and but half-atoned injustice' that England had inflicted on Ireland.[8] But he made no strenuous intervention on the issue of whether or not anything more could be done to alleviate the effects of the famine. And yet there was a moral tone in his voice that was soon to be familiar in Gladstonian Irish Liberalism; an ethical note that was to reappear when in the 1860s Gladstone adopted what might be called his first major Irish initiative: the disestablishment and disendowment of the Church of Ireland.

Gladstone had turned the Irish Church question over in his mind for some time before his ideas crystallised in the late 1860s.[9] That there were anomalies in the Church of Ireland's position could hardly be denied. In the early nineteenth century the chief grievance was the payment of tithes which, in a country where three-quarters of the population was Roman Catholic (and a substantial number, indeed a majority in the province of Ulster, was Presbyterian) was hard to defend. This question was resolved in the 1840s, but it left the second and larger anomaly: that a state church was defended in a country where most of the state's subjects professed a different religion. Of course, the Irish Church's position could be defended on the grounds that the Act of Union of 1800, which created the United Kingdom of Great Britain and Ireland, stipulated that the Churches of Ireland and England were to become one church and, moreover, linked the creation of that one church to the safety and continuation of the Union itself. To lay rough hands on the Church of Ireland would be to attack not only the whole Protestant establishment, but the very basis of the United Kingdom constitution.

Gladstone's motives in moving towards tackling this dangerously deep question were, inevitably, varied. Like all Englishmen, he had been shaken by the Fenian uprising of 1867 which, although it failed completely and even in some respects was farcical, nevertheless prepared public opinion in Great Britain for some concessions to alleviate Irish discontent. Gladstone was not motivated by this crisis;[10] but he

saw the opportunity that it offered to make a bold move in the direction of settling at least two of the major grievances of the Catholics of
Ireland: the religious grievance; and, another long-identified aspect of
Irish unrest, the land question, that is the problem of relations
between landlord and tenant which threatened to disrupt the whole
of Irish rural society. The Irish Church question offered him an opportunity to rally the forces of Liberalism and Nonconformity behind a
potentially popular and noble cause, and one that defenders of the
Church of Ireland would find hard to refute. And then here was Gladstone's own search for the high ground of morality in politics, which,
he later declared, enabled him to shape and mould public opinion on
some great issue. Care must be exercised when assessing Gladstone's
later rationalisations; but the high moral tone, which was evident in
his response to the Great Famine, is significant. There was another
motive as well, though one not yet fully formed. Professor Richard
Shannon has drawn attention to the distinction that can be made
between Gladstonian Liberalism, with its ethical language and high
moral sense, and Gladstone's liberalism, which was of a different
order: more pragmatic, and above all more conservative; and, it might
be added, more Anglocentric.

   For here, in Gladstone's Disestablishment policy, and in his Land
Act of 1870, were the outlines of what was to underlie even the most
apparently radical of his Irish policies: the policy of Home Rule. Gladstone hoped by reforming Ireland to make it more like England. The
causes of friction within Irish society must be removed, or at least
moderated. The causes lay in the relations, first of all between the
Catholic majority and the state church (which, since it was a state
church, naturally led Catholics into conflict with the state itself); and
then between landlord and tenant. This latter grew in significance as
Gladstone returned in 1880–81 to the problem of Ireland. For the
moment, Gladstone developed his strategy of resolving the ruinous
and destabilising frictions in Ireland. Thus he moved forward to dis-
lodging Disraeli's Conservative government by putting forward a
series of resolutions in the House of Commons for disestablishment
and disendowment. In this way he preempted Disraeli's plan of con-
current endowment by which the Catholic and Presbyterian churches
would be supported by the state as well. Disraeli just managed to hold
on to power for the remainder of the parliamentary session, but he
was obliged, and knew he was obliged, to defend a state church whose
position could hardly be supported without at least some reservations.
His promise of a 'great Protestant crusade' never took fire; and Glad-

stone was returned to office in the general election of November 1868 with a mandate to – as Irish Protestants saw it – plunder not only the Church of Ireland, but to break thereby 'our venerated constitution, our liberty – civil and religious'.[11] The election was a triumph for Gladstone not only in Great Britain but in Ireland itself, where the proportion of Liberals to Conservatives rose from fifty-eight and forty-seven respectively, to sixty-six and thirty-nine. It must be noted, however, that this Liberal support was mainly in the Catholic south and west; Conservative policies, and especially anti-disestablishment, found most support in the province of Ulster.[12]

Catholics rejoiced over the fall of their enemy; Protestants execrated Gladstone as having turned Ireland into a 'churchless nation'; but Gladstone believed that he had taken a major step towards settling an issue that could only remain divisive, and one that, once settled, would enable the Church of Ireland to escape the calumnies that had been heaped on it as a minority church that enjoyed state support. When Gladstone came to tackle the land question, he was equally conservative in his motives. The friction between landlord and tenant was damaging to the kind of stability that England enjoyed because of her satisfactory relations between the two classes. Gladstone's essentially conservative approach to this issue was noted by Lord Eversley, who drew attention to Gladstone's dislike of the concept of fixity of tenure (which would afford the tenant legal protection from eviction); and his hope that compensating tenants for any improvements they made to their farms would set aside any need for fixity of tenure. Gladstone made his overall motives clear: 'I hold that each successive act of justice develops feelings of content and loyalty, and narrows the circle of disaffection'.[13] Thus did Gladstone move forward from his confession in 1863 that he did not believe there was

> any way in which this House can address itself to so serious an evil. I know of no way in which this House can address itself to correct that evil except by endeavouring to do everything in its power to improve the social and economical condition of Ireland, and give its people equal rights and advantages with the rest of the kingdom in regard to the security, independence and freedom of their enjoyment and espousal of their property.[14]

This quotation alone warns against discerning any clear, undeviating line of approach when Gladstone grappled with Ireland; and it reveals that Gladstone's commitment must be seen as compatible with his concern not to overturn the rights of property, nor to set Ireland about the ears with radical social or political initiatives. Yet he used the phrase 'justice for Ireland', and it remained to be seen how far that notion would take him. It did not take him very far beyond 1874, for Gladstone's attempt to deal with the Irish University Question brought down his government, and cost him Liberal support in Ireland. Gladstone's plan was to establish an Irish national university with affiliated colleges, consisting of Trinity College Dublin, the Queen's Colleges (Cork, Galway and Belfast), the Catholic College at Maynooth, and Magee College (a Presbyterian institution), with an overall governing body. This measure was opposed by Ulster Conservatives, was supported by one Ulster Liberal, and opposed by the majority of Irish Liberals, who were Catholics, because it did not do enough for Catholic education. Gladstone had also moved too far ahead of his English Liberal supporters, who could not warm to this aspect of justice for Ireland as they had to the disestablishment of the Irish Church; the government fell and Gladstone was left to ruminate on Ireland in Opposition.[15]

Ruminate on Ireland he did. Again, this was not a major preoccupation; there were other more attractive and exciting causes, such as the Bulgarian agitation, to call upon Gladstone's political energy and his sense of moral righteousness. But he was aware of the challenge posed both to stability in Ireland and to good relations between Ireland and England by the rise of Isaac Butt's Home Rule Party, which was making headway in winning Irish seats. The Home Rulers were busily linking the cause of Irish self-government in the domestic sphere with the question of tenant right; farmers' clubs came out in support of the party's aims. When candidates presented themselves to the electors they offered Home Rule, fixity of tenure and fair rents, followed by denominational education and an amnesty for Fenian prisoners. The general election of 1874 saw two Home Rulers returned for the province of Ulster, and fifty-eight for the rest of Ireland; this was a sharp contrast to the results of 1868 when sixty-six Liberals had been returned; it signified a dissatisfaction of most Irish voters with the constitution, and a desire to change it.[16]

Gladstone, for his part, pondered on the ways in which, yet again, Ireland might be reconciled to the Union. Now he turned over in his mind the question of local government reform. He returned to the moral problem that Ireland posed to England, writing to Lord Granville in 1870 that 'to this great country the state of Ireland after 700 years! of our tutelage, is in my opinion so long as it continues, an intolerable disgrace, and a danger so absolutely transcending all others, that I call it the only real danger of the noble Empire of the Queen'.[17]

Could such a small adjustment as local government reform be turned into a moral issue? Gladstone was of course capable of turning anything into a moral issue, but his language showed that he saw this possibility was some kind of real and significant recognition of Irish nationality. This was revealed when Gladstone at last made the visit to Ireland which he had promised himself to do (he informed Guizot in 1872) in 1845.[18] In 1877 he made his long delayed visit, receiving the freedom of the city of Dublin, and suddenly (it seemed) deciding to unmuzzle himself and abandon his resolution not to make a major speech in a country whose politics made it sensitive ground for major, or even minor, political speeches. He indicated two broad areas of policy for Ireland. One was what he called 'local government, not only in the shape of municipal institutions, but in all those other shapes in which it is known to our history'. Parliament was failing in its duties; the kingdom's government was overcentralised. The three kingdoms of England plus Wales, Scotland and Ireland 'should be one nation to the face of the world'; but the people should be trained in their public duties locally so that they could all the more effectively carry them out nationally. This was an extension of political liberty.[19]

The second political topic was land and Gladstone once again mused on the differences between England and Ireland. In England it was essential that the land should be owned by one sort of men and tilled by another; and anyway the mass of the population did not aspire to purchase the land. But in Ireland the case was different. Tenants in Ireland needed security and confidence, and Gladstone declared that 'for my own part, attaching small importance to the acquisition of small proprieties in England, I attach great importance to it in Ireland'. It was of the greatest consequence: 'The creation of a class of small propriety in Ireland will give new views and new ideas to the proprietors'. There was in Ireland a sharp division between the interests of the cultivators and those of the proprietors. 'The best cure for that', Gladstone claimed, was that 'in a good and appreciable number of instances the same man shall be cultivator and proprietor too.' He then would learn to look at the whole case, and realise that there was no necessary conflict between these two classes, but that they ought mutually 'to assist and support one another'. Gladstone then rather surprisingly claimed that he had refrained from 'entering on the politics of the future'; and he concluded that the Liberal Party, however

much it had lost ground in the last two elections in Ireland to the
Home Rulers, would have its policies governed by the idea of 'justice
for Ireland' – which sounded very like looking into the politics of the
future.[20]

Gladstone's ruminations on local government reform, therefore,
were not a recognition of Ireland's nationalist claim but an attempt
to reconcile Irish with British nationality; and in 1880 he claimed that
what he called the 'true supporters of the Union' were those who
'fairly uphold the supreme authority of Parliament, but exercise that
authority to bind the three nations by the indissoluble ties of liberal
and equal laws'.[21] This could mean establishing Grand Committees of
the House of Commons, as Gladstone considered in November 1880;
or it could, again, be local government reform, but reform which he
now seemed to regard in a highly flexible way. He wrote to Granville,
on 16 September 1881, of local government reform 'to which I shall
affix no limits except the supremacy of the Imperial Parliament and
the rights of all parts of the country to claim whatever might be conceded to Ireland'.[22]

By February 1883 he was discussing the difficulty in so reorganising
the government of the United Kingdom that imperial could readily
be separated from Irish affairs: 'I will not undertake to say what
decision this House might arrive, provided a plan were before it, under
which the local affairs of Ireland could be, by some clear and definitive
line, separated from the Imperial affairs of Ireland'. In the same
month he spoke of his 'strongest objections' to the centralising tendency of English government: local institutions were 'a great source of
strength' and the only limit to their powers was 'the adequate and
certain provision for the supremacy of the central authority'. Irish
control of Irish affairs would not necessarily be separatist.[23]

All this showed that Gladstone's mind was moving on Ireland;
though the direction was not yet defined as Home Rule. But, meanwhile, Gladstone's government was engaged with the somewhat less
obviously liberal task of restoring order in Ireland, and of dealing with
the rural organisation, the Land League, which was formed in the last
months of Disraeli's administration. It was a task for which they had
little preparation and not much sense of engagement. Irish affairs
were absent from the British political scene throughout most of Disraeli's government, and it would be an unlucky party that won power
just at a time when Ireland was moving from side to centre stage; and
from peaceful politics to what looked like revolution. Gladstone's idea
of creating a small class of prosperous tenant proprietors seemed as

far as Liberals need go on the land question; but the Liberals were confronted with the landlords' serious difficulty in collecting rent, and the growing intimidatory powers of the Land League. The growing seriousness of the agrarian crisis was compounded by the rise of Charles Stewart Parnell to the leadership of the Home Rule Party in May 1880, which would give it a vigorous edge that Butt and his short-lived successor as leader, William Shaw, signally failed to achieve. The government brought in a Compensation for Disturbance Act which gave compensation for 'unreasonable' evictions; but this in due course led the government into defending any evictions that might be deemed 'reasonable', and thus the legislation took on more of a law and order character, and less of a protection of tenant farmer character.[24]

Gladstone took no part in these proceedings. His Irish Chief Secretary, W.E. Forster, supported powerful coercive legislation to restore order, but Gladstone disliked the method of suspending Habeas Corpus, which itself reflected his deeper feeling that law and order were not merely, and perhaps not only, matters of applying coercion through the state, but rather the moulding of society in such a way that the community could police itself – with especially the propertied classes taking the lead in this regard. This fitted in with Gladstone's view that possessory right was an important settling influence, hence his remarks in Dublin in 1877; but he had no desire to rob the landlords. The Land Bill would remove the causes of rural crime, he believed; and to tackle the cause (rural discontent) rather than the effect (agrarian crime) was his intention. The way forward was a union of property, with contented tenant farmers living in harmony with the landlords. Hence his belief that neither landlord nor tenant should make unrealistic demands for rent, or for the reduction of rent. But he was moved forward to the idea of the Three Fs (Fixity of Tenure, Fair Rent and Freedom of Sale), though, having accepted this, he was now prepared to assert the government's authority against what he saw as Parnell's attempts to wreck the Land Act. In Leeds, in October 1881, he declared that disorder would be met with measures to prove that the 'resources of civilisation' were not exhausted.

The government's decision to arrest and gaol Parnell stands oddly with Gladstone's scruples about coercion; its decision to release him, a year later, seems even more at variance with any consistent thread. But the Gladstonian approach to Ireland was now taking shape, a shape that was influenced by the events that the government was obliged to respond to. To imprison Parnell was to acknowledge that this was, in the overall view, a political problem. To admit this was to suggest, what Gladstone already believed, that rural disorder could only be resolved by ending the conditions that gave rise to such disorder. Disorder was expensive to suppress; and Ireland had too long relied upon English money and support to suppress it. The idea of finding some means to bring Ireland to her senses – to remind her, and especially her propertied classes – of their responsibilities in giving Ireland normal life was growing in Gladstone's mind. But for this to take the form of a landlord counter-attack, and even victory, would (Gladstone's Cabinet colleagues convinced him) only compound the problem.[25]

Small wonder that Gladstone was inclined to leave Ireland alone again, especially since tenants were working the 1881 Act, and order was being restored in Ireland. But the problem with Ireland was that it was necessary at times to develop policies that went far beyond their original limits. The government could not ignore the fact that it was facing a closer alliance between the Conservative Opposition and the Home Rulers, a new mood that seemed in a few years' time to suggest that Tory and Nationalist might ally against Liberal. Therefore the government moved towards the idea of releasing Parnell from Kilmainham Gaol and breaking up the possible nefarious compact.[26] The Phoenix Park murders in May 1882 seemed to put an end to any clear direction in the government's Irish policy, which had now swung between coercion and conciliation, and to such a degree that it induced a form of political dizziness in the Cabinet and Gladstone, who were now glad to let it all go for a while. Imperial policy and Parliamentary Reform formed his personal political commitment. Yet certain elements in Gladstonian thinking about Ireland can be discerned. The dislike of a policy of thorough coercion; the revulsion against its cost, in money and English prestige; the hope that some form of stability could be worked in Ireland in such a way that the law would be seen as the instrument of public opinion, and not the means of subduing and coercing it; the hope that landlord and tenant might yet be shown their common interest; overall, the hope that there was a Conservative solution to the Irish problem, one that respected rights in property, and safety in power, was at least raised. The dead end of 1882 was, it turned out, more apparent than real.

Were these possibilities based on a realistic assessment of Ireland? Did Gladstone understand the deep division between landlord and tenant, the force of nationalist sentiment, the aggressive tactics that it employed, the violence of its language? Like many English statesmen, he failed to appreciate the fear that existed between rival people and communities in Ireland, above all between the two brands of Christian. His return to local government likewise can be seen as an enlightened response to the problem of Ireland; yet his belief that it would help create one British nation was, to say the least, one that had yet to be based on anything other than Gladstone's own perception of what that nation could be like: 'one nation for every purpose of duty and power'.[27]

The shift in Gladstone's thinking, from local government reform to Home Rule, can be traced in various ways. In his February 1883 ruminations, quoted above, to which J.L. Hammond gave great credence, and which indeed indicate a growing flexibility of mind, words like 'no limits except the supremacy of the Imperial Parliament' certainly appear to justify Hammond's claim that, even when Gladstone was not a Home Ruler, 'anybody who studied his speeches, or his letters to his colleagues, could see that if conditions changed he might well become one'.[28] Yet when considering the position of the Parnellites in the British Parliament in 1883 he dismissed their influence with the somewhat disagreeable comment that they were like vermin about a man's body: certainly irritating but hardly life-threatening.[29] The key year in the history of Gladstone and Ireland was therefore 1885; for it was then that the desirability, indeed the inevitability of Home Rule for Ireland forced itself upon him, and drove him towards the revolution in British politics that was to shape parties, Parliament and policies for the next three decades.

Gladstone's moves towards this revolution were complex: moralism, political calculation, and a certainty that England and Ireland had reached a turning point in their relationship all provided the general context of his thinking. The details lay in the working out or engaging of all these trends. Gladstone, when dealing with coercion in the early 1880s, had come to the conclusion that it was an expensive and ultimately self-defeating exercise; that it was better to find means to obviate the need for coercion, and that those means must be political. He still doubted whether a responsible political leader could be found in Ireland who would work with him towards this desirable end; though the Kilmainham Treaty with Parnell in 1882 suggested that he was prepared, however gingerly, to deal with Irish nationalism. When considering the franchise reforms which the government passed in 1884, Gladstone weighed up the possible consequences for the Union if Ireland were to benefit from these changes. Although he acknowledged in a letter to Lord Hartington in 1883 that nationalists would take twenty-five seats from the Liberals in Ireland, and increase their representation from forty to nearly eighty members, he concluded that 'to withhold franchises from Ireland while giving them to England and Scotland, and to proclaim the principle of an unequal union, is the greatest blow that can be struck by any human power at the Act of Union'.[30]

It was ironic, therefore, that in June 1885 a caretaker Conservative administration under Lord Salisbury took office, following a Tory and Irish Nationalist voting combination that turned Gladstone out, and governed until elections should be held under the new franchise. There followed a brief Conservative-Parnellite rapprochement, as the Conservatives seemed inclined to consider a federal settlement for Ireland, with Lord Carnarvon exchanging ideas with Parnell about the possibilities of such a scheme. This encouraged Gladstone in another step towards Home Rule: the possibility that the Conservatives might be induced to accept such a measure, and bring it in with Liberal support, as Peel had acted in 1846 when he repealed the Corn Laws. Then there were the undeniable results of the general election of December 1885, which saw the Parnellites winning eighty-five Irish seats, plus one in Liverpool. 'Ireland has now spoken', he concluded, and 'an effort ought to be made by the Government without delay to meet her demands for the management of an Irish legislative body of Irish as distant from Imperial affairs.'[31] Gladstone, as a firm believer in parliamentary government, had no doubt that Westminster could resolve Ireland; that the parliamentary system was one that could contain and domesticate this problem. He was not the only one, for in 1885 Joseph Chamberlain was also engaging on the question of what could reasonably be offered to Parnell. His 'central board' scheme for the reform of Irish local government was discussed by the Cabinet before the government fell, but failed to find favour. In any case Gladstone was a significant step beyond local government reform (and not unwilling to part with Chamberlain over Ireland, for reasons of keeping moral values alive in politics, an ambition which was not entirely unconnected with Chamberlain's developing role as potential successor to Gladstone).[32]

Yet it was local government reform that the Parnellites anticipated,[33] even though in November 1885 Gladstone requested a copy of Parnell's proposed constitution for Ireland.[34] Gladstone was determined that his hand would not be forced by Parnell, whatever the cautious contacts between them: he told Lord Spencer that an 'immense loss of dignity in a great crisis of the Empire, would attend the forcing of our hands by the Irish, or otherwise'.[35]

The general election of 1885 suggested, however, that a certain forcing of hands might prevail, for the Liberals won 335 seats, the Conservatives 249, and the difference between the two exactly equalled Parnell's number; Parnell could thus keep either British party out of office, but he could only put the Liberals in. While the consequences of this remarkable result were being digested, there came the sensational news, released on 17 December 1885 by his son Herbert, that Gladstone had reached the conclusion that Ireland should have Home Rule.[36]

Gladstone accepted this precipitate action with equanimity, for he was convinced of the moral rightness of his move from local government to Home Rule. Ireland must be brought to a sense of her responsibilities, which she had escaped for far too long. Of course, England had to bear her share of the burden for bringing about the present undesirable state of affairs; the Union, carried by corruption, had brought the corruption of Irish politics, and of Anglo-Irish relations in its wake. Moreover, if landlord and tenant could be persuaded to work together, instead of standing at odds with each other, Ireland would again enjoy social peace, and social responsibility, the corollary of social peace. Parnell, he believed, was by no means as anti-landlordism as he seemed (a view with good foundation in fact). Gladstone's coupling of the land question with Home Rule, his acceptance of what he had hitherto disliked – land purchase – was probably because of his need to retain the support of Spencer and John Morley, key figures in his party;[37] and partly it may have been a kind of consolation prize if the Home Rule Bill should fail. But there can be no doubt that Home Rule was his real goal, his governing passion; for it was only through the policy of Home Rule that government by consent could be rooted in Ireland, and law in Ireland made integral to its social attitudes, as had happened in Scotland.[38]

When Gladstone took office with Parnellite support in January 1885, he therefore did so with conviction. His Home Rule Bill still excites admiration for the boldness of its conceptualisation. Yet it was a much less bold measure than a casual glance through the document might suggest. Yes, Ireland was to have control of her domestic affairs, and (a frightening prospect to many Liberals let alone Conservatives) Irish Members of Parliament were to be removed from Westminster altogether: a confession by Gladstone of the difficulty in separating 'Irish' from 'Imperial' affairs, and of allowing Irish MPs to vote on matters which might be construed as purely domestic to England, while also having the privilege of dealing with Irish affairs, which English MPs must be excluded from. But the constitution that Ireland would enjoy reflected Gladstone's conservative intentions for Ireland. There were to be two legislative 'orders' in Ireland. The first would consist of twenty-eight peers and seventy-five others meeting high property qualifications (a minimum of £4000 or an annual income of £200), elected by voters meeting a £25 qualification. The second order would consist of 204 Members elected under the existing United Kingdom franchise. Both orders would normally sit as a single chamber, but either could demand a separate vote on any particular issue and exercise a veto. The first order could exercise its veto for a three year limit. The Land Purchase Bill (which Gladstone dropped after the failure of the first Home Rule Bill) would ease the landlords' fear by offering them an alternative, if they did not trust their property to the new political regime in Dublin.[39]

Gladstone's Home Rule Bill was introduced in the House of Commons on 8 April 1886, and fell before the ranks of Conservatives, and dissident Liberals led by Hartington and Chamberlain, in June. The contrast between the essentially conservative intentions of the measure, and the high hopes placed on it by Gladstone (and by posterity) still strikes the observer. Gladstone brought to bear all his formidable powers of persuasion; and the history of Anglo-Irish relations, especially between 1912 and 1922, helps explain why the Bill has been charged with such significance. If posterity thinks, as Gladstone said they must, not only of now but of the years to come, then the years to come suggest that Gladstone's wasted breath was of serious consequences for the people of Britain and Ireland. Yet, from a contemporary perspective, there were formidable obstacles in the way of success. Even if the Commons had passed the Home Rule Bill, it would surely have fallen in the Lords; and for Gladstone to lead a crusade against the Lords would have been a tricky enterprise and not one that he would have found congenial. But Gladstone did succeed in one of his greatest aims: to domesticise the Irish problem, to bring the Irish Nationalist MPs within the British constitution, indeed to bind them to the Liberal Party. Gladstone embraced the party spirit eagerly, remarking in the course of the debate on the Home Rule Bill that those on the Opposition benches who claimed that Ireland was best dealt with in a non-party spirit were profoundly mistaken:

What is meant by this? Is it meant that the Party spirit is to be expelled generally from the circuit of English politics? Is that so? Is there a dreamer who, in the weakness of his dreams, has imagined that you can really work the free institutions of this country upon any other principles than those in the main which your fathers have handed down to you and which have made this country what it is?[40]

Parnell for his part responded in kind: the Home Rulers were now in the Liberal alliance in what facts, as well as intentions, reveal was a pervasive and durable relationship. Gladstone may have failed in his Home Rule Bill, and again in 1893 in his second Bill; but he had achieved another great goal: that of making the Irish question a 'creature of parliamentary politics' and thus 'containing it for thirty years'.[41] Nowhere was this shown more clearly than in Parnell's distancing himself from the 'Plan of Campaign', which launched a new, if more limited, period of agrarian agitation, and his eager embracing of his role as the lion of Liberal society. Parnell was given a 'perfect ovation' at a dinner of the Eighty Club attended by various English political luminaries; in July 1889 he was given the freedom of the city of Edinburgh, at which he made what his Nationalist critics called a 'disgustingly moderate speech', calling for the concession to the Irish people of the power to work out their own future, and assuring his audience that this could do no harm, but only good, to the United Kingdom and the Empire.[42]

Yet if Gladstone seemed in a fair way towards domesticating all but the most extreme Irish nationalists, he was by no means so successful in reconciling Unionists to his policy of Home Rule within the sovereignty of the British Parliament. It is easy to overestimate the importance of this, however, in the light of the Ulster Unionist rebellion of 1912–14.[43] Ulster and Irish Unionists were but poorly organised in their opposition to the first Home Rule Bill; even in the case of the second, they were by no means the determined people that they were by 1914. The Gladstonian generation of Unionists in Ireland shared the characteristics of Gladstone, in their determination to offer only the force of public opinion, the strength of a moral opposition, the power of a people united in demonstrating their hatred of Home Rule; but a hatred that would only take political expression.[44] Yet the fact remains that Gladstone was unwilling to regard the Ulster Unionists as anything more than a local variation of the Irish people, as the Highlanders were in relation to the Scottish people: he considered that some provision might be made for the minority; but a minority was what the Protestants of Ulster were, and they could not stand in the way of the Irish majority. This was a clear-cut response to the problem; but it raised the question of how that minority could be brought to live by, and under, laws made by a Parliament that they regarded as destructive of their lives and liberties. Gladstone believed that Home Rule would reconcile the Irish Catholic to the law, for the law would now be his; but, in so doing, he inverted the problem, creating a new set of people in Ireland who would not regard the law as theirs. But Gladstone believed that by settling the main, Nationalist grievance he would serve the interests of the United Kingdom as a whole; and this was what Gladstone wished to serve, by means of an Irish settlement.

Gladstone's fundamental desire to make Ireland like England was expressed in a speech he made after the defeat of the first Home Rule Bill. In Birmingham, on 7 November 1888, he claimed that Ireland suffered from a system of unequal laws; thus you had in England 'a law of combination which permitted working people to combine without exposing them to the charge of conspiracy'; 'but in Ireland, on the contrary, they may not practise the very same expedient of endeavouring to place themselves in collective action, which is prohibited under the name of inducing others to exclusive dealing'. The law of public meeting was likewise different in both countries; so was the law of prison discipline; and the question of payment of arrears was likewise troublesome, with Scottish tenants enjoying more protection in the matter of remitting rent. Worse, the Conservative government was itself abusing the law, in the case of the Mitchelstown shootings in which several men died as a result of police firing. And the origin of all this was the Union; the Union entailed coercion against the Irish people, but this trial must not go on for ever. We must not become the slaves of that particular generation, and it was the Liberal Party's duty to establish in Ireland 'that first condition of all good government the tolerable satisfaction and contentment of the people'. A system of permanent coercion could not secure that great end.[46]

The price of making Ireland into England involved satisfying English public opinion that Parnell was indeed, as he now claimed to be, a mediator between Ireland and England; the man who could deliver a peaceful Ireland into a system that involved Ireland remaining under the sovereignty of Westminster. This seemed to be moving towards a successful conclusion in 1889; but Parnell's being cited as co-respondant in the O'Shea divorce case placed that in great jeopardy. Parnell assured his supporters that he would emerge from the affair with his reputation unblemished; and he initially received the full support of his party, at a meeting held in Dublin on 18 November 1890. But there were signs that the Liberal Party could not let the matter rest there. On 21 November John Morley reported to Gladstone that Nonconformists would insist on Parnell's resignation as leader of the Irish Parliamentary Party. Gladstone would not go so far as to request the Home Rulers to drop their leader; but he did point out the difficulty of his leading his own party, since he, Gladstone, was so closely identified with the presentation of the Irish cause. The Irish Parliamentary Party at a meeting in Westminster on 25 November reelected Parnell as its chairman for the coming session, but it did so without knowledge of Gladstone's position. When his views were disclosed, on 26 November, the party was forced to choose between its leader and its goal. A meeting in Committee Room 15 witnessed a bitter and acrimonious debate, in which Parnell sought to postpone a decision on his future. But on 6 December Justin McCarthy, vice-chairman of the party, called on those who thought Parnell should stand down to leave and follow him. Forty-three left; twenty-seven and Parnell stayed behind.[47]

This did not end the Liberal alliance. On the contrary, it strengthened it, for Gladstone had now been given a new mandate to retain that alliance and lead it towards the promised land. In March 1891 Gladstone turned again to Ireland, emphasising that the great achievement of his policy so far was to inculcate and familiarise the Irish with the doctrine that Parliament was the organ through which redress of grievances was to be obtained. The Irish Parliamentary Party had accepted this and advanced it in the Irish mind. Again Gladstone insisted on the connection between Home Rule and social order in Ireland; the Irish were deprived by the present administration 'of the privileges which Englishmen enjoy'.[48] Thus it was with the utmost conviction that Gladstone led his party into office following the general election of July 1892. His second Home Rule Bill differed from the first in providing for the retention of Irish MPs at Westminster, thus assuming a less 'separatist' character. This time it was passed by the Commons, only to be rejected by the Lords with a vote of 419 against to only 41 in favour. Gladstone contemplated action against the Lords; but the vote for Home Rule in the Commons was narrow, following eighty-two sittings and an extended session. Gladstone was left to contemplate his greatest fear: that the 'struggle ... must survive me, cannot be survived by me'.[49]

It is hard, even at this distance, to make any definitive judgement on Gladstone and Ireland. His Land Bills made important inroads into the rights of property in Ireland. Yet he disliked, and ultimately abandoned, the resolution of the land problem which the Conservatives embraced: that of land purchase, whereby the state would buy out the landlord, and the tenant farmer would become an owner-occupier, repaying the state over a period of time. He disestablished the Church of Ireland, and thereby strengthened the Liberal Party in Ireland; yet within a few years of his being hailed as the Moses leading the Irish people into the promised land, he saw Irish Liberalism losing ground to the new Home Rule Party, which by the end of the 1870s was clearly the choice of the vast majority of Catholics in Ireland. He introduced the policy of Home Rule, only to see it twice rejected in the British Parliament. He also saw his successors as Liberal leaders, Rosebery – and Asquith in particular – bound by his pledge, tied to his inheritance, and unable either to deliver on Home Rule, or to slough it off as a policy that could only lead the Liberals into a dead end: and Ireland and Great Britain into civil war.

Yet Gladstone and Ireland have made their enduring mark on the politics of the British Isles. If politics are about creating new contexts, providing new ways of thinking, then Gladstone was remarkably important in his attitude to Ireland. If he did not leave behind Home Rule, if he failed to grasp the importance of land purchase to the tenant farmers of Ireland, then at least he left behind some highly charged, ethically focussed phrases: 'justice for Ireland'; 'the government of Ireland by Irish ideas'; 'Ireland stands at your bar expectant, hopeful, almost suppliant', and, above all, his great conclusion to his speech when introducing the first Home Rule Bill. 'Think, I beseech you, think well, think wisely, think not for a moment, but for the years that are to come, before you reject the Bill'.[50] These phrases cast into pallor the machinations, the political calculations, the deviousness, the long period of disinterest that also characterise Gladstone's connection with Ireland. Gladstone gave Irish nationalism and its demands a liberal and democratic character and a parliamentary tradition, that transcend the immediate context of his policies. He gave the Irish Question the kind of moral dimension that he, and he alone of British politicians, could give it. Whether this was for good or ill remains in dispute. The best epitaph for his Irish policy was perhaps that written by Gladstone himself, when he ruminated on the affairs of men: 'We live . . . in a labyrinth of problems, and of moral problems, from which there is no escape permitted us'.[51]

7

Gladstone, Wales and the New Radicalism

Kenneth O. Morgan

Gladstonianism was a powerful factor among the Liberals in rallying and reuinifying them down to the 1906 general election, with its great imperatives of freedom of trade, religious equality and international peace founded on national self-determination. It remained of import-ance in building up the tradition of Liberal 'guiding principles' after 1918 (Lloyd George's memorable onslaught on Herbert, Viscount Gladstone notwithstanding). In the Liberal schisms of the 1920s the Gladstone tradition was still important in the reconstruction of 'the immortal principles of the great Liberal Party' and its various regional bases.

Even in the 1980s the tortuous attempt to construct a viable rela-tionship between the Liberals and the Social Democrats within the Alliance, was marked in the case of Roy Jenkins, himself an eminent historian of Liberalism, by frequent Gladstonian references to a 'union of hearts' and to there being no limit to the onward march of a nation (the European Community notwithstanding).

To an extent that is often forgotten, Gladstone was also a potent force in the birth and early growth of the Labour Party. He had a profound influence on Labour pioneers like Arthur Henderson, Philip Snowden and George Lansbury. Keir Hardie, in effect the founder of the Labour alliance in 1900, had an intense devotion for Gladstone as a great liberator of the masses: 'God bless him! May he be spared to accomplish the great work to which he has put his hand', he wrote in 1887.[1] He wrote a passionate tribute to Gladstone in the *Labour Leader* when the great man died in 1898, including in his eulogy the liberation of Ireland, and the challenge to the House of Lords and vested inter-ests generally. 'Gladstone's work has made Socialism possible', Hardie wrote.[2] The Liberal heritage was a vital factor in the history and ideas of the Labour and socialist movement at least down to 1945, as the writings of men such as Tawney and Laski indicate. In some respects, as in the attempt to redefine socialism as personal freedom, it had its relevance even in the 1980s, almost a century after Gladstone's death.[3]

Nor was Gladstone's legacy, real or assumed, confined to the political left. Where radicals saw the great emancipator, new Conservatives (sometimes christened neo-Liberals) extolled the great economist, even while they made Disraelian genuflections to 'one nation'. The prolonged attempt by Mrs Thatcher and her followers in the 1980s to restore faith in strict economy, private enterprise and market forces was a concentrated attempt to elevate once again the principles of Gladstonian economics after years of harassment and heresy by the aberrant followers of Keynes. With all these factors in mind, therefore, there is every justification in looking anew at Gladstone's style and principles.

A most important light is shed on Gladstone's abiding influence by his attitude towards the politics, culture and nationality of Wales. There is no doubt that in his later years Gladstone became a great national hero to the Welsh, amongst whom he made his home in Hawarden in Flintshire – witness the immense acclaim given to his mass address at Singleton Abbey in Swansea in 1887, or his dramatic speech at Cwmllan, at the foot of Snowdon in 1892.[4]

Yet it has been widely assumed, both by Conservative churchmen and by several Welsh Nonconformist radicals of the quasi-nationalist *Cymru Fydd* (Young Wales) school, that Gladstone was basically hostile to the Welsh Nonconformist presence that emerged in the Liberal Party between the 1860s and the 1890s. There is often assumed to have been a fundamental tension between the high church squire of Hawarden and the great mass of Welsh Nonconformists. William George, Lloyd George's brother, called Gladstone 'a drag on the wheel'; the Unionist squire of Trevalyn Hall (not far from Hawarden), Arthur Griffith-Boscawen, said much the same.[5]

Furthermore, it has been claimed that this is a symptom of a wider weakness endemic in the Liberal Party in the later nineteenth century – the pressure upon Gladstone by 'faddists' or purveyors of 'crochets' in the party, especially after the split over Irish Home Rule in 1886.[6] The supreme symbol of this is taken to be the 1891 Newcastle Programme (which had Welsh disestablishment as the second in its lengthy list of items), which Arthur Balfour derided as 'a programme of varieties'.[7] The Welsh radical element in the Liberal Party is taken as a symbol of the sectionalism that created turmoil within the late Victorian Liberal coalition. The influence of the so-called Celtic Fringe is considered to be a damaging factor down to 1914, and thus a major cause in the ultimate death, 'strange' or otherwise, of Liberal England (and Wales). I wish here to examine this view, which seems to me basically mistaken.

Wales, in fact, played only a marginal and episodic part in British political life from the Tudor age down to the 1860s. There were only occasional noises off in the valleys, as in the Merthyr uprising of 1831, the Rebecca riots or Chartism. Welsh politics, wrote the radical Henry Richard in 1866, were essentially 'feudal'.[8] Even so, Gladstone, as he emerged to full political stature, encountered an important range of influences which kept him in close touch with Welsh affairs. He married a Welsh woman, Catherine Glynne. He lived in Hawarden. In 1866, he was much impressed by the *Letters* published by Henry Richard which drew attention to the public neglect of Welsh interests.[9] Gladstone was also increasingly drawn into the Welsh political and cultural scene, as in his memorable attendance at the Mold *eisteddfod* of 1873 when he praised 'the ancient history, the ancient deeds and the ancient language of your country, the Principality of Wales'.[10] Through Henry Austen Bruce, his Home Secretary in 1868–74, he became involved in Welsh education and the campaign for a national university.

Above all, there was Stuart Rendel, the member for Montgomeryshire from 1880 to 1894.[11] He became a particularly close friend of Gladstone. He was his host several times at his villa on the French Riviera; his second daughter, Maud, married Gladstone's third son, Henry; he was a pall-bearer at Gladstone's funeral. Rendel was neither a great intellectual nor a powerful orator. But he was a very shrewd political strategist. Although an Englishman, an Anglican and (remarkably) a wealthy arms manufacturer, he had a clear conception of the need to recognise the Welsh political identity, focusing on the supreme issue of the disestablishment of the church in Wales, and of how to merge Welsh national causes of various kinds with a wider organic Liberalism.

After 1890, Rendel became somewhat out of touch with some aspects of Welsh politics, as his concern with the tithe riots of the late 1880s indicated. He had scant sympathy with the aggressive, almost separatist, nationalism of younger men like David Lloyd George. But Rendel retained a powerful influence on Gladstone right down to 1894, when he went to the House of Lords on the premier's retirement. Stuart Rendel was in many ways a genuine radical – witness his later strong support for Lloyd George during the Boer War and the campaign for the 1909 'People's Budget'. He remained a benevolent influence in Wales, notably as a generous benefactor of the University College of Wales, Aberystwyth, where several chairs and a hall of residence bear his name to this day. By educating Gladstone in the national and political needs of Wales, he played a notable and creative part in transforming the social and political outlook of the Liberal Party.

Gladstone's direct contact with Welsh politics down to the Irish Home Rule schism of 1886 was intermittent, though important. In particular, as a deeply committed Anglican, he viewed with great anxiety the rise of a popular Nonconformist movement in Wales to disestablish and disendow the Anglican Church there. Gladstone maintained that there was no parallel with the Irish Church which he himself had disestablished in 1869. He spoke strongly against Welsh disestablishment on Watkin Williams' motion in the Commons in May 1870. The Prime Minister emphasised that the Welsh Church enjoyed 'a complete consitutional, legal and historical identity with the Church of England'.[12] A separate measure to disestablish the church in Wales was, therefore, unthinkable.

On the other hand, Gladstone did also appreciate the perceived inadequacies of the church in Wales at the time. After all, fully three-quarters (perhaps four-fifths) of the worshipping population of Wales attended Nonconformist chapels, not the mother church. As Colin Matthew has shown, he accepted and endorsed the growing religious pluralism within the United Kingdom, developing since the 1840s. He made the significant admission that there was indeed a Welsh Church problem – and a Welsh political problem extending far beyond it. He devoted, therefore, much time and trouble to selecting a Welsh-speaking bishop for the see of St Asaph in 1870, and again for the see of Llandaff in 1882. He took it very seriously. He had also evidently totally changed his view on the Welsh language which had created 'unfavourable impressions' in his mind back in 1856.[13]

Thus in January 1870, he wrote: 'I have not since taking my present office felt more strongly the gravity of any matter of duty requiring to be done than this of the Welsh bishopric'.[14] In December 1882, he added complainingly, 'A vacancy in a Welsh see costs me more trouble than six English vacancies'.[15] The effects could be comic. He wrote to Henry Bruce in January 1870: 'If you read in the papers some morning that I have been carried to Bedlam and that a straight waistcoat is considered necessary, please to remember it will be entirely owing to the vacancy in the see of St Asaph'.[16]

The personal results were not altogether happy. Joshua Hughes, eventually appointed to St Asaph in 1870, was not a distinguished bishop. He had, it emerged, acquired only a B.D. (Lampeter) not a B.A. (Cambridge) as recorded in *Crockford's*.[17] Richard Lewis, appointed to Llandaff in 1882, was termed a '*pis aller*', and 'an inferior Basil Jones' (a reference to the Bishop of St David's, himself by no means an intellectual giant).[18]

Even so, Gladstone's concern with Welsh church appointments had indirectly a most powerful effect on the movement for Welsh disestablishment and church reform, even if this was largely accidental. In paying such intimate attention to the need for a Welsh-speaking bishop, sympathetic to Nonconformists, Gladstone was making a notable public concession. He was acknowledging implicitly that the disestablishment of the Welsh Church was justifiable, not on the Liberationist argument of freeing all churches everywhere from the trammels of the state connection, but on the specific grounds of Welsh nationality. Wales, it emerged, could be recognised as a nation, as Ireland had been in 1869. By 1885, when thirty of the thirty-four Welsh constituencies returned Liberals and greatly helped Gladstone back to Downing Street for the third time, the great majority of the Liberal Party, especially of course in the principality, was in sympathy with Welsh disestablishment. Gladstone was coming to accept the great tide of popular feeling – which he himself had indirectly stimulated. By 1885, indeed, he was making private admissions that he might well have to reverse his view on Welsh disestablishment,[19] as his son Herbert's 'Hawarden Kite' was dramatically to show he had also done on Irish Home Rule.

Gladstone also stoked the fires of Welsh national sentiment elsewhere. He made, as we have seen, a powerful emotive declaration of support for Welsh cultural nationalism at the Mold *eisteddfod* in 1873. He also intervened strongly in the Commons on behalf of the Welsh Sunday Closing Bill in 1881, which he justified on national grounds as a sanction for separate Welsh legislation on a matter on which Welsh Nonconformists had particularly strong feelings.[20]

Above all, he was pushed by Bruce, Rendel and others into endorsing the Welsh crusade for higher education. He publicly endorsed Hussey Vivian's motion on behalf of Welsh intermediate schools in the Commons in 1879.[21] He appointed the epoch-making departmental com-

mittee on Welsh higher education in 1880–81 which, led by its chairman Lord Aberdare (formerly Henry Bruce), called powerfully for a
Welsh intermediate school system and for two Welsh university colleges.[22] Gladstone also reluctantly provided some state funds for the
new colleges at Cardiff and Bangor in 1883. Even more reluctantly,
he endorsed support for a third college, the University College on the
seafront in Aberystwyth which had existed since 1872 and which had
already produced such distinguished students as O.M. Edwards and
Tom Ellis.[23] Unforeseen at the time, the social and cultural base for
a Welsh national movement had thereby been provided. The schools
and colleges created by the Welsh educational crusade – involving
such emotional symbols as *Sul y Brifysgol*, when poor chapel-goers gave
their pence to a national university on 'University Sunday' – were to
provide the new middle-class elite that dominated Welsh political,
commercial and cultural life down to 1914. The University of Wales,
Prifysgol y Werin ('The People's University') by its very existence challenged the hierarchical, static world that Wales had known over the
centuries.

By the mid 1880s, the change in the tone of Welsh politics was very
pronounced. The older type of Welsh Liberal, men like Henry Richard,
Lewis Dillwyn, George Osborne Morgan and Hussey Vivian, was being
supplanted by younger, more radical, more intensely nationalist figures such as Tom Ellis and the very youthful Lloyd George. By 1885
Wales had become the most Liberal part of the British Isles. It was,
of course, particularly affected by the Reform and Redistribution Acts
of 1884–85. With thirty Liberal Members it had become an uncon-
querable bastion of the British left.

Most significantly, in the Irish Home Rule schism of 1886, it
responded overwhelmingly to endorse Gladstone's position on Ireland.
Despite the impact of Joseph Chamberlain and the radicalism of his
Unauthorised Programme, which had an especial appeal for Nonconformists and disestablishers, the Protestant Welsh in their thousands
turned decisively towards Gladstone.

Only a small minority flirted with Liberal Unionism – and several
of those few, including Sir Hussey Vivian, the editor-publisher Thomas
Gee of Denbigh, and (almost) the youthful David Lloyd George, swung
back to Gladstonianism soon after the polls.[24] In Montgomeryshire,
Rendel, who clung on to his marginal seat with much difficulty, urged
Liberal activists to 'say as little as they can' about Ireland, and to
concentrate on disestablishment, land reform and the towering personality and moral leadership of Gladstone.[25] The relative unanimity

of Wales in 1886 (and again in 1900 during the Boer War) was in marked contrast with the divisions of Liberalism in Scotland and its large-scale retreat in much of southern England. It was Welsh national consciousness that largely contributed to this result.

After the Irish Home Rule split in 1886, there was a major transformation of the Liberal Party. There was the new prominence of labour and the unions, of agrarian radicalism, of urban progressives in London – and of Welsh and Scottish nationalists. It was, contrary to what many historians have alleged in Dangerfield-like terms, an optimistic, forward-looking period, the years which gave birth to the New Liberalism of Hobhouse and Hobson, of Rowntree, Masterman and Chiozza Money, of Churchill and Lloyd George.[26] Political developments in Wales were an important part of this optimism.

There was the creation of a distinct Welsh Parliamentary Party, with its own whips, chaired by Stuart Rendel from 1888 onwards. There were the emergence of distinct Welsh political priorities: church disestablishment, education, temperance, land reform, a qualified form of governmental devolution. There was a new political structure in Wales, with the North Wales and South Wales Liberal Federations coming into being – both of them affiliated to the National Liberal Federation in London, unlike their comrades in Scotland. There was also a new elite of political leadership – Tom Ellis, Herbert Lewis, Sam Evans, D.A. Thomas in the mining valleys and, above all, Lloyd George, returned to Parliament for Caernarfon Boroughs in a by-election in 1890. Others, like Ellis Griffith and Llewelyn Williams, were following on. Even Rendel himself was gradually being phased out. Gladstone was being forced to respond, and respond positively, to their pressure.

Certainly the Liberal leader was far from happy about some aspects of this. He was worried about the growth of agitation over the land tenure system in Wales, with its alarming parallels with the Land League of Michael Davitt in Ireland. He kept silent over the tithe disturbances and the government's various Tithe Bills of 1889–91 – an almost unique act of self-denial on an ecclesiastical topic. He was, however, forced to acknowledge that there was, if only on cultural grounds, a separate Welsh agrarian question, with largely Nonconformist, Welsh-speaking tenant farmers deeply alienated from their Anglican, Tory, anglicised landlords. Great dynasts like Sir Watkin Williams Wynn, Lord Penrhyn or Lord Cawdor were finding that the sands of time were running out. Gladstone, somewhat characteristic-

ally, appeared to give public support to Tom Ellis's Welsh Land Bill
of 1892 – even though in the end he voted against it. He also strongly
endorsed Rendel's Welsh Intermediate Education Bill of 1889, which
many of the clergy, and St David's College, Lampeter, viewed with
intense suspicion.[27] The eventual Act of 1889 was a powerful one, creating a nationwide network of secondary 'county' schools, and making
Wales a bastion of state secondary education which it remains to this
day. Gladstone also caused a sensation by a particularly emphatic
endorsement of the Welsh language and its value, at the Wrexham
national *eisteddfod* in 1888.[28]

He also made a decisive shift on Welsh disestablishment. After 1886
one prominent Liberal after another came out in support of it in principle: Morley, Harcourt, Rosebery, even Spencer. Francis Schnadhorst,
the party organiser, encouraged the growth of the North Wales and
South Wales Liberal Federations, both of which had disestablishment
as their first objective. Gradually, indeed delphically, Gladstone also
responded. As an Anglican, he was repelled by the anticlericalism of
men like Sam Evans and Lloyd George, notably when the latter
attacked the 1891 church congress at Rhyl for 'floating on barrels of
beer'. But, almost imperceptibly, in a sea change as it were, Gladstone
moved to a complete reversal of his views on Welsh disestablishment.
It might be noted here that his son, the Reverend Stephen Gladstone,
the Rector of Hawarden, became a committed disestablisher.

Thus we have Gladstone in June 1887, in terms of remarkable
obscurity even for him, stating that he was 'endeavouring to give to
the demand for information that is not unnaturally entertained whatever satisfaction the question may permit'.[29] In 1890 Gladstone actually voted on behalf of Scottish disestablishment and declared that the
question in Wales was 'ripe for decision'. In February 1891 he both
spoke and voted for it in the Commons. He placed his argument on
the firm ground of Welsh nationality. He declared that the Welsh
Church had become the church of the few, and the church of the
rich.[30] Wales was a nation of Nonconformists. A great intellectual
crisis had thus been overcome. At Newcastle in October 1891, as
noted, Welsh disestablishment was the second item on the Liberal
programme, with Gladstone's benevolent assistance.

When he formed his fourth and final government in August 1892,
Gladstone was very aware of the problems of Wales. After all, he had
a majority of only forty; the Welsh Liberal members numbered thirty-
one and theoretically held the balance of power. He actually formed
his government in Rendel's elegant home at 1 Carlton Gardens, just

behind Pall Mall. He accepted all the three main points that Rendel put to him. He went ahead with a charter for a national university of Wales, ignoring the clerical protests that emanated from St David's, Lampeter. With some reluctance, he appointed a Royal Commission, rather than a mere committee, to inquire into the Welsh land question.[31] Finally he drafted a Suspensory Bill to suspend the vested interests created within the Welsh Church, an earnest of goodwill regarding future disestablishment and disendowment. In addition, a talented young Welsh MP, Tom Ellis of Merioneth, was made a junior whip.

Despite much sceptical criticism from the Welsh newspapers, Gladstone was now clearly moving towards the framing of a Welsh Disestablishment Bill. 'Vote! Vote! Vote! for Irish Home Rule and Welsh Disestablishment', he shouted at Lord Randolph Churchill in the House.[32] In the late autumn of 1893, a Welsh disestablishment measure was being drawn up by government draftsmen, and indeed was to be introduced by Asquith, the Home Secretary, the following May, after Gladstone had retired as Premier.[33] It is worth noting, incidentally, that despite much political and historical controversy on the point, Monmouthshire was firmly included as being part of Wales in this Bill.

Gladstone retired as Premier in early March 1894. He was followed by Lord Rosebery, a change greeted with some rebelliousness by Welsh Liberals who had little regard for an imperialist peer as Prime Minister. It seemed as if an important chapter in Welsh politics was at an end. However, it was not quite over. In June 1895, *The Times* announced, quite unexpectedly, that Gladstone had cancelled his 'pair' with Villiers over the Welsh Disestablishment Bill now going through its committee stage in the House. It emerged that Gladstone objected to two disendowment provisions, notably the secularisation of cathedrals. (Gladstone's grandson, W.G.C. Gladstone, MP for Kilmarnock, also objected on this point when the 1912 Disestablishment Bill was being discussed, and that the provision about cathedrals was eventually removed.)[34] However, Gladstone assured a Welsh Liberal MP that he still accepted the justice of the broad principal of disestablishment for Wales. There seems no reason to doubt this. Gladstone, after all, had come to recognise that Welsh nationality existed – but also that the Welsh national movement differed fundamentally from that in Ireland. The land question in Wales was more amenable to a compromise settlement. The pressure for separatism was much less intense. Cultural nationalism did not necessarily lead to a demand for political separation or Home Rule. Welsh rural society was not scarred by the endemic violence of tenant-landlord relations in Ireland. The religious denominations were less antagonistic since there was no Welsh Ulster. Wales was, above all, stimulated by a desire for national equality within the United Kingdom as a whole. It was a part of the wider democratisation of British society as a whole.

By the time of Gladstone's retirement, the influence of the Welsh within the Liberal Party, and on the British political scene, was much enhanced. It was to remain powerful until after the First World War, with Lloyd George becoming Premier himself in 1916 and passing the eventual disestablishment and disendowment of the Welsh Church (with general all-party endorsement by this time) in 1919. But several major questions, however, remain to be asked about the process we have outlined.

First of all, was the role of the Welsh a symbol of a wider, disastrous movement towards sectionalism, parochialism and eventual disintegration for British Liberalism? This seems a very doubtful view. After all, the Liberal Party had always been a coalition of divergent interests, a kind of popular front, ever since it came into existence in the latter period of Palmerston's reign in the early 1860s. As early as the 1870s, the stresses between the old Whigs, middle-class mercantile Liberals and scattered groups of working-class and other radicals, and between all of them and their parliamentary leadership, were evident. Dr T.A. Jenkins's study has shown how the defection of the Whigs was under way from 1874 onwards,[35] and that a range of popular clubs and local Liberal associations was emergent, not least in London. In these circumstances, Liberals had to work out their ideological positions pragmatically as they went along – indeed, this is what they always had done. Attempts to impose a single great, overarching theme on the party had always been misguided, let alone efforts to 'wipe the slate clean' as the Liberal Imperialists tried vainly to do after 1900.[36]

The Welsh, indeed, were a vigorous element in the many-faceted radicalism and pluralism of the *fin-de-siècle* Liberal Party. Further, the causes of Wales were wide-ranging in their implications. They were not promoted by single-issue pressure-groups, like the Liberation Society or the United Kingdom Alliance, which cared only for their own sole, obsessive concern. The Welsh embraced religious, agrarian, educational, temperance and labour reform, without any necesary feeling of incompatibility or a battle for primacy existing between them. Thus Welsh disestablishment after 1880 merged into a wider nationwide campaign for democratic reform, instead of being the dogmatic

narrow theme as propagated by the Liberationists. Gladstone's positive response to the Welsh is a tribute to this outward-looking quality.

Secondly, it may well be questioned whether Gladstone's positive
reaction to the pressures of the Welsh Liberals was the product simply
of 'political blackmail'.[37] Of course, political pressure by the Welsh
played its part, as it always does in politics. Liberal votes among the
Welsh, the Scots and religious Nonconformists generally were an
important consideration, especially after 1886 when Liberalism
appeared to have lost its majority in England with the defection of
the Chamberlainites and the Whigs simultaneously. There was the
proclaimed policy, too, of 'filling up the cup' so that the challenge to
the House of Lords from a Liberal government would be as comprehensive as possible.[38]

But there was more to it than that. There was also the force of
nationalism – an elemental, almost sacred force for Gladstone in continental Europe and in the United Kingdom as well since his famous
protest against Neapolitan tyranny in 1851. Thus it was that his perception of the triumph of nationalism in Italy or the Balkan countries,
along with his first-hand observation of communal endeavour in the
small nation of Norway which he witnessed in 1885, played its part in
Gladstone's mounting understanding of the needs of Wales. He was
also aware of the wider social forces released in his party from the
1870s onwards, and only inadequately reflected in the Newcastle Programme. These forces needed sustained, moral leadership.

On balance, he saw Welsh radicalism as a source of strength for his
principles and for his party – 'it is not the Irish case all over again'.[39]
Welsh radicalism was not self-contained or exclusive. The rural areas
made common cause with the mining valleys of the south. The Welsh
could build bridges between the Old Liberalism of democracy, civic
and religious equality and the New Liberalism of social reform, with
its links with organised labour. It could straddle Tom Ellis in the
agrarian uplands of Merioneth, and 'Mabon' in the coal-mining
strongholds of the Rhondda. Lloyd George's own career down to
1914 – perhaps later – showed vividly how a Welsh outsider, from a
distinct and possibly more classless society, could fuse the Old Liberalism and the New in political action. There was, indeed, a basic
strength about British Liberalism in the 1890s, masked by policy divisions first over Ireland and then over southern Africa, and by tensions
over the leadership when Gladstone retired – just as the condition of
the Labour Party was more robust in the 1951–64 period than its
schisms over foreign policy and the leadership struggle after Attlee

departed might suggest at that time. The Welsh fitted naturally into this pattern of growth in the 1890s and Gladstone recognised it.

Finally, what light do the activities of the Welsh shed upon 'faddism', that nebulous concept on which important books by Professors Shannon and Hamer have focused? In practice, I would argue, 'faddism' brought important new elements of vitality into the Liberal coalition. It helped to extend the Liberal appeal to agricultural voters and to industrial workers alike after 1885, as well as to the long dormant and semi-colonised 'Celtic Fringe'. The analogy Gladstone frequently drew was with the United States, a land which much influenced him, and where he had close contacts such as with the radical Republican Sumner and the tycoon Andrew Carnegie. In such writings as 'Kin Beyond the Sea', Gladstone lavished praise on the United States as a buoyant democracy and the land of future.[40] He told John Morley in 1891 that the 'history and working of freedom in America' was 'the first object and study for every young man'.[41] He was much struck by how the American constitutional and social system could recover from the disruption of civil war after 1865 and adapt to a dynamic democracy.

Despite his own early declaration of support for the secessionist South in 1862 – which later much embarrassed him and which he totally recanted – he admired the USA as a pluralist, popular society with diverse cultural traditions, vibrant religious communities (all disestablished) and varied ethnic constituents. It was moving in the right direction – 'the stream of tendency' was satisfactory and healthy. The late Victorian Liberal Party to Gladstone was, in many ways, the United States writ small. It, too, embodied the collective will of 'capable citizens', of 'the masses' rather than 'the classes'. Wales, no less than Midlothian, played a vital part in his understanding here. It was a crucial target for his moral rhetoric and popular oratory. It helped make him a democrat, 'the People's William' indeed.

Time was to show that by 1914 the Liberals, revived by the 1906 election and driven by a powerful programme of major social legislation thereafter, had absorbed many of their sectional strains – with the omnipresent exception of Ireland, which was a problem apart. By 1914 there was some renewed confidence in Liberal ranks, *pace* Dangerfield's 'Strange Death' thesis. The troubles surrounding labour, insurance and the suffragettes seemed to recede even if Ireland remained insoluble. Ministers commented that 'time is on our side' and that they were 'nearly out of the wood'.[42] Gladstone's legacy was the forging of a new Progressive Alliance, of which the Labour

Party, so close in its outlook to late Victorian Liberalism especially in its economics and links with the chapels, was an outgrowth. Had not Keir Hardie himself – 'Labour's Grand Old Man' – paid tribute to it?

The strength of Liberalism down to 1914, like that of the Labour Party after 1931, lay in the fact that it was not monolithic. It was a sectional party with diverse traditions. The relationship of the lively, obstreperous Welsh with their leader, Gladstone, was thus a symptom of a wider renewal, an infusion of new life. Out of apparently arid, outdated arguments about such arcane matters as the origin of tithe, the purpose of educational charities, the title to Welsh land or the lineal components of the concept of Welsh nationhood, can be seen emerging a pattern of politics recognisably modern.

8

Gladstone and Garibaldi

Derek Beales

There can be few among his contemporaries with whom Gladstone would have preferred to be linked than with Garibaldi. A year after Garibaldi's death in 1882, Gladstone spoke of 'the marvellous effect produced upon all minds by the simple nobility of his demeanour, by his manners and acts . . . his splendid integrity . . . his wide and universal sympathies . . . that seductive simplicity of manner which never departed from him, and that inborn and native grace which seemed to attend all his actions'. Garibaldi, he said, united 'the most profound and tender humanity with his fiery valour'. Gladstone wrote too of his illustrious name, 'inseparably connected with the not less illustrious name of the great Cavour, and . . . with the name of Victor Emmanuel'.[1] All that, let me acknowledge, is from Morley's *Life*, and one of the subsidiary points that emerges from this story is how wonderfully Morley selected, organised and presented material which would have overwhelmed almost any other writer.

At the time Morley wrote, Garibaldi unquestionably qualified for a red-letter day in the Liberal Calendar of Saints, with perhaps George Washington and Abraham Lincoln, to mention only foreigners.[2] In Italy he was all but deified in his lifetime. Artists depicted him crucified and ascending, and, according to one of his modern biographers, this expressed 'no more than the feelings of the great mass of the Italian people, especially in the southern provinces'.[3] The nuns of a Palermitan convent, promising to love him and pray to Santa Rosalia for him, compared him to St George, 'sweet and beautiful as a seraph'; and a Milanese crowd gasped at his resemblance to St Ambrose.[4] Many relics are preserved and venerated: for example, some of his red shirts, locks of his hair, the bullet that pierced his ankle at the skirmish of Aspromonte in 1862, and the stretcher, stained with blood, on which he was carried wounded from the field.

Italians might perhaps be expected to go to extremes in their devotion to their national hero. More surprising was – and is – the adoration of the English, Welsh and Scots, especially as shown during Garibaldi's visit to England in 1864.[5] For the great Evangelical, Lord Shaftesbury, Old Testament references were as heavy with significance as prayers to Santa Rosalia were for Palermitan nuns: he likened Garibaldi to Gideon, Solomon and Judas Maccabaeus.[6] Notwithstanding Garibaldi's lack of religion and his notoriously casual attitude to matrimony, he was considered a fit recipient for gifts of English, Scottish and Italian Bibles and of *The Pilgrim's Progress*.[7] A prominent Nonconformist divine, the Rev. Newman Hall, one of Gladstone's principal Free Church contacts, described his life as 'a most powerful lesson of moral and political right and of true practical religion'.[8] A Methodist minister, preaching in Bedford, went further. He took his text from Jeremiah:

> Thou art my battleaxe and weapons of war; for with thee will I break in pieces the nations, and with thee will I destroy kingdoms ... And I will render unto Babylon and to all the inhabitants of Chaldea all their evil that they have done in Zion in your sight, saith the Lord.

The Lord's battleaxe was Garibaldi. Babylon represented the papacy with its temporal power, pernicious not only to the world at large but to Catholicism itself.[9] For many people in Britain, Garibaldi stood 'for the worshipful and holy cause of a nation's redemption, and for the hope of religious liberty through the downfall of the Papacy'.[10]

There were other grounds of attraction, of course. He was worshipped by many of the most exalted British ladies, at least three duchesses among them, so that Cavour thought it worthwhile to send to Emanuele D'Azeglio, his Minister in London, for distribution to the more influential of these admirers, a lock of the hero's hair.[11] When he went to the opera at Covent Garden, the Floral Hall through which he passed was packed, at 10s. 6d. a seat, with an audience composed of five women to one man. According to the *Scotsman*:

> Women, more or less in full dress, flew upon him, seized his hands, touched his beard, his poncho, his trousers, any part of him that they could reach ... They were delirious with excitement and behaved in the proverbially barbaric manner that Englishwomen of the middle class always do when

they are unduly excited and bewildered by anything that they consider splendour ... Would any class of people in any other country under the sun – always, of course, excepting America – conduct themselves in such an indecent manner?[12]

His popular appeal was not confined to self-conscious Protestants and women 'temporarily a little out of their minds'.[13] Many other influential groups looked to him as a model and champion. The Volunteer Rifle Clubs, founded during the war scare of 1859–60, treated him as a patron, and some of them imitated his dress in their uniforms.[14] Freemasons knew him for one of themselves.[15] Working-Men's Associations, including trade unions, had no doubt that he belonged among them and that their class was 'the class whom [he] loves and delighteth to honour'.[16] Lord Granville, Leader of the House of Lords at the time of Garibaldi's visit, explained to Queen Victoria:

> [He] has all the qualifications for making him a popular idol in this country. He is of low extraction, he is physically and morally brave, he is a good guerilla soldier ... he has a simple manner with a sort of nautical dignity, and a pleasing smile. He has no religion, but he hates the Pope. He is a goose, but that is considered to be an absence of diplomatic guile. His mountebank dress ... has a certain dramatic effect ... His political principles, which are nearly as dangerous to the progress and maintenance of real liberty as the most despotic systems, are thought admirably applicable to foreign countries.

Granville's condescending cynicism told only part of the story. To an extent unmatched by any other figure, historical or contemporary, Garibaldi combined the attributes of a film star with those of a successful revolutionary, general and dictator. He had been a real-life cowboy hero in South America. He almost had won wars singlehanded. He had exhibited a saint's self-denial in quietly retiring to his island of Caprera after conquering two kingdoms, and had won a martyr's crown when wounded by the soldiers of his own country – the country he had himself made – at Aspromonte. His deeds had been widely publicised in Britain by the *Illustrated London News*; and *Punch*'s coachman – a more articulate version of *Private Eye*'s taxi-driver – despised him as 'a revolootionary leeder, similar to those in the penypapers'.[17] He reminded the educated of Cincinnatus and Joan of Arc.[18] To the radical working-class *Reynolds's Newspaper* he ranked as 'the greatest man by whom England has ever been visited'.[19]

His red shirts and blouses became fashionable, and biscuits and sweets were named after him.[20] During his stay in London, his hosts' servants sold at exorbitant prices soapsuds supposed to have come from his wash-basin.[21] Among numerous artefacts made to represent him were several Staffordshire figures.[22] There are or have been Garibaldi Streets in Grimsby, Liverpool, Manchester and Woolwich; and Garibaldi pubs in Yarmouth, Redhill, Guildford, Staines, Slough, Bourne End, Burnham, St Alban's, Northampton, Worcester, Stourbridge, Swansea, Manchester, Oldham, Haltwhistle – and certainly elsewhere. I know of only two other non-royal foreigners who had pubs called after them in the nineteenth century, Blücher and Lincoln. There appear to have been more British inn-signs depicting Garibaldi than either Gladstone or Disraeli.[23] Among modern British historians he is as much a hero to Denis Mack Smith as he was to G.M. Trevelyan. And I have myself heard him set up as a paragon of Christian leadership from a Yorkshire Baptist pulpit.

It was on Monday 11 April 1864 that he made his astonishing triumphal entry into London. He arrived at Nine Elms station, near Waterloo, at 2.30 p.m. *The Times* in the morning had announced that he was expected at Stafford House, now Lancaster House, then the town palace of the Duke of Sutherland, at 4 p.m. He eventually reached it, by the natural direct route, at 8 p.m. The fact that it took his procession more than five hours to cover roughly three miles testifies to the density of the crowds.[24]

The most vivid account of the scene was written by Arthur Munby, the well-connected clerk in the Ecclesiastical Commission Office who made a fetish of observing the behaviour of the working class, especially its women.[25]

I went out about 3.40. . . . By four o'clock the crowd was impassably dense as far as one could see, from Trafalgar Square to Parliament Street. It was a crowd composed mainly of the lowest classes; a very shabby and foul smelling crowd; and the women of it, young and old, were painfully ugly and dirty & tawdry . . .

Yet for three hours, from four till seven – for I stood on the steps of a tobacconist's shop all that time – this coarse mob behaved with the utmost good humour and peacefulness, though their patience must have been taxed to the utmost . . . [At last Garibaldi appeared.] The excitement had been rapidly rising, and now, when this supreme moment came, it resulted in such a scene as can hardly be witnessed twice in a lifetime. That vast multitude rose as one man from their level attitude of expectation: they leapt into the air, they waved their arms and hats aloft, they surged and struggled round the carriage, they shouted with a mighty shout of enthusiasm that took one's breath away to hear it: and above them on both sides thousands of white kerchiefs were waving from every window and housetop ... One would have known that heroic face among a thousand: and in his bearing and looks there was a combination utterly new and most impressive, of dignity and homeliness, of grace and tenderness with the severest majesty ... Ralston [Munby's friend] was converted on the spot by that grand countenance, and says ... it was 'by many degrees more beautiful than any face he ever saw'.

This of today has been the greatest demonstration by far that I have beheld or, probably, shall behold. No soldier was there, no official person: no King nor government nor public body got it up or managed it: it was devised & carried out spontaneously by men and women simply as such; and they often of the lowest grade. It was the work of the rough but law-abiding English people, penetrated with admiration for something divine, and expressing themselves as usual in a clumsy earnest orderly way ... How rare, and how beautiful, to see hundreds of thousands of common folks brought together by motives absolutely pure, to do homage to one who is transcendently worthy!

This passage is as remarkable for what it reveals about the attitudes of the educated civil servant, Munby, and his friends, as about the welcome itself. They see Garibaldi as spotless, even divine, deserving the capital H in 'He'; His beauty and manner overwhelm them; implicitly, the cause associated with Him is equally immaculate.

People searched for precedents for such a vast, enthusiastic yet peaceful demonstration. In 1851 the exiled Hungarian national leader, Lajos Kossuth, had attracted large crowds, but not on this scale.[26] An obvious comparison was with the huge turnout for the arrival of Alexandra, the new Princess of Wales, in 1863, but Munby contrasts 'the shouts of simple welcome' produced on that occasion with the 'ardour and the sort of deep pathetic force about' the cheering for Garibaldi.[27] Lord Palmerston, the Liberal Prime Minister, who kept only a sparse and laconic diary, wrote in it for this day: 'Garibaldi met with such a reception as no one ever had before.'[28] The welcome became celebrated in Liberal historical writing:

The western world [wrote Morley in his *Life of Gladstone*] was in one of its generous moments. In those days there were idealists; democracy was conscious of common interests and common brotherhood; a liberal Europe was then a force and not a dream.[29]

Garibaldi spent twelve hectic days in London, receiving notable welcomes wherever he appeared. The 'Establishment' overwhelmed him with hospitality, and Palmerston had decreed that the government itself 'ought not to show a cold shoulder to a man to whom the whole nation are about to give a warm reception'.[30] As well as being feted whenever possible by the Sutherlands and Seelys in whose houses he stayed, Garibaldi dined with Palmerston, with Gladstone, then Chancellor of the Exchequer, and with the Marquess of Clanricarde, one of the most infamous of Irish landlords but also the son-in-law of the great Canning. He lunched with the Foreign Secretary, Lord Russell, breakfasted with the Reform Club and was banqueted by the Fishmongers' Company; he received the freedom of the City, went twice to the opera and twice to huge demonstrations at the Crystal Palace, and was shown over Woolwich Arsenal; he visited both Houses of Parliament, where he met Lord Derby, the Leader of the Conservative Opposition, and sundry bishops; he was painted by G.F. Watts, called on Tennyson and Florence Nightingale, and was finally himself called on – to the fury of the Queen – by the Prince of Wales.[31]

Palmerston boasted that the welcome had 'afforded great pleasure to the bulk of the nation, as a proof of the community of feeling among all classes'.[32] But the applause was not universal. *Punch* put into the mouth of its coachman remarks which must have reflected, even while caricaturing, the feelings of some conservative observers. They refer to the damage done by the pressure of the crowd to the Duke of Sutherland's carriage, which was almost pushed off Westminster Bridge into the Thames:

> *Dis-gusting!* the karrige of the *Dook of Sutherland*, K.G., *torn in peeces*, if I may be aloud so strong an eggspression, by the beestly mob, drored together to welcum *General Gariballdi*, wich I ave reason to beleeve he have no regular Kommishun. [It was] about the beestliest, wust-dress't, and I may say haltogether workin-classedest mob . . . as I ever see . . . That 'ere karrige was the British Konstitooshin, the Dook cheek by jowl with a man of low eggs-trackshun and revolootionary principles represented the Lords a-forgittin theirselves and the ouse of Kommons sich as Reform Bills and anti-Corn Law Leegs has made it.[33]

A group of Tories succeeded in preventing the Commons from adjourning in his honour.[34] Catholics were bound to feel offended by the strident anti-papalism expressed by many of Garibaldi's hosts. The future Cardinal Manning wrote a condemnatory pamphlet, and the Marquess of Bath, a Conservative Whip in the Lords, resigned

PUNCH, OR THE LONDON CHARIVARI.—APRIL 9, 1864.

" THIS IS THE NOBLEST ROMAN OF THEM ALL !"

Fig. 21. Garibaldi.

in protest at his leader's joining in the celebrations.[35] Disraeli, busy cultivating the support of Irish Catholic MPs, refused to meet Garibaldi.[36] Manning declared that for the Catholics of Ireland the welcome was 'the most refined and deadliest insult which could be directed against all that they cherish on earth, and dearer than life itself'. From an utterly different standpoint Karl Marx derided such popular enthusiasm for 'a pitiful . . . donkey'.[37]

I have spent so long in establishing the unique force and breadth of the impact made on British society by Garibaldi and his visit in order to make sense both of Gladstone's role in it and of the remarkable response it evoked from him.

Garibaldi reached England early in April, still suffering from his wound sustained at Aspromonte. He had received numerous invitations from every level of society, from the Duke of Sutherland down to working-men's organisations.[38] The government had made no attempt to prevent the visit, although Garibaldi was regarded by many continental rulers as the most dangerous of revolutionaries. Palmerston, when approached, had rather encouraged the idea, remarking that Garibaldi might be doing much worse mischief elsewhere.[39] However, among his British sympathisers serious differences of approach were evident at every stage; and the aristocracy and the government took care to keep control of the arrangements, explicitly in order 'to keep Garibaldi out of dangerous hands'.[40] While he was in England, one provincial town after another invited him to visit it, and a protracted tour of much of Britain was planned for him. Then suddenly, on 18 April, it was announced that he would soon be leaving the country because his health did not permit him to accept any of these invitations.

This decision had been taken on the previous day, Sunday 17 April, at Stafford House, and a conversation with Gladstone had played an important part in deciding Garibaldi to leave. In consequence, Gladstone was much criticised, as was the whole government, on whose behalf Gladstone was assumed to have been speaking. Peter Taylor, the Radical MP for Leicester, claimed to have information about the incident that would 'go near to *smash* Gladstone'.[41] There were demonstrations, protest meetings, letters to *The Times* and questions in the House.

Gladstone and the Government gave explanations which proved acceptable to many. But a nasty taste was left behind, and historians have naturally pursued the matter, because it is a mysterious and even murky story. To judge Gladstone's role aright is important both for an understanding of his developing attitudes and for the sake of his general reputation.

The Radical leader, John Bright, summed up popular suspicions of the Government in his diary:

> He is going away. It is said, and doubtless truly, that the Government wants him out of the country. They fear he may excite political feeling in the provinces; or his presence here be annoying to the French or Austrians; or the Queen is irritated at the manner in which he has been received. Perhaps there is truth in each of these stories.[42]

There was certainly *some* truth in them. The Queen constantly complained to Ministers about 'the extravagant excitement respecting Garibaldi, which shows little dignity . . . in the nation, and is not very flattering to others who are similarly received'.[43] Of the members of the diplomatic corps in London, only the Turks and the Americans would attend functions in Garibaldi's honour.[44] Radicals were confident that he would excite political feeling in the provinces.[45] And pressure was undoubtedly brought to bear on him to hasten his departure.

Those mainly concerned were a group who thought of themselves as his 'friends', Sutherland, Shaftesbury, Seely – and Gladstone. We know of a meeting of some of these 'friends' at Stafford House while Garibaldi was lunching at Teddington on 17 April with Herzen, the great Russian revolutionary. But that was clearly not quite the beginning of the story. At that meeting it was arranged that in the evening much the same group should return to Stafford House, to be joined this time by Gladstone. They were to consider what action to take on a medical opinion provided by the distinguished surgeon, William Fergusson, who had been attending Garibaldi since his arrival in England, to the effect that his contemplated provincial tour would overtax his strength.[46] (Professors Vincent and Shannon are mistaken in thinking that Garibaldi's health needed the attentions of Dr Robert Ferguson, the obstetrician.)[47] The tour, as now planned, included a round of official functions in all the principal towns of Great Britain – thirty at least, according to some accounts sixty.[48] But earlier in the day, when approached on the subject, Garibaldi had inconveniently declared that his health had never been better, and doctors could be found who differed from Fergusson and had even written to *The Times* to say so. A spokesman was needed to talk the great man round. The 'friends' wanted Gladstone to try, but he at first refused. Then Garibaldi himself asked to speak to him.

Several accounts exist of the meeting of 'friends', but only two of the crucial conversation between Garibaldi and Gladstone, which apparently took place in another room and in Italian. One of these accounts is Gladstone's own and was repeated with only minor variations to the House of Commons and to Radical deputations. The other is by the hero's secretary, Guerzoni, who claims to have been in a position to take notes. The accounts tally in most respects, and Guerzoni's generally has the ring of truth, though he is obviously anxious to show Gladstone in a bad light.[49]

This is Guerzoni's. Gladstone said:

> he was speaking as a friend, not as a minister; he rejected, as unworthy of refutation, any suspicion of foreign pressure or ulterior political motive: he assured the General that whatever his decision no Englishman could allow himself to be wanting in the duties of hospitality; he merely wished to impress upon him that, London visited, the principal object of his journey had been accomplished, and that these same splendid ovations which were one of the most marvellous events of our time, instead of growing, might with endless repetition decrease in dignity and splendour: anyway no one could claim that the engagements he had made had to be considered irrevocable and absolute; so that if he did not mean to give them all up there remained always the expedient of restricting his visits to the more important places, taking advantage elsewhere of the conclusive argument of his health and of his need of rest, which would cut short all protests and complaints.

Guerzoni continues that Gladstone's powers of persuasion were by no means yet exhausted, but Garibaldi was beginning to understand, for

> the more carefully Mr Gladstone steered around the principal reason that had moved him to speak, the more clearly this reason, as by a chiaroscuro effect, stood out; the further away he struggled to keep the shadow of the government from his speech, the nearer that shadow approached and the nearer his thoughts came to the surface.

According to Guerzoni, Garibaldi, inferring that Gladstone was speaking on behalf of the Cabinet as well as for his friends and hosts, rose from his chair and announced that he could not choose between his engagements; it was all or none; he would go tomorrow. If Guerzoni's version is right, there had to be further discussion to prevail upon Garibaldi to complete his programme in London. But both accounts agree in ascribing to Garibaldi himself the decision to abandon the whole tour: both depict Gladstone mentioning the possibility of a shortened tour, which the General rejects, cancelling all the arrangements. Even Mazzini complained that Garibaldi had given his word too soon, and so could not withdraw when he was later assured that the government had had no part in the approach.[50] As Lord Shaftesbury wrote to *The Times* in carefully chosen words, 'it was ... the General's own and unsuggested decision to give up the provincial journey *altogether*'.[51]

The fact that Gladstone took such a prominent part in the business naturally strengthened suspicions that the government was involved, especially since Garibaldi plainly shared them.[52] But Gladstone hotly denied the charge, and so did Palmerston and Clarendon in Parliament.[53] Maybe Shaftesbury, Sutherland and Seely deliberately exploited the duality of Gladstone's position as a 'friend' who spoke Italian and as the Chancellor of the Exchequer; perhaps his classical Italian proved difficult for Garibaldi to follow; certainly his talent for circumlocution was unequalled. But Gladstone himself, despite the impression he created on Garibaldi, clearly supposed that he was acting in a private capacity and felt aggrieved that Garibaldi did not at first accept his assurances to this effect.[54] One can see both their points of view.

The way in which Palmerston and Granville reported Garibaldi's change of plan to the Queen seems conclusive that they, and Ministers as a body, were innocent of complicity in the intrigue. Neither claimed for the government any of the 'credit for getting him away', despite the fact that the Queen would have strongly approved their taking such action. Palmerston ascribed it to Shaftesbury, Granville to Sutherland. Neither mentioned the role of Gladstone. Further, although both welcomed the cancellation of the tour, neither seems to have felt much apprehension about it.[55]

If the government's motives are not in point, those of the 'friends' who suggested the curtailment of the tour certainly are. According to their own public statements and to Palmerston in the House of Commons, action had been taken 'purely and entirely on the score of a regard for [Garibaldi's] health'.[56] This concern must have been genuine. Seely seems to have set about trying to reduce Garibaldi's commitments after seeing him apparently exhausted and even fainting at the end of a crowded day, and Fergusson was supposed to have threatened him with 'parilesis' if he continued to overtax his strength.[57] It must seem very questionable whether he could have stood such a strenuous programme as the provincial tour would have entailed. However, there is no doubt at all that considerations other

than Garibaldi's health weighed with the 'friends'. Gladstone's suggestion that the repetition of popular welcomes in town after town might
cheapen them was reasonable and harmless enough to be echoed even
by some Radicals.[58] Much more damagingly, Palmerston told the
Queen that 'those who have taken an interest about him, and especially Lord Shaftesbury, thought that politically, and with regard to
his health, it was very desirable that these visits should not be made'.[59]
Unfortunately, the Prime Minister did not explain what he meant by
'politically'. James Stansfeld, an MP who had just been forced to resign
his post in the government because of his Mazzinian sympathies and
who was involved in some of the meetings of the 'friends', stressed
their fear that Garibaldi might encounter in the provinces hostile
Irish demonstrations leading to violence, such as had occurred in
London and Birkenhead two years earlier, after the hero had received
his wound at Aspromonte.[60] This was a threat more recently visible
than any from domestic radicalism. But even the 'friends' cannot have
felt desperately alarmed about the political situation, or they would
not have been content with proposing the curtailment, rather than
the cancellation, of the tour.[61]

Among the historians who have attributed a variety of discreditable
motives to Gladstone in this affair, two deserve particular mention.
D.M. Schreuder, in a provocative article, described the visit as 'a disaster, as far as Gladstone was concerned', claiming that he 'had little
time for and some considerable fear of the great revolutionary'.
'Clearly Garibaldi was exciting the urban masses in a most unwelcome
manner: Gladstone's Liberalism did not extend, as yet, to the methods
of popular democracy.'[62] Richard Shannon, on the other hand, has
claimed that he saw in Garibaldi a dangerous potential rival to himself
'as former and director of public opinion'.[63] I concede that on one view
of Gladstone – or given some of his attitudes – his ostensible admiration for Garibaldi is surprising. Gladstone was one of the most irre-
deemably civilian of men, and Garibaldi one of the most indiscrimin-
ate of *condottieri*. Garibaldi's Reaganesque simplicities and vaguenesses
of expression contrasted sharply with Gladstone's studied rhetoric and
administrative precision. Gladstone admitted, soon after the visit, to
feeling 'surprise and concern' at the revolutionary sentiments Garibaldi uttered at Herzen's lunch, and 'the deepest sorrow and concern'
at his 'attenuated belief'.[64]

These two men were the chief charismatic heroes of the nineteenth-
century Englishman, especially the nineteenth-century Protestant and

Liberal Englishman; and the bases of their popular appeal were remarkably similar. Both were regarded as men of the people. We may think Garibaldi, the half-educated fisherman's son, rather better entitled to be seen in this light than Gladstone, Etonian and Oxonian, son of one of the richest of British merchants. But so pervasive was aristocratic influence in nineteenth-century British politics that anyone not actually a lord – Canning and Peel, as well as real outsiders like Disraeli and Chamberlain – could exploit the feeling that his success represented a rare triumph of merit and talent over birth and privilege. Hence Gladstone could be nicknamed 'the People's William'. Further, he had already attracted astonishingly wide and committed support from working-class activists, including Garibaldians, for his policies of free trade, low taxes, tiny government expenditure and therefore limited social reform.[65] Gladstone might declare himself 'an out-and-out inequalitarian' and Garibaldi claim to be a socialist, but they were agreed that class should not be set against class and both espoused the gospel of Self-Help.[66] Most important, they had in common a passionate and bitter hostility to the Pope and his temporal power. Garibaldi's went even further than Gladstone's of course: he had little sympathy with dogmatic Christianity of any brand, whereas Gladstone professed himself a (non-Roman) Catholic. But even now, despite the notable work of Colin Matthew and Jon Parry, it is doubtful whether enough weight has been given to Gladstone's anti-papalism.[67] He wrote of the Papal States as 'a foul blot upon the face of creation'.[68] It was in a letter to Manning that he admitted his concern at Garibaldi's secular and religious attitudes, but he went on: 'I need not repeat an opinion, always painful to me to pronounce, as to the principal causes to which it is referable, and as to the chief seat of the responsibility for it'.[69] That meant the errors, follies, intransigence and corruption of the papacy.

Admittedly, Gladstone was slow to recognise Garibaldi as a worthy representative of anti-papalism. It is not easy to follow the early stages of the process. The riches of the *Gladstone Diaries* are unavoidably presented in a form which still leaves historians with work to do. Garibaldi, for example, figures in the list labelled 'Dramatis Personae', in the index volume, where he is stated to have been first mentioned on 10 April 1864. In fact he is not mentioned in that entry. So far as I can see, the first reference Gladstone ever made to Garibaldi was in his diary on 20 July 1849. He was then travelling in Italy in pursuit of evidence to justify Lord Lincoln divorcing his wife. He found himself caught up in the turmoil of repression that followed the revolutions of 1848. In Genoa, he records, he saw in the shop windows portraits of 'Kossuth, Garibaldi, Mazzini, Charles Albert (rare), Napoleon – no Pius IX'. Two days later in Rome he heard the guns of Napoleon's troops sent to restore the Pope – Garibaldi had left the Eternal City on the 2nd and the French had entered it on the 3rd.

I can find no comment from Gladstone on Garibaldi during this period. In so far as he was yet aware of the Italian question, his mind was concentrated with its notorious intensity on the connected issues of the papacy, the papal state, Rome, the future of Roman Catholicism and that of Catholicism more generally. He must still have regarded Garibaldi's politics with the deepest suspicion – though, on the same day that he travelled from Naples to Rome in 1849, he had read Mazzini's *Address to the Pope*.[70]

One might have supposed that he would have begun to pay more attention to Garibaldi when he visited Naples in the winter of 1850–51. It was then that the plight of the political prisoners of the Neapolitan regime so stirred Gladstone that, in his *Letter to the Earl of Aberdeen*, he denounced it as 'the negation of God erected into a system of government', thus aligning himself for the first time with liberal opinion on foreign policy and implicitly attacking the Austrian hegemony in Italy.[71] This was presumably what Garibaldi was referring to when in 1864 he addressed Gladstone as his 'precursor'.[72]

Moreover, during his visit to Naples Gladstone seized upon the four volumes of Farini's *Stato romano*, a critical history of the papal state between 1815 and 1850. The book is first mentioned in the diary when he started reading it on 27 November 1850. He began translating it on 21 December. While in Leghorn on 20 February 1851, on his way home to England, he finished what he called 'the first operation' by translating twenty-two pages in under six hours. Even for him this was an extraordinary feat of physical and intellectual endurance. He had arrived at Leghorn between 5 and 6 a.m. that morning after a sea journey of eleven and a half hours.[73]

Back in England, he did a lot more work on the translation with the aid of his Italian literary friends, Antonio Panizzi, the Librarian of the British Museum, and Giacomo Lacaita, and the first two volumes appeared before the end of 1851. Meanwhile he was working on the third volume, which he finished revising on 27 November and which came out in 1852.[74] But then the head of steam ran out. The fourth volume did not appear until 1854, having been translated, the title-page tells us, by 'A Lady' under Gladstone's direction, i.e. by his cousin, Mrs Bennett.[75] It is not clear that he took much interest. Whereas the first three volumes of the Italian original in St Deiniol's

Library are heavily annotated in Gladstone's hand, the fourth is virgin. And it is only in the last volume that Garibaldi's exploits are described. Farini was as opposed to republicanism as to reaction, but – as Trevelyan noticed – the tone of the book grows steadily more favourable to Garibaldi. He was said at one point in the account of the defence of Rome to have shown himself 'void of all judgement', and the table of contents has a heading 'his self-will'. But he was also stated to be 'an honest man' and to have the 'highest reputation amongst the volunteers in the army, and the insurgents in the city'.[76] All this, I fear, passed Gladstone by; and when, as authors did in those indulgent days, he reviewed his own translation in nearly forty pages of the *Edinburgh Review* of April 1852, he had no occasion to mention Garibaldi.[77]

In the course of his correspondence with Panizzi about the translation, he wrote on 21 June 1851 that he was still unready to take a stand on the question of Austrian control of Italy. 'For *me*', he said, 'it is no small matter to have come to a conclusion about the papal power.' He remarked in the same letter:

> I do however *most deeply* grieve over the silence of Parliament about the Expedition to Rome in 1849. That was a great and a sacred opportunity and should not have been missed. It was missed, out of a misplaced regard to democracy, the sham democracy of France.[78]

In denouncing the French expedition he might appear to have been supporting Garibaldi, but I doubt that he yet intended to do so. He was still concentrating on the temporal power.

By 1855, however, his position had clearly changed. In that year he took part with Panizzi in promoting and funding an expedition to free the Neapolitan liberals imprisoned on an island in the Bay of Naples. He must have known and approved the choice of Garibaldi to take command.[79] Yet Schreuder alleges that Gladstone regretted Garibaldi's successes of 1860 in Naples and Sicily: 'Garibaldi's legendary "Thousand" were a thousand too many for Gladstone'.[80] No evidence is quoted, and none exists, for this absurd claim. On the other hand, Schreuder either ignores or misrepresents the following statements of Gladstone, which destroy his case:

> I wonder whether the stars and Garibaldi will let you finish your month by the Dee in peace. That fine fellow has three mouthfuls to swallow yet: 1. Naples 2. The Pope and 3. Venetia. The first of these I suppose he will very soon manage and the second not long after.
>
> (To Russell, 16 August 1860).

At home the aspect of things is so singularly chequered, and the causes of rejoicing so balanced with those of lamentation, that I hold my mind for the most part in suspense, but in Italy, thanks be to God, ground has been gained and is being gained for all the great and solid interests of humanity, and if all shall end as it has begun, then the Italian movement of our day, will count as one of those [upon] which every one who has shared in it, and even those who have but wished it well may look back with joy, whether while he frets and stirs as an Actor in this untranquil scene, or when upon his deathbed he feels himself about to pass into the unveiled presence of the God of truth justice and good will.   (To Massari, 30 August 1860)

The affairs of Italy inspire at once Joy and tremblings. The downfall of the King of Naples is a great triumph over unrighteousness but clearly I must hope with you that Garibaldi may exhibit more self-command than ever by refusing to provoke an unequal contest either in Rome or for Venetia. As to Rome, I conclude that if he gets the territory, some arrangement about the City will before long be made. As to Venetia, I stand abashed in the presence of brute force backed by impenetrable stupidity. Until Austria is out of Venice the Italian question remains unsolved, the danger to the peace of Europe continues, and Austria will never, I suppose, be able to square her accounts.   (To Russell, 15 September 1860).[81]

Schreuder's account of Gladstone's attitude to Garibaldi's visit depends partly on this misrepresentation of his views in 1860. It requires also a misreading of the diary for 1864. In the entry for 14 April, made famous by Morley, Gladstone wrote: 'Went by a desperate push to see Garibaldi welcomed at the opera. It was good, but not like the *people*.' Until Schreuder, this passage had been taken to mean that Gladstone thought the welcome from the opera-goers, though notable, was less impressive than the earlier welcome of the people at large. In other words, Gladstone already appreciated popular enthusiasm, and was on the way to preferring, in the terminology of his later years, the masses to the classes. Schreuder turned this interpretation on its head. Removing without any warrant Gladstone's underlining, he wrote: 'It was "not like the people", Gladstone recorded unhappily'.[82] Fortunately, Shannon has found more than one earlier instance of what was obviously a standard Gladstonian usage of 'the *people*', referring admiringly to large crowds.[83]

As for Shannon's allegation that Gladstone was jealous of Garibaldi's popular appeal, there is no evidence for that either. It is at least as plausible to suggest that Gladstone, because of his own almost unique experience of addressing a succession of vast meetings, was particularly aware of the strain the provincial tour would place on Garibaldi's health.

The truth of the matter is that Gladstone by now greatly admired Garibaldi and his achievements, that he was thrilled by the visit and that, in acting as the spokesman of those who urged the curtailment of the planned provincial tour, he saw himself acting as a private person concerned for a guest's health and wellbeing. The visit was not so much a political manifestation as a personal triumph for Garibaldi and a Protestant festival for the British. In 1850 Russell as Liberal Prime Minister, in condemning the establishment by the Pope of a regular Catholic hierarchy in England, had evoked a violent outburst of anti-papal feeling and destroyed for a generation the long-standing political alliance between Whigs, Liberals and Irish Catholics. Palmerston's leadership of the Liberals from 1855 only widened the split: his foreign policy, especially over Italy, was explicitly anti-papal; he pointedly withdrew all government patronage from Irish Catholics; and when, in July 1864, he was threatened by defeat in the Commons on his foreign policy, 'he saw greater advantages in being defeated by Popery, than in conciliating it'.[84] As we have seen, there was now more reason to fear religious than political riots. In this atmosphere Gladstone felt little, if any, difficulty about joining in this greatest of all anti-papal demonstrations.

Garibaldi's visit is usually thought of as an extraordinary incident that dominated the British scene for three weeks in April 1864 but had no significant effects then or later. In fact it was important in the short term because it strengthened the position of Palmerston and his government, the Whigs and the aristocracy. And it was significant in the longer term since it contributed to the Liberal revival that made possible the landslide election victory of 1868 – and to Gladstone's own development as a Liberal statesman.

The organisation both of the welcome and of the protests against Garibaldi's departure anticipated and influenced future Liberal activities. In Birmingham, though the committee on the projected visit was supported by almost all sections of opinion, an attempt to dominate it was made by the young Joseph Chamberlain and colleagues such as George Dixon, William Harris and the Rev. R.W. Dale, who would soon be working together in the larger tasks of running the Birmingham Liberal Association (1865), the National Education League (1869), their city corporation and the National Liberal Federation (1877). Foreshadowing their later techniques, they were already talking in 1864 of forming committees of 200 and even 1000 members.[85] Among the active participants elsewhere are to be found great Liberal names of the future, such as Forster, Goschen, Edward Miall and John and Samuel Morley.[86] After the police had dispersed the first London protest meeting, 'the committee at once adjourned to a tavern at the foot of the hill, and determined to start a Reform League'. They could not carry through their intention at once, but they continued to work together and helped to found the Reform League in the following year, with Garibaldi as honorary president.[87] The same Edmond Beales who presided over the protest meetings, and who figured in almost every radical organisation of the period, was 'in the chair' when the league defied the government by holding two huge meetings in Hyde Park in 1866 and 1867, which contributed both to establishing the right of assembly there and to the passage of the Second Reform Act in the latter year.[88]

For Gladstone himself the visit was one of the landmarks in the process by which he was drawn towards a more radical position. Italian affairs had already played a notable part in the development of his views.The impact of his visit to Naples in 1850–51 has already been mentioned. When he accepted the Exchequer from Palmerston in 1859, his main point of agreement with the Prime Minister had been enthusiasm for the Italian cause.[89] In the early 1860s he was discovering and eliciting sympathy for his moralist approach to politics outside the ruling classes, among the people at large. He was beginning to have dealings, as Chancellor, with trade unions;[90] and his cultivation of relations with Nonconformists, particularly in the person of the Rev. Newman Hall, became serious at almost exactly the time of Garibaldi's visit.[91] Disraeli rightly guessed that Gladstone had been stirred by the popular welcome for Garibaldi – by the enthusiam of 'the *people*' – and that his feelings helped to account for his notorious Commons speech of 11 May on Baines' Parliamentary Reform Bill:[92] Gladstone, hitherto considered unsympathetic to extending the franchise, now declared that all men 'not presumably incapacitated' deserved to 'come within the pale of the constitution'.

When criticised by Palmerston and eulogised in the radical press for what he had said, Gladstone denied that it was anything new; but the impression that it was could not and cannot be effaced.[93] He had actually told a deputation at the end of March that he intended soon to make an important statement on parliamentary reform.[94] Since then he had seen the welcome to Garibaldi, and been embarrassed by having to justify to a working-class deputation on 10 May his role in bringing the visit to an early end.[95] The strength of his pronouncement on Reform no doubt owed something to both experiences.

In declaring himself an active parliamentary reformer, Gladstone was setting himself up against Palmerston and his system of domestic politics in a manner certain to be applauded by Garibaldi and the British working-class movement. But at virtually the same moment he began to show signs of another shift of position which was both more surprising in the light of his own previous career and more problematic in relation to British politics. It was at a Stafford House reception for Garibaldi, on 13 April, that Gladstone and Bright first discussed the Irish Church question: '[Gladstone] thought, when the Liberal Party is restored to life, that question would come up for settlement, and he should regard it as one of the great purposes of the Party, altho' it would necessarily separate him from [his constituency] the University of Oxford'.[96] In the following year he publicly abandoned his support for preserving the Irish branch of the Church of England intact, a departure from views with which he had been particularly identified for over thirty years. He duly lost his seat at Oxford.[97] As Trevelyan pointed out, the conversation at Stafford House was the first proposal of the terms of the pact which in 1868 reunited the Liberal Party after two years of internal disagreement over parliamentary reform and enabled it to win its massive election victory under Gladstone's leadership on the issue of the disestablishment of the Church of Ireland.[98]

In April 1864, however, to contemplate action that would please Roman Catholic Irishmen and anger Protestants was to defy the spirit both of Palmerston's system and of the welcome to Garibaldi. But already by the end of the year, partly in reaction to the Protestant extremism displayed during Garibaldi's visit, a National Association had been founded in Ireland, with the blessing of Bright, which brought together British Nonconformists and Irish Catholics in a programme including Irish disestablishment, and was to become one of the pillars of the triumph of 1868.[99]

Gladstone's Protestantism was infinitely more subtle than Palmerston's. He persuaded himself that the disestablishment of the Irish Church, as well as pleasing Irish Roman Catholics and British Nonconformists, would actually improve the prospects of the Irish Church itself, by permitting it to develop as a voluntary religious body untrammelled by association with the state.[100] But he remained, as his pamphlet of 1874 on *The Vatican Decrees* showed, the virulent enemy of the papacy, its temporal power and its claims to infallibility.[101] This was the strongest of the bonds that linked him with Garibaldi.

9

Gladstone and Grote

David Bebbington

George Grote was that rare phenomenon, a historian who makes an impact on the period in which he lives. Born in 1794 and so fifteen years older than Gladstone, he was a banker and a Member of Parliament. He was well known in his time as a philosophic radical, member of the group of intellectuals who in the 1830s were pressing for further constitutional changes following the Great Reform Act. But Grote is most famous now for his *History of Greece*, published in twelve volumes between 1846 and 1856. A host of contemporaries recognised the greatness of the book. The younger historian Edward Freeman spoke of reading Grote as 'an epoch in a man's life'.[1] John Ruskin was one of the many aesthetes inspired by Grote's depiction of myth as the product of the Greek imagination.[2] German historians of ancient Greece in the later nineteenth century were divided between those who were for and those who were against Grote.[3] So abroad as well as at home Grote's *History of Greece* was an immensely celebrated work.

The historian's relations with Gladstone have hitherto been little explored in their own right. John Morley's *Life of Gladstone* calls Grote 'that admirable man', but makes only four brief references to him.[4] Hugh Lloyd-Jones, in his fine sketch of Gladstone's classical achievement, merely alludes in passing to Grote.[5] The one extended treatment of the two, in Frank Turner's volume on *The Greek Heritage in Victorian Britain*, concentrates on aspects of their debate about the political significance of antiquity.[6] Although very illuminating, Turner's study does not place the controversy in the context of their other engagements with each other or of Gladstone's early thought as revealed in his unpublished memoranda in the British Library. That is what is attempted here.

Turner treats Gladstone's detailed classical work as an outgrowth of his efforts to reform the University of Oxford during the 1850s.[7] That view is mistaken, because the statesman had been hard at work on the poet Homer in the previous decade. Gladstone started the systematic examination of the Homeric world in 1846, the year in which Grote issued his first two volumes on early Greece. Grote had published in the spring; Gladstone began his studies in the autumn. There is no clear evidence of Gladstone reading Grote before March in the following year,[8] or even of his seeing the evaluation of the work in the *Quarterly Review*, but he must certainly have been aware of the scholarly publishing sensation of the year. It is virtually certain that part of the original stimulus for Gladstone's research on the poet was Grote's provocative treatment of the Homeric age. Much of the statesman's subsequent work on Homer, which generated five distinct books and innumerable articles, was composed in debate with Grote. A programmatic essay of 1857 culminates in a carefully understated explanation of Gladstone's target:

> The name of Mr Grote must carry great weight in any question of Greek research: but it may be doubted whether the force and aptitude of his powerful mind have been as successfully applied to the Homeric as to the later periods.[9]

In his *Studies on Homer and the Homeric Age*, a massive work in three tomes issued in the following year, Gladstone trains his fire directly on Grote in the passages discussing political institutions; and as late as 1890, in his last published volume on the ancient poet, *Landmarks of Homeric Study*, Gladstone still takes issue with his erudite predecessor. Why did Gladstone choose to spend so many of his leisure hours in trying to confute the historian? There are several answers, which can usefully be considered in turn.

First there was a basic political antagonism between the two men. George Grote's background, like Gladstone's, was commercial. George's paternal grandfather had come from Bremen as a general merchant, subsequently, in 1766, establishing a banking house in London. But whereas Gladstone's father had ensured that his son was co-opted into landed society through Eton and Christ Church, the Grote family had remained wedded to the counting house. George's father put him in the family bank at the age of sixteen and shortly afterwards expected him to take over much of the responsibility for running it. Only on his father's death in 1834, when he inherited a substantial fortune, did George slacken his ties with the bank, and it was not until 1843 that he snapped them entirely.[10] It was therefore as an experienced manager of financial affairs that Grote entered the Commons in 1832, immediately after parliamentary reform, sitting, appropriately, for the City of London. He had long been committed to a programme of additional reforms springing, as he explained in his 1832 election address, from suspicion of the social elite:

> The oligarchical interest hitherto predominant in our Legislature have kept up an exorbitant scale of public expenditure, fruitful in corrupt influence, and oppressive as well as demoralizing to the nation. This long-standing course of abuse it will be among my earliest endeavours to rectify.[11]

Grote was an outright moderniser, dedicated to sustaining an onslaught on 'Old Corruption'. All this was anathema to the young Gladstone, who in the same year became an MP as the nominee of the Duke of Newcastle, an arch-defender of the old order that Grote had in his sights. Gladstone was as much as ardent anti-reformer as Grote was a virulent advocate of systematic reform.

It is not surprising that the two men came into collision during the decade that together they sat in the Commons. The only reason it did not happen more often was that, at this early stage in his career, Gladstone was a very junior member of a Tory Party that had been reduced to a rump by the crisis of reform. Grote was by far the more prominent figure. The banker was not an extreme radical, being willing to make terms with the moderate Whigs in power much more readily than some of his more fire-eating colleagues, particularly those from Ireland.[12] Yet at times he appeared extreme. In the summer of 1837, for example, *The Times* referred to him as 'the frontispiece of a revolutionary code':

> He has become the representative and peculiar organ of whatever is most chimerical in theory, most reckless in experiment, most fatal and revolting in hostility to our national institutions. Mr Grote personifies the *movement* system. He concentrates in himself the destructive principle, of which he is, substantially at least, if not vociferously, the most obstinate and incorrigible doctrinaire.[13]

Gladstone, who had been selected for Parliament by Newcastle precisely because he was resistant to change, was necessarily on the opposite side on most issues: over the abolition of property qualifications for the vote in boroughs, over rejecting Lords amendments to bills carried by the Commons and over much else. Of the major legislation of the period, little but the New Poor Law of 1834, which attracted their support, found them on the same side.[14]

The most direct clashes were over colonial questions. Grote favoured a policy of quiet withdrawal from what he saw as unnecessary drains on the Exchequer. Gladstone, whose father had profited enormously from trade with the colonies, wanted them to remain in British hands. Particularly over Canada, where there was rebellion in 1837–38, the two differed sharply. 'Spoke (in a way) on Canadian matters', recorded Gladstone in his diary for 22 December 1837.[15] In fact he argued that there was no parallel between the rising in Canada and the American War of Independence: whereas the Americans had possessed grievances of principle, the Canadian rebels could offer no reasoned case. Grote rose immediately afterwards to deny the point: on the contrary, he contended, the Canadians were activated by the same point of principle that had stirred the Americans, the right of the British government to take the people's money. The two crossed swords again over Canada in the Commons only a month later.[16] Thus Gladstone came to see Grote as a natural political opponent.

Grote, however, was particularly identified with a single cause: the secret ballot. The new technique was designed to replace the time-honoured system of voting at parliamentary elections by means of a public declaration on the hustings. As early as 1821, the banker had issued a pamphlet on parliamentary reform in which he had argued in favour of secret delivery of the vote in order to avoid harassment by social superiors.[17] 'Without a ballot', he announced in his 1832 election address, 'free and conscientious voting is unattainable.'[18] Accordingly, on 25 April 1833, he proposed a Commons motion in favour of the ballot, contending that half the electorate could not call their votes their own because of the pressure brought to bear on them. He answered various objections, such as the consideration favoured by contemporaries that the franchise was a trust for which a voter should be publicly accountable to non-electors.[19] Gladstone entirely shared this objection, believing in addition that nobody deserved the vote unless he were prepared to make a manly avowal of his choice on the hustings. Although in 1871 Gladstone was to claim never to have been a vehement opponent of the secret ballot, in 1833 he had gone to the trouble of composing a letter to the *Liverpool Standard* denouncing the idea on the authority of Cicero and charging it with causing the downfall of the Roman republic.[20] In 1838, having read a pamphlet on the subject by an old college friend, he composed a brief memorandum setting out the case against the ballot.[21] That was to prepare himself for the debate that, two days later, Grote raised in the Commons. It was the fifth time he had proposed the ballot, and, although on each occasion Gladstone voted in the majority against it, the minority supporting it crept steadily upwards. In 1839 the government, by then in a profoundly weak position, was so fearful of defeat that it allowed a free vote on the issue.[22] Although the ballot was once more rejected by a comfortable majority, the question had been thrust to centre stage. It was a subject which singled out Grote to Gladstone's notice as the persistent advocate of an apparently dangerous innovation.

What is more, Grote publicised the cause of the ballot by methods that seemed distasteful. Sir Robert Peel, as Conservative leader, had argued that it would be impossible to preserve the secrecy of the ballot. Grote wished to demonstrate unequivocally that this objection was invalid. In this enterprise, crucially, he involved his wife. Harriet Grote was a *femme formidable*, bold in conversation and masculine in appearance, with none of the shrinking then thought proper in a woman. In her family she was nicknamed 'The Empress', and even a close friend admitted her 'grand and haughty manner'.[23] She contrasted markedly with her husband, who was diffident and retiring by disposition, a bookish man who felt most at home in the seclusion of his own library. 'I like the Grotes', remarked the clerical wit Sydney Smith. 'He is so ladylike and she is such a perfect gentleman.'[24] Gladstone, preoccupied in the later 1830s with finding a wife and so prone to evaluate female qualities with a discerning eye, must have been dismayed by Harriet's notorious forwardness. In 1836 she and her husband were together responsible for inventing an answer to the problem of security for the voter's privacy. It was a version of the ballot in which the elector stabbed the name of his preferred candidate with a dagger – what Sydney Smith called 'political acupuncturation'.[25] The couple had forty or fifty ballot boxes made and distributed them, at the cost price of twenty-four shillings each, round the country for display.[26] The joint enterprise of the Grotes excited ridicule and contempt. Here was self-advertising that appeared to reflect Mrs Grote's powerful and pretentious personality. The ballot box seemed a symbol of all that was wrong with radicalism: its perennial itch for novelty, its demagogic ways and, through Harriet's undue prominence, its ultimate threat to the social system. To a Tory traditionalist such as Gladstone the venture must have looked highly alarming.

There was another symbol that represented Grote's radicalism: the *History of Greece*. It was a long-standing project, going back long before his parliamentary career. Harriet claimed to have suggested in 1823 the idea of writing an account of ancient Greece, but George did not need much urging: 'he could not dissemble', according to his wife, 'the indifference he felt for everything that was not books'.[27] Before their marriage, in acts of male supremacy that seem to have decreased in number after their wedding day, George set Harriet essays on various subjects and gave her books to read, requiring a digest.[28] Perhaps because he had been forced into the uncomfortable groove of banking by his father, Grote was incorrigibly devoted to scholarship, and that still meant primarily the classics. So to write on Greece came naturally. He was applying himself to the task in the 1820s and even during the reform crisis of 1831.[29] To quote Sydney Smith once more, 'I never go into Grote's dining-room without expecting to find an altar to Zeus'.[30] For such a fastidious scholar, the hurly-burly of politics was uncongenial. Already, after only a single parliamentary session, Mrs Grote was reporting his 'disgust' at the lack of 'purity of principle' in public men.[31] Successive failures with the ballot proposals increased his frustration. By the 1841 general election he was glad to escape from the Commons. After a continental tour, in 1842 he set to work once more on the history, which began to appear four years later. The book was therefore an alternative to parliamentary life, a continuation of politics by other means. It is hardly surprising that Gladstone should look on it with grave suspicion. Gladstone's attitude to the *History* was coloured by the political polarity between the two men during the 1830s.

The gulf between Gladstone and Grote was more than a matter of sitting on opposite sides of the House of Commons. It was also, secondly, a question of ideology. The philosophy that made Grote a philosophic radical was another cause of offence to the young Tory statesman. Grote was a Utilitarian, a member of the circle who, under the influence of Jeremy Bentham, wanted to apply the principles of the Enlightenment, understood in radical fashion, to any and every institution so as to promote the greatest happiness of the greatest number. Grote was at the heart of the group, regularly attending and even hosting its social gatherings. He was drawn by the writings of Bentham into the company of the ageing oracle himself.[32] More influential over him, however, was James Mill, the Scottish political writer who was intensely devoted to Bentham's principles. It was Mill who set out in an article of 1830, published in the radical *Westminster Review*, the convictions on the ballot that Grote subsequently championed in the Commons.[33] George became a close friend of Mill's son John Stuart, who, famously, after a model Utilitarian education that entailed beginning Greek at the age of three and a subsequent private rebellion, settled into the advocacy of a more sophisticated brand of the philosophy. Grote was even thought to have suggested modifications to the second edition of Mill's greatest work, *A System of Logic*. The banker sat from 1827 to 1831 on the first council of what became University College, London, an institution in part inspired by the Utilitarians, and he was eventually to become its president.[34] *The Times* branded Grote's ballot box publicity schemes 'exhibitions of ultra-Benthamite foolery',[35] and it was entirely right to associate him with the name of the patron saint of Utilitarianism.

Grote adopted Benthamite views wholeheartedly. In 1823, for example, he urged his sister-in-law that, whenever in her reading she met a vague expression, she must 'resolve it into the principle of utility'.[36] The underlying premise was that any concept could be reduced by analysis into unambiguous terms. Only then could its tendency to promote or retard happiness be accurately assessed. This technique was the essence of Benthamite method, what Grote called applying first principles in the manner of Lord Bacon. If suitable terms did not exist, they must be coined. Grote actually introduced a number of neologisms, including the words 'autonomy' and 'hegemony' that in due course were to enjoy immense vogue. In 1865, near the end of his life, Grote was still to avow that utility was the sole criterion of what is morally right.[37] On Utilitarian principles, self-interest, what will lead to an individual's happiness, is necessarily the guide of that person's actions. In 1823 he rejoiced that his sister-in-law shared his acknowledgement of '*amour de soi* being the universal mover, variously modified, of the human race'. He was not denying that people derive pleasure from the happiness of others, but claimed that 'the best way of getting others to make us happy is to exert ourselves in making them happy'.[38] At root all are out for their own ends. Human beings, in Grote's estimate, are unavoidably individualists.

A political inference of great importance followed. The legislature, Grote held, should be an organ for representing individuals rather than groups. That was to deny an axiom held in common by Tories and Whigs in the age of reform. The two major parties of state, whatever their differences, agreed that groups, what were usually called 'interests', were the basic units to be represented in Parliament. So long as their interest – the commercial interest of the East India merchants or whatever – had its spokesman in the Commons, there was no need for individuals to have direct representation. This view was expounded, for instance, by the Whig Sir James Mackintosh in the *Edinburgh Review* for 1820. Grote's first venture into print was to criticise Mackintosh's assumption. For groups such as merchants or landlords to be championed in Parliament was to prevent individuals from expressing the preferences that reflected their own self-interest. The existing system ensured that the community as a whole, which on Benthamite principles was nothing but the sum of the individuals who composed it, could not have its interest advanced. Grote evinced a deep-seated hostility to all secondary associations, groupings intermediate between the individual and the total community, that is reminiscent of Rousseau. Parliamentary constituencies, according to Grote, should be so arranged as not to consist of people with the same sectional bias – the very opposite of contemporary presumptions and even of the guidelines given to boundary commissioners in the twentieth century. Rather, each voter was to pursue his own private interest.[39] Here was the theoretical rationale for the secret ballot. Here, too, was a political philosophy of strident individualism.

Gladstone could hardly have differed more sharply from Grote's position. His great undergraduate speech at the Oxford Union in 1831 denouncing the Reform Bill contained a barb directed against the Utilitarians, who, in his view, provided some of the intellectual impetus for so destructive a scheme.[40] The young Tory's private memoranda of the 1830s are peppered with trenchant strictures on their theory. A note of 19 November 1836 is typical: 'Utilitarianism deceives itself more than any other philosophy, and seems in its disappointments more an object of rebuke than pity'.[41] Happiness, he argued, though the goal of Utilitarianism, is left undefined by that school of thought. Virtue, not happiness, should in any case be the object of Christian endeavour. Utilitarian claims to be scientific, furthermore, are spurious because the methods of science suit physical phenomena but not human beings. 'The question is', Gladstone wrote in one memorandum, 'useful for what?'[42] All these objections have carried weight with subsequent philosophers of other schools who have found fault with the Utilitarian position. Gladstone was in private a most determined foe of the convictions Grote espoused. And in public Gladstone identified not with the secular, Utilitarian-inspired University College, London, but with the rival King's College, loyally attached to the Church of England. He was profoundly hostile to Benthamism in all its expressions.

Consequently, Gladstone disagreed totally with Grote's inferences from Utilitarian premises. Gladstone's own starting points were Christian teaching and the ancient philosophers, especially Aristotle. From them he drew an insistence on the importance of community. Appealing to Aristotle in a manuscript of 1835, he argued that society is 'naturally formed, not optionally'.[43] Human beings do not exercise choice in order to belong to a community; rather, they are born into one. Indeed, before they rise to consciousness, as Gladstone put it, they are debtors to society for their early nurture.[44] The bonds between individuals are part of the order of nature, not, as the Utilitarians believed, the expressions of calculated self-interest. Hence human beings properly form groups, and these manifestations of solidarity must be recognised in the constitution. Every government, Gladstone argued, should promote 'the *interests* of all classes of the community'.[45] The system of representation must allow these interests to have a voice – exactly, Gladstone noted, as it already did.[46] Groups, and not just individuals, should have their spokesmen in Parliament. Gladstone was a decided communitarian and that made him a principled opponent of Grote's version of political individualism.

Gladstone knew that he would discover much to censure on these grounds in the *History of Greece*. Grote, for all his devotion to scientific method, was not the man to write a dispassionate narrative eschewing his own presuppositions. On the contrary, his whole aim was to correct received opinion about ancient Greece from a Benthamite perspective; and so, in turn, to shape policy in his own day. The object of a historian in his field, he asserted in an article of 1826, should be 'to bring to view the numerous illustrations which Grecian phenomena afford, of the principles of human nature'.[47] The achievements of the ancient Greeks could be located on the scale of improvement which, in the wake of James Mill, Grote believed had marked the history of mankind.[48] It was a typical programme of the radical Enlightenment. Within this framework, the *History* hinted at the undesirability of secondary associations. In the primitive heroic age of Greece, Grote wrote, politics was unduly 'guided by family sympathies'. People, that is to say, operated as family units under their chiefs, and the consequence was the widespread pursuit of sectional interests. In the admirable classical age, by contrast, the sectionalism of families had given way to the collective sovereignty of the civic community.[49] Here was the infusion into the *History* of a lesson entirely repugnant to Gladstone, that even family connections should count for nothing in the ideal policy of rational individuals pursuing their own self-interest.

It was a message Gladstone must have expected from a man professing Grote's beliefs. There was a fundamental ideological incompatibility between the two.

Because the foundations of their positions were so different, the superstructures contrasted equally sharply. Grote's views on monarchy, thirdly, were not those of Gladstone. The Utilitarian was a republican, inheriting currents in the tradition of civic humanism that had flowed powerfully through western Europe since the Renaissance. The state, he believed, should be governed by law rather than a king. The collective sovereign of ancient Greece, the city consisting of active citizens, was his model. In such a community men would take turns in command and obedience: there was no question of permanent leadership by a monarch.[50] In public life Grote's republicanism, though veiled and sometimes ambiguously expressed, was apparent to the discerning ear. He commented in the Commons that a defence of Peel's first Conservative administration of 1834–35 by reference to the royal prerogative would soon lead to the prerogative itself being questioned. In 1837 he was more direct, protesting against the grant of an additional £8000 to the Duchess of Kent, the mother of the young Queen Victoria.[51] Grote saw no reason why relatives of crowned heads should be a drain on the public purse: the republican corollary was evident. He was no friend to monarchy right down to his final years. When Gladstone read Harriet's biography of her husband published in 1873, two years after his death, the statesman rightly noted: 'A speculative republican to the last'.[52]

Gladstone thought Grote's republican connections worthy of remark because he disagreed with them so strongly. At the time of making the comment, Gladstone, as Prime Minister, was trying to shore up the throne of Victoria, then under criticism for her neglect of public duties since the death of Prince Albert.[53] Gladstone had originally entered the political fray partly to champion the crown, the traditional *raison d'être* of the Tory Party. The evidence of the memoranda from his early career, however, shows that he was never reactionary on this question. He was, on the contrary, an advocate of what he called 'moderate monarchism'. He upheld 'a mixed and tempered government' in which any element under threat was to be defended.[54] Yet he was persuaded in conscience of the suitableness of monarchical institutions to the national character.[55] In 1840, while studying the seventeenth-century republican Algernon Sidney, he ruminated that the appointment of Saul to be the first king over Israel, an Old Testament passage cited by opponents of monarchy, was in fact a testimony in its favour. The elevation of Saul was censured in the Bible only because it substituted human for divine government. Because there was no other ground of condemnation for the change, monarchy must be the proper form of government, enjoying the tacit endorsement of scripture.[56] It was a typical piece of Gladstonian casuistry. The statesman's notoriously poor relations with Queen Victoria are ironical in view of his devotion to the crown as an institution.

Grote's *History*, as Gladstone would have supposed in advance, was critical of kingship. The author's purpose, as he explained in the preface to the first volume, was to rectify both the errors and the point of view in the most influential previous history of ancient Greece.[57] This work had been published between 1784 and 1818 by William Mitford, a Hampshire country gentleman and backbench Pittite MP. The point of view that Grote disliked was moulded to an extraordinary extent by Mitford's conservative political stance. Mitford was prepared to defend tyrants, but reserved most praise for states like Phaecia, which possessed a 'mixture of monarchy, aristocracy and democracy not less marked than in the British constitution'.[58] Athenian democracy by contrast was, in Mitford's view, a dress rehearsal for the mob rule of the French Revolution. Grote launched his first attack on Mitford in the *Westminster Review* for 1826. The earlier historian of Greece, Grote complained, had been 'devoted to kingly government, and to kings, not only with preference, but even with passion and bigotry'.[59] So Grote set out to undermine his standing, assembling materials such as a passage in which Mitford had credulously declared that Homer leaves us in no doubt that there was once a 'Grecian prince' called Hercules.[60] When Grote's *History* came to be issued, a good deal of its impact was due to its successful confutation of the previous authority in the field, William Mitford.

Kingship is therefore depicted by Grote in an unappealing light. The king of archaic times, supremely Agamemnon, was a ruler without responsibility to his people. Although Grote admits that there existed bodies, the council and the assembly, that would later develop into checks on royal power, in Homer's account, he argues, they existed merely at the king's whim and for his purposes.[61] Agamemnon exercised a purely personal ascendancy and so was clearly an unconstitutional monarch. Kingship, according to Grote, is intrinsically arbitrary. This is the view that Gladstone tried to refute when he began publishing on the Homeric world. In his three-volume work of 1858, *Studies on Homer and the Homeric Age*, the political section is a counterblast to Grote. Kings as described by Homer, Gladstone urges, are not

to be equated with tyrants. They receive the free assent of their subjects. The Homeric king should be, although he not always is,
'emphatically a gentleman'.[62] His subjects possess rights, Gladstone
insists, even if these rights are indeterminate.[63] As late as 1890, in his
Landmarks of Homeric Study, the statesman still takes up the theme.
Grote had relied on a spurious half-verse in Homer, Gladstone claims,
to contend that Agamemnon enjoyed the power of life and death over
his people. 'But', the statesman concludes, 'there is no such thing in
Homer . . . as arbitrary power'.[64] Kings were far less black than Grote
had painted them.

Furthermore, according to Gladstone, monarchy as presented by
Homer was definitely limited. The assembly had been described by
Grote as having no constitutional function, without the power to take
votes or pass resolutions. Gladstone homes in on this remark in his
work of 1858. Resolving issues by numbers is not necessarily the best
way, he observes, no doubt with Grote's ballot campaign in mind.
'Decision by majorities', he goes on, 'is as much an expedient, as light-
ing by gas.'[65] Only wisdom and virtue, not numbers, have the right to
command – a strange remark for a man who in the following year was
to join a Liberal Cabinet. Nevertheless, Gladstone contends, Grote
was mistaken about the importance of the assembly. Its members
could resist Agamemnon's will, as did Achilles and Diomedes. They
could indicate their attitude to royal proposals by a chilly silence or a
loud cheer – and acclamation rather than arithmetic, Gladstone tartly
points out, is the normal way of settling issues in deliberative bodies.
There were actually the equivalents of parties in the assembly because
we are told that people who thought together sat together. Speechmaking could sway opinion and there was even a rudimentary form of
public opinion among the Greeks, though not among the Trojans.[66]
Therefore, there existed the elements of a constitution with a large
role for the equivalent of the House of Commons. 'The position of
Agamemnon', he concludes, 'bears a near resemblance to that of a
political leader under free European, and, perhaps it may be said,
especially under British institutions.'[67] The parallel with the modern
world could hardly be more explicit. Gladstone was trying to establish
that Homer's limited monarchy was entirely compatible with freedom
for the people. Even the editor of Grote's minor works, the like-
minded Alexander Bain, had to admit that, through drawing on his
personal experience of parliamentary life, Gladstone had made out a
persuasive case against the Utilitarian.[68] It was a blow struck in the
royalist cause.

A further contrast, fourthly, between Gladstone and Grote lay in their attitudes to aristocracy. Grote had absorbed from James Mill a stern hatred of the hereditary social elite that remained so power-ful in early nineteenth-century Britain.[69] Harriet was something of a social climber and so desperately wished to cultivate friendships in aristocratic society, but for many years George exerted all his resources of marital authority and refused. Only in 1840 did he relent so far as to visit Holland House, the centre of Whig high society.[70] His aversion was so strong because it rested on a cherished point of political principle: the landed interest had preyed on the state and should do so no longer. 'No conqueror', he wrote in 1831, 'ever wrung from vanquished and despised aliens so severe a tribute as the English Aristocracy have extorted from their subjects and fellow-countrymen.'[71] The top echelon of society, he believed, con-sisted of greedy parasites.

Following Bentham's views in his later years, Grote saw democratic rule as the remedy for aristocratic pretensions. The democracy he favoured was of that peculiar type often endorsed by the progressive but fastidious wealthy. In 1818, at a dinner party with a few cronies, he enjoyed, according to his own diary, 'some excellent conversation upon the ignorance of mankind in general'.[72] Lack of education was in Grote's eyes, as in those of J.S. Mill, a barrier to the vote, and so he had no sympathy with the demands of the Chartists for manhood franchise. In 1831, when the population of the United Kingdom was about 24,000,000, he called for an electorate consisting of only one million.[73] Yet he was convinced that democracies were intrinsically superior to any other form of polity. Their securities for good govern-ment were admittedly inadequate, but oligarchies and monarchies, he insisted, afforded no such securities at all. His thinking on this subject was largely the result of an evaluation of the classical models, and the fruit of admiration for Athens in particular. 'It is to democracy alone', he wrote in 1826 '(and to the sort of open aristocracy which is, practic-ally, very similar to it), that we owe the unparalleled brilliancy and diversity of individual talent which constitutes the charm and glory of Grecian history.'[74] Like many a historian after him, Grote was dazzled by Athenian democracy.

Gladstone maintained very different opinions. Eighteen months after going down from Oxford, he was asked by a former undergradu-ate acquaintance to outline a speech for delivery at the Union against the proposition 'that an hereditary aristocracy is an evil'. Gladstone was pleased to oblige and, being Gladstone, also penned a long memorandum on the subject for his own future use. He set out an elaborate case in favour of the aristocracy (and this is merely a summary):

1. Scripture sanctions hereditary rule.
2. Human equality is a 'monster'. Whereas inequality may not give people their deserts, equality cannot give them their deserts and so must be faulty.
3. Men of merit should be allowed to lay up benefits for their successors.
4. The sons of capable men are likely to be capable themselves.
5. If mixed governments are desirable, a third element is needed to balance the monarchy and the populace.
6. Hereditary aristocracy is a necessary buttress to hereditary monarchy.
7. The 'moderate aristocracy of England' was open to fresh talent (a point recent historians have challenged).
8. Finally, the history of England showed the merits of the aristocracy: it was a force balancing the monarchy and the papacy.[75]

Although much of this polemic is typically theoretical, it constitutes a powerful battery of arguments. Gladstone supplemented them from time to time with other bits of evidence revealing the shortcomings of democracy. Burke had shown, he noted in a memorandum of 1831, that the majority was not necessarily right. Since the majority of men are swayed by passions, there is a presumptive case that at any given point the majority will be in the wrong.[76] Plato's *Republic*, he recorded in the following year, was 'very pungent' about the character of democracy.[77] And Dante's *Purgatorio*, according to a memorandum of 1835, vividly illustrated democratic instability.[78] So there was no doubt about Gladstone's stance on these issues. The democracy to which Grote leaned was fickle and dangerous; the aristocracy which Grote disdained should hold a principal role in society and government.

Battle was joined betweeen the two men over ancient history. One of Grote's achievements in his later volumes was to rehabilitate Cleon and his fellow-demagogues of Athens, even if they are portrayed rather too much in the guise of radical MPs.[79] Similarly, in the early part of his *History*, the chieftains of the Trojan War are depicted as almost politically redundant. The council, where they assembled to advise the king, lacked, according to Grote, any power to restrain Agamemnon.[80] Gladstone's Homeric works concentrate their fire on this assertion. On the contrary, he insists in *Studies on Homer and the Homeric Age*, individual members of the council can resist Agamemnon.

Gladstone conceives Homer's council to be very like the Cabinet in the British constitution. The council is:

> a most important auxiliary instrument of government; sometimes as pre-
> paring materials for the more public deliberations of the Assembly, some-
> times intrusted, as a kind of executive committee, with its confidence;
> always as supplying the Assemblies with an intellectual and authoritative
> element, in a concentrated form, which might give steadiness to its tone,
> and advise its course with a weight adequate to so important a function.[81]

The chieftains are far from political nullities, but instead act as a brake on popular turbulence. By the time of *Juventus Mundi*, a simplified version of *Studies* issued in 1869, Gladstone idealises the Homeric chieftain:

> Simple yet shrewd; passionate, and yet self-contained; brave in battle, and
> gentle in converse; keenly living in the present, yet with a 'large discourse'
> over the future and the past; as he is in body 'full-blooded and tall', so is
> he in mind towering and full-formed.[82]

Almost his only vice, Gladstone suggests, is a willingness to cheat at chariot-racing.[83] Gladstone took readily to the round of country house parties arranged by the Whig grandees.[84] The aristocracy of the land supplied many of his friends and colleagues. One of the purposes of his Homeric study was to vindicate, against Grote, the right of the leisured heads of landed society to take the lead in national life.

A fifth area of divergence was religion. Grote's maternal grand-
father had been a minister in the Countess of Huntingdon's small but fervent connexion. The grandfather had named Grote's mother 'Selina' after his patroness the countess. During Grote's boyhood, his mother shunned worldly society, and it may be that her son imbibed an overdose of religion. He certainly reacted against this aspect of his family inheritance. Reading Lucretius, Lessing and Voltaire as a young man confirmed him in an irreligious course, and James Mill's strident anticlericalism pushed him further along the road.[85] In 1822, at Bentham's request, he published a summary of the master's critical views on religion, but under a pseudonym for fear of the consequences.[86] Grote valued his connection with University College, London, precisely because it offered education without religious appendages.[87] His irreligion found expression in politics. His 1832 election address promised support for efforts to extinguish the abuses of the Church of England, and from his first parliamentary session he regularly demanded greater ecclesiastical reform in Ireland as well as

England.[88] Grote was a freethinker carrying his views into the public arena.

Once again that stance entailed confrontation with Gladstone. The young Tory was already in the early 1830s moving from his family's Evangelicalism to his later high churchmanship, but throughout there was a keen interest in religious issues of all kinds.[89] The Irish Church was the key battleground of the period, actually causing an influential group under Lord Stanley to cross the floor of the Commons from the reformers to the Tories. The established Church of Ireland was Anglican, whereas some four-fifths of the Irish population were Roman Catholics. Reformers could see justification for its continued establishment only if its endowments were drawn on to provide secular education for the Irish people. Some radicals wanted to go further by disestablishing the Irish Church altogether. Tories, however, were resolved to preserve its privileges and emoluments intact. Gladstone in particular wished to provide a fresh defence for its establishment, a task that would culminate in the appearance of *The State in its Relations with the Church* (1838). In the persistent skirmishing of the 1830s over the issue, Gladstone held that because the church existed 'to promote the glory of God by saving the souls of men' it was wrong for the state to hinder its mission by appropriating part of its property, even for education.[90] Consequently Grote's attitude to the Irish Church touched Gladstone's rawest nerve.

As Gladstone must have expected, Grote's free thought coloured his analysis of Greek history. Another of his achievements as a historian was the favourable reevaluation, for the first time, of the sophists who are denigrated in so many of the sources.[91] In their arguments he recognised the first flowering in European civilisation of freedom of enquiry. Their time, the fifth century BC, was the Athenian golden age. The much earlier epoch of Homer, by contrast, had been a period of darkness, not least in morality. Grote insisted that there were no ethics taught in Homer and that in Homeric society, apart from private ties, there are 'scarcely any other moralising forces in operation'.[92] Like other Utilitarians, Grote supposed that morality is not innate.[93] Only gradually, between the eighth and the fifth centuries BC, had it arisen in ancient Greece. As the veneration of the gods lost its hold, that is to say, moral standards steadily developed down to the time of Socrates. Homer's age had been marked, according to Grote, by homicide, fraud, brutality, robbery, perjury, neglect of orphans, mutilation and vengeance.[94] A religious society was utterly immoral.

This censure was another that Gladstone tried in his writings to wipe away. Gladstone believed that all ancient nations derived their religious and moral convictions from the disclosure made by the Almighty to Adam and then to Noah, the fathers of the race. The closer to the dawn of human history, the purer the religion and morality must be. Hence it was axiomatic for him that the moral tendency over time was downwards.[95] He could not abide Grote's assertion that Greek terminology hardly possessed ethical meaning until the time of Socrates – a perception subsequently reinforced by those scholars who have seen archaic Greece as a 'shame society' rather than a 'guilt society'.

> I ask permission [bursts out Gladstone in his *Studies*] to protest against whatever savours of the idea that any Socrates whatever was the patentee of the sentiment of right and wrong, which is the most precious part of the patrimony of mankind. The movement of Greek morality with the lapse of time was chiefly downward, and not upward.[96]

The treatment of women, an instance of moral behaviour explored by Gladstone at some length, supplied specific evidence. He suggests, for example, that in the *Odyssey* Nausicaa is free to marry her own choice of husband. That illustrated the elevated position of women in Homeric times and so formed a confutation of those who saw in human history a law of moral progress.[97] Although it was unfair to saddle Grote with that opinion, he was once more the chief writer in Gladstone's mind. Homeric society was both religious and moral. The coupling of freethought with virtue was an illegitimate ploy.

There was, sixthly, a basic disagreement about method between the two scholars. Grote's scepticism was carried over, in Gladstone's view, from religion into classical studies. There was, in the first place, the question of the authorship of the epics assigned to Homer. In Germany in the previous century F.A. Wolf had propounded the view that the poems could be broken down into different blocs by various hands. Gladstone's first venture into print on a Homeric topic was to repudiate the more extreme version of this theory, put forward by Karl Lachmann, that the epics were consolidated from as many as eighteen originally distinct sources.[98] Grote was much less adventurous. He held merely that the *Iliad* had grown from an original corpus of only thirteen books, and that there was probably more than one author.[99] But Gladstone is not content with this more moderate position: 'There is no limb of the *Iliad*', he argues, 'separable from the body without destroying the symmetrical, masculine, and broad development of its general plan.'[100] The consistency of the poem, in Gladstone's view, invalidated Grote's conclusion. Gladstone wished to re-establish the plausibility of believing in a single Homer.

That aim was subordinate to a more fundamental issue separating him from Grote. The banker had learned from the great German historian of Rome, B.G. Niebuhr, to discern in the misty stories of early times not history but a mass of what was coming to be called myth. Grote concluded that the period before 776, the first Olympiad, was irrecoverable to the historian. All, therefore, that could be done for early Greece was to record the tales that subsequently circulated about the remoter past. Grote rejected the traditional enterprise of trying to distil the essence of real events from the stuff of myth. He simply recounted the legends 'without presuming to measure how much or how little of historical matter these legends may contain'.[101]

So sceptical a conclusion was repugnant to Gladstone. The historians Herodotus and Thucydides had disagreed, he pointed out, and yet Grote was willing, with good reason, to trust the enquiries of the latter. In a similar way research could make progress in uncovering the reality of archaic times if it was sufficiently rigorous in method. Homer, in particular, must not be conflated with other sources, but should be treated as a distinct testimony to a vanished world.[102] The issue here was whether or not there could be any reliable evidence at all for the early period. If not, then Grote's conjectures about political and moral change might be unassailable. If so, however, the other arguments that Gladstone wished to mount against Grote might carry weight. Hence a preoccupation with vindicating the essential historicity of Homer became the driving force of Gladstone's classical scholarship from 1846 until his death. It led him, for example, to give more credence and publicity in the 1870s to the discoveries of the semi-fraudulent archaeologist Heinrich Schliemann than the man's character or achievement warranted.[103] Schliemann's excavations seemed to supply independent evidence to confirm the authenticity of Homer's account of Troy. If Gladstone was betrayed into misjudgement by his desire to reinstate the authority of Homer as a witness to the earliest phase of western civilisation, it also led him to a major perception. The main question, he insisted, was not whether Homer had carefully recorded 'a certain series of transactions', but whether he had faithfully represented 'manners and character, feelings and tastes, races and countries, principles and institutions'.[104] It did not matter enormously whether or not Homer had managed to compose an accurate narrative of political events. What he had done was to preserve a treasury of materials for the social historian. Subsequent scholars have generally agreed that Homer is an invaluable source for the way of life of archaic Greece rather than merely a tissue of imaginative fables. To that extent they have decided the question of method in favour of Gladstone rather than Grote.

In any summing up it must not be supposed that there was nothing in common between the two scholars. Apart from sharing many of the concerns of rough contemporaries, they were both trustees of the British Museum, both enjoyed felling trees and both sat several times to the painter J.E. Millais – Gladstone four times and Grote, as Gladstone noted with interest, as many as twenty times.[105] As Prime Minister in 1869 Gladstone wrote offering Grote a peerage, but the historian refused it. Morley interpreted this gesture as an act of magnanimity by the Prime Minister to a man of no religion, and no doubt that is true.[106] Yet, as with most of Gladstone's political acts, there was more than one purpose, and it would have been deeply satisfying to have induced Grote to join the ranks of the aristocracy that the Utilitarian had once reviled. In declining the honour, Grote referred to his 'peculiar feelings' on the subject, and so it is evident that his anti-aristocratic sentiments persisted;[107] and, as all who knew him avowed, he was a man of rigorous consistency. After Grote's death in 1871, Gladstone paid several vists to his widow, who survived her husband by seven years. Harriet thought Gladstone wise, discerning and self-respecting, but verbose.[108] She gave Gladstone a volume on Arab philosophy as a memento of George, and then a copy of her husband's 1822 critique of religion.[109] It is clear that Gladstone had respect for his former antagonist. Indeed even in the *Studies* he had acknowledged the 'general authority' of Grote and habitually treated him as such – to the extent, remarkably, of accepting an aspect of his interpretation of early Greek religion.[110] The dissent that Gladstone registered against some of Grote's views was offered in a spirit of scholarly interchange.

Yet there is no disguising the strength of feeling underlying the dissent. The editor of Grote's minor works justifiably remarks that Gladstone's criticism of his subject's views on Greek ethics is expressed 'with some warmth'.[111] Gladstone, for all his courtesy of debate, disagreed fundamentally with Grote's premises. In politics, as we have seen, the radical Grote contrasted with the conservative Gladstone. In ideology, the Utilitarian Grote contrasted with the communitarian Gladstone. Over the monarchy, the republican Grote contrasted with the royalist Gladstone. Over the aristocracy, Grote the democrat contrasted with Gladstone the defender of landed society.

In religion, the freethinking Grote contrasted with Gladstone the churchman. And over method, the sceptical Grote contrasted with Gladstone the champion of Homer. Classical studies, as recent writers have reminded us,[112] were still a vehicle for discussion of contemporary issues in early and mid-Victorian Britain, and so it is not surprising that the understanding of Homer was the field on which their many-sided controversy was fought. Grote revealed his commitments fully in his *History*, showing by his breadth of vision why he is rightly charac-terised as a philosophic radical. But for Gladstone studies it is import-ant to appreciate the extent to which the statesman's scholarly preoc-cupations were shaped by his Utilitarian opponent. Gladstone felt compelled to meet Grote's contentions at many points along an extended front. A broad intellectual vista may also be justly claimed for the Gladstonian side of the debate. Both antagonists intertwined their politics and their scholarship to a remarkable degree. That is why Gladstone, in his earlier career, may properly be called a philo-sophic Tory.

10

Gladstone and Ruskin

Michael Wheeler

Looking back now, one hundred years after the last decade of their lives, we tend to think of Gladstone and Ruskin as Grand Old Men. Perhaps the photograph at the foot of the stairs at St Deiniol's Library comes to mind, and the late photographs of the 'Sage of Brantwood'. But a glance at the frontispiece portraits in the multi-volume Gladstone diaries, or the numerous portraits of Ruskin taken during his long life, remind us of the many different stages that marked the development of these two titans of the Victorian Age, each in his different way a great controversialist and, intellectually, a polymath. This essay connects two men who came to know one another only late in life, in rather strained circumstances. I will be looking at Ruskin's visit to Hawarden Castle in January 1878 in some detail, and considering the significance of the conversations that took place during the visit. By way of introduction, however, we will 'call in' on both men in selected years leading up to 1878, choosing all the 'eights' in the nineteenth century (1808, 1818, and so on), as a number of these happen to provide illuminating parallels and contrasts between Gladstone and Ruskin.

Modern scholarship provides us with masses of detail, a positive embarrassment of riches, on which to work as we attempt to reconstruct the working of these men's minds. At the same time, modern media treatment tends to distort and trivialise complex historical figures, so that in the popular consciousness Gladstone is associated with fallen women, and Ruskin with an unconsummated marriage. The danger of applying modern slogans and politically correct ideas to such figures was dramatised a few years ago in Sheffield, where the city council decided not to name a new piazza Ruskin Square, because ethnic minority groups had discovered that Ruskin was a 'racist'.[1]

The recovery of the past in some ideal true, accurate and complete record, or version of reality, is ultimately impossible, as historians know. Even eye-witness accounts of events are inevitably flawed or limited in some way, and facts are open to a wide range of interpretations, both in the past and in the present from which we look back. This is what prose fiction, and indeed the higher criticism, were largely about in the nineteenth century. But even a diary entry represents a shaping, a selecting from the mass of sense impressions that an event or series of events generate. Significantly, among literary critics the theoretical debate that set the agenda for the 'crisis in English studies' is now swinging away from philosophical and linguistic issues relating to the nature of language and reality towards pressing questions relating to history, and the 'reading' and rewriting of the past.

In literary scholarship the new historicism concerns itself with ideology, language and power, often starting from some obscure particular instance and extrapolating from it. The brand of 'old historicism' which I myself espouse also concerns itself with minute particulars (my sub-title might have been 'Why was the Curate Nervous in Hawarden Church on the First Sunday After the Epiphany, 1878?'), but it seeks to relate those particulars to the larger and dominant cultural forces of the age, and to the Victorians' version of 'grand narratives' that are in fact transhistorical. It is religion that provided for men like Gladstone and Ruskin the grand narrative against which they measured themselves and their (fallen) world. Let us turn, then, to these unique and yet in certain ways representative lives and intellects, and first to a series of snapshots, taken every ten years from 1808 to 1868.

My first snapshot, taken in 1808 (and thus anticipating photography by some years), is like one of those blanks that come back from the processing lab, exposed before the film was wound on to the first frame. (Tennyson might have talked about the great deep of prenatal existence.) For Gladstone – rather annoyingly for my purposes – was not even conceived in 1808; he was to be born on 29 December 1809. His father, John Gladstone, had moved to Liverpool from Scotland over twenty years earlier, and was now an established merchant magnate. Meanwhile Ruskin's father, John James Ruskin, who had moved to London from Scotland, was a partner in a wine importer's business. He was to become engaged to Margaret Cock in 1809, the year of William Gladstone's birth.

By 1818 John Gladstone was a Liverpool MP, a Canningite Tory. An Anglican since 1804, he had built Seaforth Church and worshipped

Fig. 22. John Ruskin by H. S. Uhlrich (1879).

regularly there. His roots, like Mr and Mrs Ruskin's, were Scottish Presbyterian. John James Ruskin, while remaining a High Tory and an Evangelical, was to attend a number of different churches in south and central London over the coming years, dissenting and Church of England.[2] Both Anne Gladstone (an Episcopalian) and Margaret Ruskin remained Evangelical in outlook, and based their religion upon close and regular reading of the Bible – a tradition that was to be passed on to their sons, both of whom were to move away from Evangelicalism later in life. But whereas Gladstone was to move from the Tory benches, John Ruskin (born on 8 February 1819) was to remain, like his father before him, a 'violent Tory of the old school', while also claiming (in July 1871) to be a 'Communist of the old school – reddest also of the red'.[3] Coleridge reminded the nineteenth century of the adage 'extremes meet',[4] and they were certainly to meet in Ruskin, who would announce in 1880 that he hated Liberalism as he did Beelzebub.[5]

Let us return to our chronology, and to 1828. Gladstone was now eighteen, and during the summer his sister Anne helped him to accept the high church doctrine of baptismal regeneration, signalling an important shift in his churchmanship in readiness for the step he took in October down the familiar path of future members of the Victorian ruling class, from Eton to Christ Church.[6] (In two years' time he was to distinguish himself as President of the Union and, in 1831, to graduate with a double first.) Meanwhile in Herne Hill the nine-year-old Ruskin read the Bible daily at his mother's knee and enjoyed a family tour of the west country, one of many such trips that the family were to make together, combining business (ever more successful business) with pleasure.

Ten years later, in 1838, it was Ruskin's turn to be an undergraduate at Christ Church, but in his case not having withstood the rigours of Eton, and now not greatly enjoying Oxford. He remained under the vigilant eye of his mother, who lodged in the High. Unlike Gladstone, who had graduated in glory seven years before, Ruskin left Oxford two years later through ill health (probably tuberculosis) and eventually returned to take a 'complimentary double-fourth'.[7] But he was awarded the Newdigate Prize for poetry, and introduced to the Poet Laureate, Wordsworth. He also deepened his understanding of drawing, natural history and geology under Dr William Buckland, Canon of Christ Church, who claimed to have 'eaten his way through the animal kingdom'. (Ruskin was always to regret a 'day of unlucky engagement' on which he missed a 'delicate toast of mice'.)[8] Young

John Ruskin's first extended publication, *The Poetry of Architecture*, was concluded in serial form in Loudon's *Architectural Magazine* in 1838. More pressingly, he was deeply and (so it proved) hopelessly in love with Adèle Domecq, daughter of his father's partner.

In contrast, Gladstone, for the past six years Conservative MP for Newark, was more hopefully in love with Catherine Glynne, sister to his contemporary at Eton and Oxford, Sir Stephen Glynne of Hawarden Castle. (The following year William and Catherine were to share in a double wedding at Hawarden.) On a continental tour he was captivated by Miss Glynne, but managed to correct and return the proofs of his first major publication, *The State in its Relations with the Church*. On Christmas Eve, while Ruskin entertained the Domecq girls at Herne Hill, Gladstone met his fellow MP Macaulay, who was soon to review (or rather dismember) his book. Four days later, on his twenty-ninth birthday, Gladstone attended Mass with Henry Manning, whose own first book, *The Unity of the Church*, dedicated to his friend, was to take up Gladstone's theme of church and state four years later.[9] (Manning was to become Ruskin's friend, too, and Ruskin was to write on Manning's and Gladstone's theme in *Notes on the Construction of Sheepfolds* in 1851.) For all three writers, as for their contemporaries in the years of the Oxford Movement and the Catholic Revival, the most pressing question was that of authority – the authority of state and church, laity and clergy, priest and bishop, scripture and tradition.[10] Years later Gladstone was to look back on this period, writing of Macaulay in a letter to Manning: 'I had professed my loyal allegiance to two principles which in religion, at least, he appeared to regard as incompatible; freedom and authority.'[11] It is the second of these principles to which we will constantly return.

Authority of a different kind was at issue in 1848, the year of revolutions on the Continent and of Chartist riots in England. On 10 April, Gladstone, now a Peelite MP for the University of Oxford, served as a special constable in London.[12] On the same day, John Ruskin married Effie Gray in Perth. So often in the careers of these two men we see Gladstone at the heart of political debate and conflict, retiring for sustenance and renewal to Hawarden, where he worked on his books and papers, while Ruskin inhabited the more marginal and critical world of the arts and letters, and left the study only to give lectures and to make extensive continental tours. Now famous as the author of *Modern Painters*, he visited Normandy with his young wife to gather material for *The Seven Lamps of Architecture*, to be published the following year, and deplored the effects of revolutionists and restorers on

the fabric of the ancient buildings.[13] Meanwhile Gladstone returned
to Oxford to be awarded an honorary degree, and, having supported
the removal of Jewish disabilities, was greeted with cries of 'Gladstone
and the Jew Bill!'[14] In this he was on the same side as the Duke of
Argyll, who entered the Lords the previous year as a Peelite, and will
figure later on in our story. As will two figures born the previous year,
in 1847: Mary Gladstone, William and Catherine's third daughter,
and Henry Scott Holland. And it was in 1847 that Ruskin sat on a
committee for securing Gladstone's election for the University of
Oxford, and that the two men met at Lady Davy's table, and quar-
relled across Miss Lockhart over Neapolitan prisons.[15]

Of the several problems troubling Gladstone in 1848, not least was
the famous Gorham case. The previous year, when the Rev. G.C.
Gorham was presented to the living of Brampton Speke by the Lord
Chancellor, Bishop Henry Phillpotts of Exeter refused to institute
him, and in March of that year concluded many hours of interviewing
Gorham on baptism by confirming his decision. Gladstone's sensitivity
to the case had two sources. First, Gorham's sceptically Calvinist view
of the doctrine of baptismal regeneration – the grounds for
Phillpotts's action – was also his own before his sister Anne steered
him to acceptance of the doctrine.[16] Secondly, the protracted appeals
by Gorham over the next two years were to raise again the question
of state and church, and of the church's authority. Although Gladstone
was to become personally engaged in the debate, discussing the case
with Phillpotts himself as well as high church friends such as Manning, he refused to join the open Anglo-Catholic attack on the
Gorham Judgement, thus causing the first breach with Manning, by
then on the road to Rome. Ruskin was also to become sufficiently
excited by the case to write a carefully prepared but unpublished
'Essay on Baptism', in 1850/1.[17] Whereas Gladstone was to comment
as the disturbed high church insider, deeply concerned with the question of ecclesiastical authority, Ruskin wrote as a comparative outsider, taking the argument back to essentials, which for him resided
in the unique authority of scripture.

Later in the decade, however, in 1858, it was Ruskin's turn to suffer a
religious crisis, but in his case a crisis of faith. On the morning of Sunday
1 August, his visit to the Waldensian (Vaudois) chapel in Turin had a
profound effect upon him. When compared to the breadth and beauty
of Paul Veronese's vision in *The Presentation of the Queen of Sheba to Solomon*,
which Ruskin was currently studying, the narrow and exclusive preaching of the 'little squeaking idiot' who represented what Evangelicals had

always taken to be the purest Protestant community struck him as repulsive.[18] Of the several different accounts he was to write of the event, one of the most dramatic – that in *Praeterita* – stated (hyperbolically) that this day his 'evangelical beliefs' were 'put away, to be debated of no more'.[19] Rather than assume that Ruskin simply 'lost his faith', we should focus on his reference to putting away his Evangelical beliefs. By this I take him to mean his shedding of all or some of those essential doctrines – original sin, conversion, justification by faith, the authority of the Word – and of those non-essential (but, for many in the nineteenth century, problematic) doctrines – eternal punishment, millenarianism, special providence, assurance – which defined Evangelicalism.[20] It is significant that he now began work on the Bible in the 'same direction' as Bishop Colenso of Natal, whose study on *The Pentateuch and Book of Joshua Critically Examined* started coming out in parts four years later. For Ruskin this controversial publication was to be a great relief, ending his sense of working in isolation and of being 'quite unable to tell any one' what he was about.[21] On his return to England, he began to teach the ten-year-old Rose la Touche; and thus began one of the great tragic love stories of the Victorian Age, later the subject of a chapter in Gladstone's daughter Mary Drew's book on *Acton, Gladstone and Others* (1924).

For Gladstone, 1858 was the year of his great speech (on 4 May) on his motion urging the Commons and the government to uphold the cause of the Romanians against the Turks and the Austrians, and of his trip to the Ionian Islands as High Commissioner Extraordinary, starting in November.[22] In between, his *Studies in Homer and the Homeric Age*, published in three volumes in the summer, included graceful references to Ruskin's own ideas on Homer.[23] Ruskin, however, in a private letter to his father, expressed his dislike of Gladstone's work on Homer, and described him as 'an eminent Speaker of Bad English; – a peculiar master of clumsy verbiage'.[24] If the two men had met in the autumn of 1858 they would surely have discussed not only Homer, but also the Vaudois. For back in 1832 Gladstone himself underwent a shock to his Evangelical system when, during a visit to Italy, he was disappointed in the Vaudois he had earlier idealised in the *Eton Miscellany*.[25] He too wrote up different accounts of the event, one for public, the other for private consumption.[26]

Ten years after Ruskin's religious crisis, the art critic and social commentator was in 1868 on the brink of a new phase of his life. His father had died, leaving him a large fortune. So in the next decade, when he was to be the first Slade Professor of Fine Art at Oxford, the founding Master of the Guild of St George and the driving force behind the Sheffield Museum, author of *Fors Clavigera: Letters to the Workmen and Labourers of Great Britain*, published in parts by George Allen on an innovative commercial basis, owner of Brantwood on Coniston Water, and tireless traveller and writer in Italy and Switzerland, his many and varied activities were unfettered by narrow financial considerations.

For Gladstone 1868 brought his first premiership, following that often recalled incident in the grounds of Hawarden Castle, of which the main ingredients are a felled tree, a telegram, and a solemn reference to the pacification of Ireland. But how characteristic it is of him to round off his diary for 1868 with a list of the notable things that had happened in his life in December:

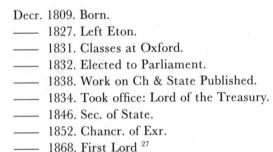

Decr. 1809. Born.
——— 1827. Left Eton.
——— 1831. Classes at Oxford.
——— 1832. Elected to Parliament.
——— 1838. Work on Ch & State Published.
——— 1834. Took office: Lord of the Treasury.
——— 1846. Sec. of State.
——— 1852. Chancr. of Exr.
——— 1868. First Lord [27]

He listed some other months, then added, 'rather a frivolous enumeration', before moving into a commentary that includes these words:

> I feel like a man under a burden under which he must fall and be crushed if he looks to the right or left, or fails from any cause to concentrate mind and muscle upon his progress step by step. This absorption, this excess . . . is the fault of political life with its insatiable demands . . .

and these:

> It has been a special joy of this December that our son Stephen is given to the Church: 'whose shoe's latchet I am not worthy to unloose'.

Ten years later, when Ruskin finally visited Hawarden in 1878, Stephen Gladstone had been rector for six years, and was to remain there for another twenty-six. In the first month of 1878, a 'tumultuous year',[28] W.E. Gladstone watched the Eastern Question coming to a head. On 8 January the Porte opened negotiations with Russia. Two days later the Shipka Pass was forced and a Turkish army overcome by the Russians. On the 23rd the British fleet was ordered to the

Dardanelles. By February, Gladstone's opposition to Disraeli's jingoism had put himself and his family in some danger, and his windows in Harley Street were smashed.[29]

Characteristically, Gladstone's steady reading continued. On 30 December 1877 (the Sunday after Christmas) he read and admired Ruskin's latest Oxford lecture, printed in *The Nineteenth Century*.[30] Ruskin's editor, E.T. Cook, later referred to a particular argument about the reality of good angels and the principalities of Satan – 'just such as would have appealed to Gladstone'.[31] But there are plenty of other passages to which one can point, such as those relating to the mystery of a future state (a favourite Gladstonian topic), on the servants of Christ, or on the need for undergraduates to take plenty of exercise in the vacations.[32] Two years previously Ruskin had answered Gladstone's call at the St James's Hall conference on the Eastern Question.[33] As Gladstone now read Ruskin's lecture, perhaps he warmed to the ironic remarks about the Englishman who enjoys 'his muffin and *Times*, and contentedly allows the slaughter of fifty thousand men, so it be in the interests of England, and of his own stock on Exchange'.[34] Like Ruskin's papers to the Metaphysical Society, including that on 'The Nature and Authority of Miracle' (1873), his high-minded contribution to Knowles's *The Nineteenth Century* was perhaps a reminder to Gladstone that they were both members of the society, that remarkably broad intellectual elite of the 1870s.[35] The first issue of the journal, in March 1877, began with a sonnet by Tennyson (still the object of some jealousy in Gladstone's mind, with regard to Arthur Hallam), followed by Gladstone's own inaugural review article on G.C. Lewis's *Essay on the Influence of Authority in Matters of Opinion*.

In any case, Gladstone was full of the lecture. So the thirty-year-old Mary Gladstone, who had met Ruskin through Burne-Jones and other mutual friends, and who loved his work, persuaded her father to have the great writer to stay.[36] The following day – New Year's Eve – Ruskin had on his bedroom chimney piece in Corpus Christi, Oxford, a letter from 'Gladstone's daughter', asking him to Hawarden.[37] Although Ruskin gratefully accepted, he was extremely nervous about the visit, and caused great hilarity among the Gladstones with the telegram he arranged to be held in readiness, in case he needed to be called away. Why did he accept? And why was he anxious?

He accepted, no doubt, for much the same reason that anyone would give for taking up an invitation from a former Prime Minister. (Immediately before the Hawarden visit, he had stayed at Windsor Castle at the invitation of Prince Leopold.) Lord Acton's later interpretation – that Ruskin was 'curious to probe the great Gladstonian mystery, not favourably prepossessed' – is perhaps a touch cynical, but may have been not far from the truth.[38] He was anxious not only because he was naturally shy, but also because he disagreed with Gladstone on many things, and had been openly critical of him in print, specifically on the subject of religion. Three years earlier, in *Fors*, he had described Gladstone in a Carlylean vein as 'nothing else than a negative system, hundred-tongued to his own confusion; the "fashionable" hairdresser, as it were, and Minister of extreme unction in the manner of pomade, to the scald and moribund English pates that still wear their religion decoratively'.[39] (Remembering Gladstone's comments on authority and freedom, it is interesting to note Ruskin's comment in this Letter 57 that for him 'Liberty' is 'only another word for Death'.)[40] He was also unwell, nervously. He wrote to his cousin Joan Severn, on 10 January 1878:

> ever since the Windsor interruption [I] have fallen into a state of confusion which is now wholly oppressive and inextricable – and I feel so exhausted that I am obliged most unwillingly to give up the Gladstone visit. It is a distress to me to feel how this will vex and disappoint my puss more than I can say. But I am sure it is wise . . .[41]

And later in the day: 'I am forced to give up Gladstone altogether . . . I'm just done up with overwork . . .'

But Ruskin did make the journey, on 'a bleak gray day' (Saturday 12 January),[42] from Oxford to Hawarden, where Gladstone was writing another paper for *The Nineteenth Century*, on the subject of 'The Peace to Come'. (The fact that Ruskin had caught a cold, which kept him in his room for much of the time between meals during the weekend, was to allow his host to get on with his work.) Mary had been walking with her younger cousin Alfred Lyttelton, famous for playing in the Eton cricket eleven at the age of fifteen, who had managed to get some 'woodcraft' in with Gladstone during the day.[43] He was later to write to Mary saying that he didn't think he would ever forget these days at Hawarden: 'if one had many such it would entirely spoil one for the coarser world'.[44]

Ruskin eventually arrived at Broughton station on the same train as Henry Scott Holland of Christ Church, known at Eton in phrenological and Darwinian terms as 'Monkey' or 'Linky' Holland, but for Mary Gladstone 'the Flying Dutchman', 'in some sense associated with wings'.[45] Holland, who admired Ruskin, accompanied the fifty-nine-year-old 'Aprile', as Mary called him, on the carriage drive, Ruskin expressing 'the darkest view possible of his host, imbibed from the "Master" Carlyle', to whose imagination he figures apparently as the symbol of all with which he is 'at war'.[46]

They arrived at 6 p.m.. Everybody was at first 'unspeakably shy', but dinner went well.[47] Mary was seated between Ruskin and Holland, and gathered plenty of material for her diary, as did Holland, for his much later (and inaccurate) reminiscences of Gladstone and Ruskin; young Ottley, the curate, for his somewhat gushing version of events;[48] and Gladstone himself, whose diary entry is to read: 'Mr Ruskin came: we had much conversation, interesting of course.' Ruskin, himself a diarist but not of the social variety, must have been aware that everything he said would probably be taken down and used in evidence for or against him; this, together with his declared inability to say what he really felt in front of Gladstone, must have been a constraint. Nevertheless, he commented on a wide range of topics – museums, newspapers, serpents (a favourite theme of his), Buckland of Christ Church, Homer, Thirlmere, the railways in Scotland, parents – several of which arose from his recent lecture, and on most of which he and Gladstone differed (they were, however, both against competitive rowing at Oxford!). Holland wrote of the 'absolute contrast between them at every point on which conversation could conceivably turn'.[49] The 'brimming optimism of Mr. Gladstone, hoping all things, believing everybody', came 'clashing up at every turn with the inveterate pessimism of Mr Ruskin', who saw 'nothing on every side but a world rushing headlong into the pit'. (Such pessimism for the world is not, of course, incompatible with the Christian hope.) Suddenly, at 10.45 p.m., and to the dismay of the company, Ruskin rose from his chair and announced that he always retired early. The inevitable post-mortem was favourable, however, and remarks were made about 'his graceful and delightful manner – bright, gentle, delicately courteous'.[50]

The fact is, though, that Ruskin felt unwell, writing in his diary the following day: 'I have seldom been more ill without serious illness; sorethroat coming on gradually and very bad when I went to bed, with feverishness and fancying I had got scarlet fever from a redfaced child in the train'.[51] (This probably explains why the hand that signed the visitors' book on Saturday 12 January was so shaky.)[52] That Sunday morning he also wrote an unflattering account of the previous night to Joan Severn, lapsing into the baby-talk he often used with her:

horrid big fashionable dinner and Miss Gladstone (whom I took in as host-ess – her mother not appearing) – though a nice girl (- and she had gathered some primroses & put in my room) yet oppressed me terribly by that macadamized manner which girls get who see everybody in the world every day; and a daughter-in-law whom Mr Gladstone took in was worse – a trained London beauty – very beautiful, and dressed like a figure in the Paris costume books – but with a face that froze one hard like this east wind, and broke one to bits afterwards – and there was a brown thin faced man who came with me from Chester – and knows me at Oxford and I don't know him and can't make him out – and Mr Gladstone talked – and is nice – but a mere shallow stream with deep pools in it that are good for nothing; and I'm fitened and borryed and misby – and don't know fot to do – only Mrs Wickham is very nice – and I hate Mr Wickham, and he's here too!

He got up 'very doubtfully and miserably', hardly knowing if he had slept; but was 'very thankful' that it was a 'mere bilious cold'. At breakfast the conversation took a truly fascinating turn, but, alas, one that did not interest Mary Gladstone, who was to record in the sole account we have of it that 'they wd go off on some dull technical point about the Colenso trial, wh. was a horrid waste'.[53] Sixteen years earlier Ruskin had written to Sir John Murray Naesmyth, taking his stand with the bishop,[54] whose daughter, Ellen Colenso, became his pupil at Winnington Hall and later a member of the Guild of St George. And just over three years before, Colenso had been present at one of his lectures.[55] In the *Fors* of January 1875 Ruskin took the Bishop of Oxford to task for preventing Colenso from preaching at Carfax, asking whether Dr Mackarness himself believed 'every statement in the Bible'.[56] In 1887 he was to present the Natural History Museum with a large uncut diamond, to be known as 'The Colenso Diamond', 'in honour of his friend, the loyal and patiently adamantine First Bishop of Natal'.[57]

Like Ruskin, Gladstone read Colenso on the Pentateuch as the parts came out in the 1860s and 1870s. His special interest in the Colenso affair, however, stemmed from the bishop's having brought an action against him and other trustees of the Colonial Bishoprics Fund in 1866, calling upon them to set aside a sum of £10,000 for the purpose of securing the income of the Bishop of Natal.[58] The Master of the Rolls found in favour of Colenso. Gladstone had written the previous year, 'I would rather see Oxford level with the ground, than its religion regulated in the manner which would please Bishop Colenso'.[59] So in the previous five years, Gladstone had kept in touch with the

Colenso debate, reading the Bishop's own defence of his position in Natal and going back to his *Argument before the Supreme Court* (1867).[60]

Although Gladstone would have been interested in Ruskin's Coleridgean advice to the undergraduates the previous month about reading the Bible as they would 'any other book – with strictest criticism, frankly determining what you think beautiful, and what you think false or foolish' – he surely would not have raised the matter with him that morning.[61] Mary's reference to a technicality about the trial indicates a safer, and to Gladstone equally important aspect of the Colenso case. For in his eyes, and in those of many of his fellow churchmen, the case, like the Gorham Judgement, undermined the authority of the Church of England. One would give a great deal to have been at that breakfast, attending where Mary switched off. And to have known whether Gladstone and Ruskin discussed two other matters during the visit: their mutual friend, Cardinal Archibishop Henry Edward Manning; and the theme which in my view underpinned both their (very different) theological positions – the eschatological doctrine of divine judgement. But we must return to our house party, and glean what we can from our team of amateur reporters as they go to 11 o'clock service.

Mary had a difficult time on her walk to church with Ruskin, whose 'conversation is often baffling as he presupposes you well up in Scott, Dante, etc.'[62] It was the First Sunday after the Epiphany and Gladstone read the lessons. Isaiah 51 ('My righteousness is near; my salvation is gone forth, and mine arms shall judge the people') seemed to him 'as if written for them in the East: and just after the Shipka pass'.[63] (Verse 5, quoted here, also highlighted the judgement theme, incidentally.)

The curate, Mr Ottley, according to Mary, preached 'well, tho' not his best as he was so nervous'.[64] This is hardly surprising, when one considers that the congregation included the greatest statesman and the greatest critic of art and society of the day, and that both of them knew the Bible (and one of them theology) better than most of the bishops. Ottley's twenty-fifth birthday was the following Friday. He had been an undergraduate at Keble College (which Ruskin refused to look at as it must have been hideous, if it was new),[65] and had been ordained deacon only two years before. He was to be priested in 1878, and two years later to become Principal of Salisbury Theological College, and later Canon of Rochester. His preaching was later to be much admired, although even his devotees admitted that he had 'his good and his bad days'.[66]

He was clearly then a young but able man, somewhat overcome by the occasion. But Gladstone liked him, describing him in his diary the previous May as 'a person of great charm'.[67] It would be interesting to know whether Gladstone had discussed with him the works of Edward Henry Bickersteth, the Evangelical Vicar of Hampstead, to whom he was related on his mother's side, and with whom Gladstone had corresponded on the subject of everlasting punishment. All we know is that Mr Ottley was nervous, and, as we do not have the sermon or a description of it, we must move on, again frustrated by the lack of firm data at a critical point in the story.

Lord Acton, a frequent guest, arrived at Hawarden some time during the morning to join the party.[68] Mary was to reflect in her maturer years that both he as a Roman Catholic and her father were 'Catholic in the deepest and widest sense of the term, both were conscious and proud of their membership in the Apostolic and Universal Church . . . Both were staunch believers in religious liberty, and both were possessed of a deep longing for the reunion of Christendom'.[69] Again, did the two of them touch on Manning in the course of conversation? And did they discuss 'Catholicism in the deepest and widest sense' with Ruskin? He was to describe his own position in a similar way nine years later, when he denied rumours that he had been received into the Church of Rome: 'I was, am, and can be, only a Christian Catholic in the wide and eternal sense. I have been that these five-and-twenty years at least [i.e. since 1858]. Heaven keep me from being less as I grow older!'[70]

Ruskin was probably rather quiet at lunch, as he believed he had got a 'fresh chill in the Park coming back from church'.[71] But Mary made a touching allusion to his Oxford lecture when she applied his biblical reference to himself.[72] Was he not glad, she asked, to have had his own dove in the Psalms 'which is covered with silver wings and her feathers like gold', to which he replied, 'Thank you so much'.[73] Perhaps this marked the real beginning of their close friendship. Little Katie Wickham, the Gladstones' first grandchild, was much taken with Ruskin, and confidingly leant against him during lunch. Incidentally, one wonders where Mrs Gladstone was all this time. She did not appear at dinner the previous night, but was in the house, as we know. (It was to her that Henry Acland wrote the following March about Ruskin's dangerous state of health.)[74]

For the moment Ruskin suffered from no more than a cold, but this was enough to prevent him from joining in the afternoon walk.[75] At tea, Lord Acton talked a good deal. Stephy and Albert Lyttelton arrived. Gladstone attended Evensong at 6.30. Dinner again went 'admirably'. Gladstone could record in his diary, 'Much conversation & good'.[76] He also added another of those tantalising references which suggest a subject that remained unrecorded:

> Looked up some of Arthur Hallam's letters to find his testimonial to [F.D.] Maurice. They are astonishing. What a bulwark he would have been, had it pleased the Most High to assign to him length of days.

How natural it would have been for Sunday conversation at Hawarden to turn from Colenso to *Essays and Reviews* to F.D. Maurice. But one must not make such wild surmises, particularly when it turns out that other associations were probably in play.

Ruskin had another bad night, 'sorethroat with roughness' keeping him awake, or 'only dozing all night'.[77] He was 'up as usual', but did not feel sure he was 'right'. At breakfast, however, Mary much enjoyed 'talking of Tennyson and F. Myers', both of whom Ruskin admired enormously.[78] Conversation could have arrived here via *The Nineteenth Century*, but much more likely through Tennyson's association with the beloved Hallam.

Again Ruskin stayed in during the morning with his cold, keeping to his room apart from joining the party for meals and having a chat with Lord Acton, Mary and Alfred Lyttelton about novels.[79] After lunch Mary played some 'lively tennis' with the Flying Dutchman, Mr Holland.[80] (We are seeing here a younger, more relaxed generation of late Victorians at play). Ruskin wrote again to Joan:

> I was obliged to stay here, Mr Gladstone being very urgent – and my throat sore besides – so that I partly feared being laid up here! . . . They're very nice in their family breakfast – the three girls – for Mrs Wickham is still a girl, and the little Grand-girl, just baby's age! and the three boys, and a nice Lord Acton – and I try to ignore Mr Wickham. Mr Gladstone is just a simple and gentle old English gentleman – very fond of talking . . . I went to church with them yesterday and Mr Gladstone read both the lessons.

It was after tea that Ruskin seemed to come back to life. Ottley joined the party about 5 p.m. to 'listen to the great master of all gracefulness'. At first all seemed to fail, with Ruskin talking 'chiefly on pathetic subjects: drunken clergy in old days, &c.', and then discussing the examination system at Oxford with Gladstone.[81] But then Mary persuaded Ruskin to come into the ante-room to show them his copies of three of the St Ursula pictures of Carpaccio. He then gave the loveliest speech Ottley had ever heard, as he explained the story

of Ursula to the company. The complex of associations the story had
for Ruskin, whose beloved Rose la Touche had died three years before,
was unknown to them; but the power of what Mary called Ursula's
'holy story' over him was obvious to all.[82] (It was Lady Mount Temple
who later told Mary about Ruskin's love for Rose.)[83] So here we have
an event which is described in some detail, but where the interpretation is (necessarily) limited.

Dinner, to quote Mary's Glynnese, was 'again a succedge'. She went
in with Holland, and afterwards played to Ruskin a good deal. (He
was to call her St Cecilia, she to call him St Chrysostom.) Mary
described how she and Alfred Lyttelton had 'all the plums', as Ruskin
sat at the piano, 'talking in the most solemn and pure and pathetic
manner of young men and maidens, love and marriage'. Mary went
off to bed 'in a glow'. Here is what Alfred Lyttelton wrote a fortnight
later:

> Ruskin talked to Mary and me all the evening, listening first to me playing,
> and winding up with Mary, and all about marriage; it was one of the most
> pathetic things I ever heard, we knowing how his home had been shattered.
> It is unfair to repeat his talk, for it loses so infinitely and seems bald in
> any one else's hands: but his view was I take it rather the old chivalric one
> ... He is very shy, but does not show it, telling Holland how he was
> shivering before coming in first.[84]

Ottley recorded that Alfred told him about this 'long sermonic talk'.[85]
Gladstone seems to have faded into the background that evening. Perhaps he was in the Temple of Peace. His diary reads: 'Walk with Ld
Acton. Worked on "The Peace to Come". Looking up passages & much
conversation. Also it was again a great day of conversation.'[86]

On the last day of Ruskin's visit, Mary went to church with her
father at 8.30 a.m. 'in much rain'.[87] Ruskin, now 'generally better', his
sore throat gone, could hardly see to write a letter to Carlyle at 8.40
a.m., as it was 'one of the true old black devil's skies closing up all
sense of morning', and the 'lovely view up to the old castle [was] a
mere dismal vista of dark green and grey, with the near boughs of the
limetrees shaking angrily across it'.[88] (Ruskin had examined the
clouds closely for forty years, and was to deliver his two lectures on
'The Storm-Cloud of the Nineteenth Century' six years later.) He
gave Alfred the letter, and later that year was to accompany him to
Cheyne Row to meet the Master.[89] He also wrote to Joan yet again:

> The reason I return on your hands so soon is that Mr and Mrs* Gladstone

had to go up to town this morning, and I suppose Mary is shy of entertaining me as hostess-: but she's got to prepare for a Lyttelton marriage on Saturday, and has enough to do doubtless . . .

*Mrs Gladstone thoroughly kind and homely, like her daughter – asked me in future only to send them word when I chose to come.

Ruskin left Hawarden at 10.45 a.m. As he stood at the hall steps, with 'Gladstone and all his family at the door', he begged publicly to recant all that he had ever said or thought against him, and pledged himself to withdraw from print the offending paragaph in *Fors*, which it now stung him with shame to remember.[90] It was, in Holland's phrase, a 'complete victory'. Ruskin was to write to George Allen on the following Friday asking him to make the necessary change to future editions of *Fors* 57,[91] and was to express in the March letter his 'great shame for some words spoken, in one of the letters of the first series, in total misunderstanding of Mr Gladstone's character'.[92] (He also, incidentally, offered the Workmen and Labourers of Great Britain a decidedly Gladstonian reading list on the Eastern Question.)[93] Meanwhile, as Ruskin took the train to Chester with 'nice Mr Holland', and thence to Preston, where he saw the new Town Hall, and so, more happily to Brantwood than he had ever known himself come, in cloudy moonlight, after sunset over sands, Gladstone finished and revised his article on 'The Peace to Come', and wrote to Knowles, concluding – somewhat ambiguously – in his diary that Ruskin was 'in some respects an unrivalled guest, and those important respects too'.[94]

There is no space here to cover the rest of the story of Gladstone and Ruskin, as it developed over subsequent months and years: of the correspondence between Santa Cecilia and St Chrysostom; of the brain fever that nearly destroyed Ruskin not long after his return to Brantwood, during which time the Gladstones prayed for him, as did many others across the nation; of his rapid recovery and visit to Carlyle with Alfred Lyttelton and the meeting with Mary Gladstone at the National Gallery (in the year of the Whistler trial); and of his second visit to Hawarden, in October 1878, when Ruskin challenged the Duke of Argyll on the subject of war (a topic on which Ruskin had lectured,[95] and on which, characteristically, a common point of reference was found in Mozley's 1871 sermon),[96] and when Ruskin accused Gladstone of being a 'leveller', to which Gladstone replied that he was 'an out-and-out inequalitarian'.[97] Instead I will briefly round off my chronology of the nineteenth century.

In 1888, the still robust Gladstone, aged seventy-eight and having been Prime Minister in two further administrations since Ruskin's visits, delivered a major speech at Birmingham, lasting nearly two hours.[98] Ruskin, ten years younger, suffered from recurrent bouts of illness, physical and mental, but managed a final tour of the Continent, and saw Italy for the last time. The following year he descended into what for his public was the last long silence. Gladstone's suggestion four years later, during his fourth premiership, that Ruskin might be Poet Laureate proved to be out of the question.[99] Gladstone himself was to spend his retirement working hard on Butler. In the *Studies Subsidiary to the Works of Bishop Butler* (1896), he robustly reminded his readers that the relegation of the traditional hell to the 'far-off corners of the Christian mind' might adversely affect morals, as a sense of the 'terrors of the Lord' could thus be lost.[100] As I suggested earlier, the doctrine of divine judgement underpinned both Gladstone's and Ruskin's (very different) theological positions. Gladstone, whose life was shaped by the belief that his every moment would be accountable on the Day of Judgement, surely recognised the weight of Ruskin's motto, 'To-day', with its tacit warning – 'The night cometh, when no man can work'.[101] It was the urgency of that challenge which drove both Gladstone and Ruskin to work, each of them in such a range of different arenas. (Consider for a moment the sheer bulk of Gladstone's diaries and papers, for example, and of the Library Edition of Ruskin in 39 volumes, the type for which weighed nine tons.) But that challenge will have to be answered one day in a state of utter singleness; hence perhaps the simple humility which lies (often hidden) at the heart of these two contrasting personalities.

In 1898, when Gladstone died after a painful illness, Ruskin wanted to write to Mary Drew, and sat 'an hour or more, pen in hand', but could get no further than the words, 'Dear Mary, I am grieved at the death of your father –', and no more would come.[102] Two years later Ruskin too was dead. Not for him the Abbey, which was offered, but Coniston village churchyard.

Let me end, not on a maudlin note, but with Ruskin's comment about Gladstone, written two years after his visits to Hawarden, which catches something of the combative spirit of the Victorian public and cultural life to which they contributed so much in such different ways. I quote from a letter that Ruskin wrote in 1880 to the President of the Liberal party of the Glasgow students, in answer to a question whether he sympathised with Disraeli or Gladstone:

Had you ever read ten words of mine with understanding you would have known that I care no more either for Mr D'Israeli or Mr Gladstone than for two old bagpipes with the drones going by steam, but that I hate all Liberalism as I do Beelzebub, and that, with Carlyle, I stand, we two alone now in England, for God and the Queen.

Ever faithfully yours,

J. RUSKIN.[103]

11

Gladstone and the Railways

John Prest

Economic and social historians are reluctant to concede that the explanation of events may be found in the motivation and actions of a single great man, while Gladstone's biographers have, perhaps understandably, preferred not to dwell upon an episode which brought the Liberal champion neither achievement nor glory in a great endeavour.[1] But the story of Gladstone and the case for nationalising the railways is woven into the whole course of his career between the 1840s and the 1880s. It is, therefore, worth another look, and I shall divide my essay into four parts. In the first I shall touch briefly (for this is the best known) upon the Railway Act of 1844, which created an option for the state to purchase the railways in twenty-one years time. In the second I shall consider Mr Gladstone's hopes in 1864–65, when the time arrived to decide whether the state should take up the option he had kept open for it. In the third I deal with events between the appointment of the Royal Commission in 1865 and the end of the Derby-Disraeli ministry in 1868. In the fourth I shall come to Gladstone's approach to the issue after he became Prime Minister.

Canals were authorised by Act of Parliament, and were used by carriers of all kinds acting in competition. In the early 1800s the first railway companies 'were not intended by Parliament to have any monopoly or preferential use of the means of communication on their lines of railway'. 'But no sooner were railways worked on a large scale with locomotive power than it was found impracticable for the public in general to use the lines either with carriages or locomotive engines; and the railway companies ... were compelled ... to embark in the business of common carriers on their lines of railway, and conduct the whole operations themselves.'[2] There was then a greatly increased danger of monopoly. In the 1830s Parliament's answer to this was to rely upon the construction of rival lines between the major centres of trade and population. A decade later the policy appeared to be losing credibility. Rival lines each lost much of the traffic and became unprofitable. One of them went under, or the two companies came to an arrangement, divided the traffic, and set fares at a level which would remunerate them both. Either way, the public were back where they started. In 1844, when Peel was Prime Minister, Gladstone, the President of the Board of Trade, in a passage which became famous, poured scorn upon the directors of railways and their reassuring talk of trusting to competition: 'he would rather give his confidence to a Gracchus, when speaking on the subject of sedition, than give his confidence to a Railway Director, when speaking to the public of the effects of competition'. He went on to cite an instance of competition between two companies, the London and Birmingham and the Grand Junction. 'But these Railway Companies were singularly philanthropic among themselves.' No sooner had they fallen out than reconciliation followed. 'Their quarrels were like lovers' quarrels, and they reminded him of a quotation once felicitously made use of by Mr Fox, "Breves inimicitiae, amicitiae sempiturnae"'.[3]

Up to the end of 1843 Parliament had sanctioned the construction of 2390 miles of railway in Great Britain and sixty-two in Ireland. In 1844, with a new construction boom in the offing, Gladstone noted 'the general and almost the unanimous opinion' of the Select Committee on Railways 'that a great error' had been committed by Parliament 'in failing to provide for the resumption under any conditions of the powers of the State over those undertakings'. The Select Committee, with Gladstone in the chair, considered it to be of great importance that an effort should be made to recover the power of the state, because this would become 'more and more difficult from year to year if it be postponed'.[4] The committee's view formed the basis of the Railway Act of 1844.[5] No attempt was made to interfere with existing lines, but henceforth all lines authorised in the present or any future session were to be liable, after a period of twenty-one years, to a revision of tolls, if their profits exceeded 10 per cent, or, whatever the rate of profits, to purchase by the state, at three months notice. 'But the most important question respected the power of purchase. If they could agree about that, they were not likely to quarrel about the rest.'[6] The Act did not commit the state to purchase the railways, and Gladstone himself would not, he told the House of Commons, have voted in favour of state purchase at the time the Bill was introduced. But a question which had hitherto been kept 'closed against the State', was being reopened, and 'it is a very different question whether I shall reserve a free agency for either the purchase or revision at any future time in case such a measure should appear desirable'.[7] In case the state did decide to purchase, terms of compensation were laid down in the Act.

Nobody could foresee exactly how the railways would develop in the course of the next twenty-one years. Still less, of course, could anyone have foreseen that the author of the Act of 1844, a young President of the Board of Trade aged thirty-four, would find himself in office at age fifty-five as Chancellor of the Exchequer, counting away the time until twenty-one years elapsed and the state approached the moment of destiny which he had reserved for it. In the meantime, while the network expanded from 2000 to 13,000 miles, the spectre of excess profits vanished, because no company was paying a dividend of anything like 10 per cent, the revision clauses became a dead letter, and the Act of 1844 did not much engage 'the attention of the public'.[8] There still remained, however, the possibility of purchase. The twenty-one year period fixed in the Act would expire on 31 December 1865. Before that time the government must make up its mind what it wished to do. For his part, Gladstone had made it clear in 1844 that the Act did not commit a future government to purchase; only to consider whether, by means of nationalisation, 'charges might be very greatly reduced and the benefits of railways proportionably extended'.[9] That, it now appeared, according to the small but active railway reform lobby led by William Galt and Edwin Chadwick, was exactly what it lay in the power of government to achieve.

Galt's interest in railways was as long-standing as Gladstone's, and had originated in a comparison of British railways with the railways in Belgium, where the state planned the layout of the system, and owned and managed many of the railroads. In Belgium fares were one-third what they were in Britain, and the safety factor was much higher.[10] For his part, Chadwick thought of the railways as a utility, comparable to the provision of water supplies, drainage and gas in the large towns. Just as there was no sense in burying two sets of pipes under every street, so there was more to lose than to gain by duplicating every line of railway. The railway, too, was a natural monopoly, and in all these areas where it had become unrealistic to think in terms of 'competition within the field', Chadwick advocated 'competition for the field', which meant that companies should be invited to tender for the right or franchise to manage a public utility upon monopoly terms for a fixed period of years.[11]

The railway system of Great Britain had been created through 1700 private Acts of Parliament, and further modified and developed by 1300 more. Both Galt and Chadwick considered that, under the existing system, the nation was faced with a crisis. The companies were caught up in a struggle for survival, and could all bleed to death together under private enterprise. In order to raise capital they were obliged to issue too many preference shares and debentures. When capital was raised they were forced to waste it in resisting invasions by rival companies and in defending territory. The consequence was that many railways could not afford to modernise track, signalling or rolling stock, and they had no alternative but to raise their charges to the point where these became, as Chadwick expressed it, an 'exaction upon necessities'.[12] In these circumstances the state should step in, seize the opportunity to purchase the railways, rationalise the system, eliminate duplication, reduce overheads, institute a uniform tariff, set fares at levels which would place the convenience of travelling within reach of the largest number of people, and use its proven capacity to raise capital at low fixed rates of interest, to continue to develop the system in the future.

In September 1864, and again in January 1865, Gladstone recorded that he had been reading Galt's book: in one of his papers he referred to the book and cited a page reference.[13] Gladstone's memoranda show that he was sympathetic to the main thrust of the argument which the reformers were developing. Dividends, he noted, were 'often reduced through improvident additions made to capital account with a view to the acquisition or preservation of territory'.[14] He considered that the high charges levied 'on the movement of goods by Railway are in very large classes of cases equivalent in their operation to taxes on raw materials', and that railway charges upon the carriage of both manufactured goods and foodstuffs acted like taxes on consumption.[15] The state had opened its ports to the whole world, and it could scarcely allow the free trade policy which had been adopted in 1846 to be subverted by the railway companies. Gladstone would have agreed with Earl Fortescue that 'an unduly heavy transport tax, though paid to companies instead of to Government, is none the less oppressive and restrictive upon that account',[16] and he was evidently looking for 'large attempts at augmentation of traffic through reduction and simplicity of charges'. 'This', he noted, 'on any considerable scale seems hopeless except through the State.'[17] 'The Penny Post', he concluded, picking up another of the reformers' favourite points, 'never could have been adopted by a body of Companies, without the aid of Govenment.'[18]

Twenty years after the Act of 1844 was passed, Gladstone was strongly attracted to the possibility of the state's taking up the option he had created for it. On 3 October 1864 he wrote to Palmerston that:

> A man named Galt has recently written a book, in which he recommends the purchase of the Railways by the State, with a view not to State Management but to a large reduction of charges and an *approach* to uniformity in the rates throughout the country, on principles partially approximating to those of the Post Office Reform.

Gladstone added that Roebuck, the Radical Member for Sheffield had 'taken up this matter with great enthusiasm' and was asking for the help of government, and concluded that he thought the proposal contained materials 'for a very great and fruitful measure'.[19]

Palmerston did not reply until 28 October, when he remarked that this seemed to be 'a large Question', and asked how it was to be done.[20] Gladstone wrote back, a little bit disingenuously, 'we have *now* an Act known as "Gladstone's Act"'. In the course of the last twenty years this Act had not been sufficiently attended to in the Bills promoted by the companies, but 'were its policy formally adopted, there would be', he assured Palmerston, 'no difficulty in choosing the form of application'.[21] On 10 December the issue was taken up in the press. *The Times* published a report that 'a large measure is now under the consideration of the Government' to effect 'a comprehensive change in the railway system of the United Kingdom'.[22] On the same day the *Economist* carried a long leading article on 'The Forgotten Act of 1844, the English Government and the English Railways'. The *Economist* contended that the railway companies stood where the Post Office did before the introduction of Sir Rowland Hill's reforms. 'They are monopolists getting a great revenue by high charges.' The editor called for 'a commission of competent persons' to 'examine our railway system' with a view to finding out whether it would be possible, 'as we think it is', to carry out a Penny Post scheme upon it.[23] On 19 December Gladstone wrote to Palmerston that he was 'endeavouring to obtain materials which will enable you and the Cabinet to judge whether we ought to institute any inquiry with a view to clearing the ground for this question'.[24] Palmerston, who was perhaps beginning to become alarmed lest the Chancellor of the Exchequer, whose notorious pronouncement in favour of a gigantic extension of the suffrage had been made on 11 May 1864, was proposing to put himself at the head of numbers in their long-awaited assault upon property, began to raise objections.

The Act of 1844 had provided for the companies to be bought out at twenty-five years' purchase of the average of the previous three years' divisible profits. Further, when a company thought this formula undervalued its worth, the Act provided for arbitration. The cost of buying out the railways, as Palmerston reminded Gladstone, could not possibly be less than £200,000,000 or £300,000,000, and might easily, if the arbitration clause was invoked, prove to be much higher.[25] Gladstone agreed that the question of purchasing the mass of railway property was a 'vast and staggering' one, and then revealed that the mode in which he was himself disposed to contemplate it 'was one which would have created no debt in lieu of stock', and looked to a distant period.[26] This was to take the Railway Passenger Tax, introduced in 1832, and use it as a bargaining counter in negotiating with the companies. If the state gave up the tax, which was 'a permanent public property carved out of the great railway estate', Gladstone thought that the railway companies could be persuaded to surrender the fee simple of their properties in return for leases of fifty, sixty or even eighty years' duration. The state would then be able to look forward, ultimately, to taking possession of 'a great reversionary estate', and the supreme attraction of this scheme to the Chancellor of the Exchequer was that it would provide a means by which 'to act effectively upon the hitherto intractable capital of the National Debt'. Instead of the state's being always in the red from borrowing, debit and credit accounts in the state's ledger could be made to balance.[27]

It is clear from this proposal, which Gladstone had already sketched out in some detail in August 1864, that there were really two quite different ways of approaching the purchase passing through Gladstone's mind. The first, as everyone would have expected, involved invoking the Act of 1844, and embarking upon a large expansion of the National Debt, in order to acquire the property, reorganise it, secure the benefit of cheap fares and remedy the complaints against the system. The second looked to a distant purchase, and to a transaction which would eventually turn the state into a great land and property owner, adding nothing to and ultimately balancing the national debt. The first formed the starting point for the proposals made by Galt and Chadwick, and appealed to the Gladstone who sympathised with the desire of all classes for cheap transport;[28] the second possessed the obvious advantage of not upsetting the money market. Gladstone's belief that the Railway Passenger Tax, which yielded the comparatively small sum of £400,000 a year,[29] could be used as a bargaining counter to persuade the companies to surrender their property may, in any case, have been hopelessly optimistic. But even if it was not, he had only the one ace. If he did not wish to add to the National Debt, he could play his ace in two ways: either to extract a reduction of charges and a rationalisation of rates now, which was what the public really wanted, or to secure the reversion of the fee simple in two or three generations time. But the one card could not have taken both tricks, and if Gladstone himself preferred the long-term reversion, then it is difficult to see how he could have secured the good behaviour of the companies in the meantime. Gladstone's memoranda, therefore, reveal a conflict of objectives. Maybe he thought that his own scheme of painless purchase could be combined with other measures calculated to secure immediate reorganisation and an experiment with cheap fares, and in his correspondence with Palmerston he hinted that 'the present system and scale of railway charges' might possibly 'admit of great reductions' even without state purchase, but there is no indication of how this was to be achieved.[30]

State purchase itself was not an easy concept to define, and Palmerston was probably happy enough to refer the whole question to a Commission of Inquiry. Gladstone himself, so he said in 1873, nominated the members,[31] and on 11 March 1865 the Royal Commission on Railways was established, with fourteen members under the chairmanship of the Duke of Devonshire charged with the responsibility of finding out whether 'it would be practicable, by means of any changes in the laws relating to Railways or otherwise' to effect economies in the system and provide more effectually for 'the safe, expeditious, punctual, and cheap transit of passengers and merchandise'.[32] Gladstone had secured the great debate which destiny required upon the option kept open by the Act of 1844, and there seems little reason to doubt that he himself was now in favour of the state's becoming the proprietor of the railways, though he consistently distinguished this from state management of which he disapproved.

From the moment the appointment of the Royal Commission was announced, the railway question assumed an Irish dimension. It was no wonder, for the Irish railways epitomised the defects of the British system. In 1865 there were approximately 1800 miles of railway in Ireland. To operate this network there were fifty-six lines of railway, supporting 430 railway directors, fifty-six solicitors, fifty-six company secretaries and over seventy managing engineers.[33] In a country with a declining population and an economy with a negligible commercial and manufacturing superstructure, an eighteenth-century system of patronage had been grafted on to what should have been a nineteenth-century method of travel. Only sixty-two miles of railway had been built in Ireland before the Act of 1844 came into effect, and if ever there was a case for state intervention to end the chaos of conflicting interests and fares, and bring the cost-cutting benefits of rationalisation, it was here. Furthermore, both sides to the great debate about state purchase had reason, while it was still uncertain what the outcome would be, to encourage the deliberations of the Royal Commission to take an Irish direction. Supporters of state purchase readily agreed to start with Ireland as an experiment. Opponents were by no means unwilling to see a distinction drawn between British and Irish railways, in order, if need be, to concede the case for nationalisation in Ireland, the better to preserve the much larger field of railway business in Britain for private enterprise.

When the names of the members of the Royal Commission were announced, the Irish MPs claimed that, with only one Irish representative, Lord Donoughmore, on the commission, 'the Irish element appeared to have been lost sight of'.[34] Gladstone did not accept the criticism, and pointed out that, in addition to Lord Donoughmore, both the chairman, the Duke of Devonshire, and Lord Stanley were 'directly and largely interested in Ireland'.[35] Monsell then gave the Irish complaints a more positive flavour by proposing that 'the Irish railway system should be considered by itself and without delay', adding that 'the definite object of his proposition was to bring into play the provisions of the Act of 1844'. Turning to face Gladstone, Monsell allowed that the Chancellor of the Exchequer was 'not one to "rest and be thankful"'. 'But even he', Monsell continued, 'might feel appalled at the idea of undertaking to touch the English and Scotch railways', with their hundreds of millions of pounds capital, whereas the capital value of the railways in Ireland was no more than £20,000,000.[36] Or, as Gregory, the Member for Galway, put it a year later, 'the difficulty of dealing with Ireland is but as the levelling of a molehill'.[37]

Gladstone met these pleas with sympathy. The members of the Royal Commission had already started work, and he did not think they could be asked to alter their agenda. But he accepted that 'the difficult and serious problem relating to the intervention of Government in the concerns of railways – is to a certain extent limited and simplified in Ireland', and he agreed with Monsell that there was no greater improvement that could be conferred upon Ireland than 'some measure taken with the view to secure to her the benefits of cheap railway transit'.[38] He asked Monsell to withdraw his motion, and promised that, in return, 'I, on the part of the government, undertake to use such measures as may be in our power to attain the object he has in view – namely, the examination of all the facts of the Irish railway system'.[39] The promise was kept. Monsell himself was added to the commission in December 1865. The examination of Irish witnesses was brought forward. Thirty-eight out of the ninety-six witnesses appearing before the commission came from Ireland, and their evidence was collected, and published separately, in 1866, a whole year ahead of the publication of the full report.[40] In 1866 the Irish Members seized upon the Irish evidence, which was almost unanimously in favour of state purchase, to press the issue upon the new Derby-Disraeli government. Speaking in the debate which followed, Gladstone, from the Opposition benches, said that he knew

> of no boon that could be conferred upon Ireland so comprehensive in its application, so impartial, so free from the taint or suspicion of ministering to any particular interest or to the views or convenience of any particular class, so far-reaching in its effect upon all classes and conditions of persons without distinction . . . so universal in its effect as a better development of the railway system of Ireland.[41]

As Sir J.C. Conroy, the historian of Irish railways said, 'These words were taken as a promise of railway legislation in the direction desired by Irish opinion, if he came into power'.[42] They were to embarrass Gladstone for many years to come.

Before Gladstone did come to power, however, a good many things happened. In the course of the evidence, taken on sixty-one days between 23 March 1865 and 31 May 1866, a great deal was said by both advocates and opponents of state purchase about the 1844 Act. Proponents admitted its deficiencies. First, it made no provision for the railways constructed before 1844. Secondly, it provided for railways constructed after 1844 to be taken over bit by bit, year by year, as they reached the age of twenty-one. Acquisition, therefore, would be as piecemeal a process as construction had been, and many years would pass before the state would find itself in a position to impose the economies which were desired. Thirdly, the term 'divisible profits', which was to be used to fix the level of compensation, did not mean 'dividends', as the framers of the Act had apparently supposed, but something much wider, and therefore more expensive. Fourthly, the companies would exploit the arbitration clauses and secure additional compensation for 'consequential profits', or the expected increase of profits in the future, thereby increasing the cost of purchase still further.[43] Not surprisingly, therefore, opponents of nationalisation preferred to treat the clauses of the Act as sacred, insisting that, if the state did decide to purchase, the Act, with its excessively generous compensation clauses, *must* be made to work. Members of the Royal Commission were brought to believe that purchase could not be effected for anything much under £1,000,000,000.

It was scarcely surprising, then, that the majority report, which was published in May 1867, came out decisively against state purchase, and concluded that it was inexpedient to change 'the policy which has hitherto been adopted of leaving the construction and management of railways to the free enterprise of the people, under such conditions as Parliament may think fit to impose for the general welfare of the public'.[44] Commenting on the Act of 1844, the majority reported that the evidence which they had heard

> warns us of the extreme difficulty of making prospective arrangements to take effect after many years. Instead of facilitating the acquisition of the railways by the State, it has rendered the operation more difficult, and indeed almost impracticable with a due regard to the guarantees it has accorded to the railway companies. It would no doubt have been easier to treat with the companies without any special law than with the conditions which the Act imposes.[45]

It was, then, the defects in Gladstone's own Act which led the members of Gladstone's own commission to determine against state purchase. The Peelites had been convicted of being bad workmen, and the commissioners' condemnation of the 1844 Act was sweeping, conclusive and, in relation to Gladstone himself, almost cruel. There was no way in which a person of Gladstone's sensibility, conditioned to taking decisions deliberately, and to accepting the consequences of his own actions, could reopen the issue.

That did not, however, mean that he had heard the end of it. The majority report drew no distinction between Britain and Ireland.[46] But Sir Rowland Hill published one dissenting report and Monsell another.[47] The Irish Members in both Houses met to give vent to their disappointment, and they were able to persuade the Derby-Disraeli government to put the views of the Royal Commission to one side, and to carry out a new and much more systematic and thorough investigation into the railways of Ireland. On 15 October 1867 five Treasury Commissioners were appointed to ascertain the financial condition of each company, and the condition of the permanent way and the rolling stock, so that, by the beginning of the new session, Parliament, should it wish 'to take up the question either of purchasing or leasing' the Irish railways, would know 'the precise sum of money which would be required to carry out that object'.[48] The Treasury Commissioners conducted their inquiries within the framework of the terms set by the 1844 Act, but, when they published their report in April 1868,[49] they received a new brief to estimate both the immediate loss that would follow upon a reduction of fares to Belgian levels and the period that would elapse before the increase of traffic would overtake the loss. It really did begin to look as though Gladstone's Act might, after all, lead to the purchase of the Irish railways.

The Treasury Commissioners' second report,[50] concluding that the relatively short space of eleven years would elapse before the increased traffic generated by a reduction in fares would overtake the loss, was presented on 7 December 1868, six days after the Queen had invited Gladstone to form an administration. Gladstone now had the opportunity to escape from the conclusions of the Royal Commission and proceed with the purchase of the Irish railways if he wished to. But it appeared that he did not. While Derby and Disraeli had been busy keeping open the possibility of state purchase, Gladstone had taken up the case of the Irish Church. The church occupied the whole of the 1869 session, and the first Irish Land Act much of that of 1870. With these two measures Gladstone became the acknowledged champion of Ireland. But the Irish Members still looked to him as being committed to meeting their wishes in the matter of state purchase. Since this was the one thing, as they continually pointed out, upon which they were unanimous, Gladstone's disinclination to take up the issue became increasingly difficult to understand. Monsell himself could no longer raise the question from the floor of the House, because Gladstone had made him Postmaster General, and appears not to have brought it up in Cabinet, and for two years the Irish Members held their peace. But in 1871 their frustration boiled over, and they raised a debate. If the Prime Minister had not changed his opinions, Mr Ormsby Gore demanded to know, why had he not 'introduced a measure dealing with the railways instead of the Irish Church Act, which injured a large portion of the community [Mr Ormsby Gore was a Conservative] and did no good to the rest'.[51] He was supported by Mr Gregory, who added that 'on that subject of railways lions and lambs had laid themselves down together and with one consenting voice landlord and tenant, farmer and shopkeeper, Whig and Tory, had expressed the most anxious desire for a reform of the railway system in Ireland'.[52] In his reply Gladstone said that he thought 'Ireland had no reason to complain of her share in the legislation of the last three years', and denied that he or his government had done anything to keep the Irish railway issue open.[53]

Before the next session began in 1872, Gregory had become the Governor of Ceylon. A new champion, Sir Rowland Blennerhassett, took up the cause and brought in a Bill for the purchase of Irish railways. Forgivingly, he did not refer to the sins of the government, or twit Gladstone with what he had said in 1866.[54] He was opposed by the Chief Secretary for Ireland, the Marquis of Hartington, who announced that he had been working for some time upon a plan to enable districts in Ireland 'to purchase . . . the Railways' for the public. Hartington added that he hoped the government would be in a position to enable the house to come to a practical issue on the question in the course of the next session,[55] and everything then appeared to fall into place for a decisive result in 1873. Hartington himself was convinced that 'the purchase . . . would be the best thing that could be done for Ireland',[56] and the Lord Lieutenant, Earl Spencer, shared this opinion.[57] Both were shaken when, on 8 February 1873, the Cabinet came to a formal decision to oppose any proposal for state purchase.[58] When Hartington remonstrated that this placed him in great difficulty,[59] and Spencer warned that 'the most profound disappointment' would be felt in Ireland when the decision became known,[60] Gladstone dealt kindly with Hartington, saying that he thought 'you and I were both implicated to about the same extent by favourable expressions not fairly yet plausibly to be construed as pledges, tho' mine happened to be of the older date and therefore less in view'.[61]

When the Irish Members brought the issue up again, as they must, Gladstone undertook to answer them himself. Led by Lord Claud Hamilton, the Irish repeated that this was a question upon which opinion in Ireland was unanimous, and reminded Gladstone that 'at one period he had upheld the doctrine that Irish affairs should be regulated in accordance with Irish ideas'.[62] Gladstone acknowledged the strength of feeling in Ireland, admitted that state purchase in Ireland need not embarrass the government in its determination to resist any such proposal for Britain, insisted that state management was out of the question, and concluded that state purchase and leasing was no longer practicable, because all the experiments that had been made with leasing had failed.[63]

This sport of trying to pin Gladstone down, and make him honour what the Irish Members professed to believe was a commitment, was repeated in 1882. Once again the Irish asked for state purchase. Once again Gladstone replied that this was a question 'about which, nearly twenty years ago, when he was Chancellor of the Exchequer ... he felt a very lively interest, and an extreme desire that some mode could be found to acquire Irish railways for the purposes of the State'.

Once again, he professed his belief that 'in the abstract, it would be a very good ideal system if it were possible for the State to be the proprietor of the permanent and fixed works of the Railways'. Once again he reasserted that state management was out of the question, and that 'all experience in this country went against the practicability of the leasing of railways'.[64]

It is not easy to make out what Gladstone's real thoughts were. From start to finish the Irish Members accepted that the costs of the operation were to fall upon the Irish themselves.[65] On the face of it, Gladstone had everything to gain from acceding to their wishes. Gladstone had made Ireland the main concern of his administration. Disestablishment removed an abuse, yes. But the Land Act did little to stimulate the economy, and state purchase of the railways was much the most constructive measure he could have taken for Ireland. Nor would the positive advantages have been limited to an expansion of commerce, for, as Lord Spencer pointed out, 'the influence of Government management would be very beneficial on all those employed on the lines. By good Selection of servants ... something of the good effect which discipline in the Constabulary has upon the Irish peasantry would be exerted all over the country.'[66] The penalties for refusal were, too, potentially enormous. In 1871 Ormsby Gore warned Gladstone that a negative would encourage 'the agitators for home rule and their dupes'.[67] In 1872 Isaac Butt, 'who was thoroughly up in the Railway question', was in communication with Galt,[68] and Hartington admitted that the long delay of seven years which had taken place in dealing with this question furnished some ground of complaint to the Home Rulers.[69] In 1873 Spencer himself said that the Cabinet decision not to purchase would be 'a welcome argument to Home Rulers'.[70]

Gladstone's behaviour was alienating many of those who were still, potentially, supporters of the Union. It was one thing for the Parliament of the United Kingdom to take decisions in matters upon which Irishmen were divided. It was quite another for the United Kingdom government to refuse to meet the wishes of the Irish Members over a matter upon which they were unanimous. Gladstone's refusal, and the refusal of the Disraeli ministry, to entertain the question in 1874, despite their obvious interest in 1867–68 (which also needs to be explained), were among the factors leading to Butt's demand for the House of Commons to begin to consider 'the present Parliamentary relations between Great Britain and Ireland',[71] and to Parnell's conclusion that 'the House of Commons could never effectually legislate for Ireland'.[72]

The option of state purchase was one which Gladstone himself had created and kept open. When the time came for the nation to debate the issue, Gladstone seized the opportunity, and looked forward to the passage of a great measure. In the course of a few months, the question of state purchase became the question of state purchase in Ireland. The Tories appeared favourable. Gladstone began to make justice to Ireland the main plank of Liberal Party policy. But at no point between 1868 and 1874, or again between 1880 and 1885, did he return to the subject himself. When compelled to do so by others, he professed himself, ideally, in favour, if only certain practical objections could be removed. Instead he took up the Irish University question, and ultimately, of course, Home Rule, and was unable to carry these either.

So what were the objections which made Gladstone set his face against the purchase of Irish railways? Although he did once say that the result arrived at by the Royal Commission ought not necessarily 'to govern the opinion of Parliament',[73] he seems to have continued to regard it as conclusive. In 1871 he referred to the disappointment which the report had brought to all his hopes.[74] In 1873 he reminded the House that the Royal Commission had come to an adverse conclusion.[75] In 1882 he said that 'it was a very laborious Commission, comprised of very able men; and they came, advisedly and deliberately, to an adverse Report'.[76] But he brushed aside the work of the Treasury Commissioners appointed by his opponents, and it seems as though there must have been some further factor working upon his mind. He did drop hints as to what it was. At various times he criticised the railway companies in Ireland for just 'waiting to be bought out', and for 'making no serious rational endeavour to realize some of those economies which were within their power',[77] for having shown not 'the slightest sign of life', and for behaving as though they thought Parliament must play the suitor.[78] To all this we may, I think, safely add Hartington's saying that he feared 'the directors and shareholders of Irish railways were looking to this operation as a means of giving them a very large bonus on their property'.[79]

The event which had queered the pitch was the Conservatives' purchase of the Electric Telegraph Companies in 1868. Upon that occasion Gladstone had agreed that 'the business now carried on by a multitude of establishments . . . might be carried on by a single establishment more efficiently and at less cost',[80] and he approved of the Electric Telegraphs being placed in the hands of the Post Office. The problem was that the moment it became known that the government intended to purchase the Telegraph Companies, the price went up, from £4,000,000, when the project was first mooted by the Chancellor of the Exchequer, to nearly £7,000,000.[81] In 1869, when the transfer actually took place, it fell to Gladstone's administration to foot the bill. The purchase turned out well, but it was not a bargain, and the general view was that the government had been obliged to buy the companies at anything up to 50 per cent above their real worth. To Gladstone this example stood as a warning against further experiments with state purchase – all the sterner, perhaps, for its having been the work of opponents. This, I think, lay at the root of his attitude towards the state purchase of Irish railways when he was Prime Minister. Some other way of effecting improvements in the railway system must be found. To that end, in 1873, he instituted the Railway and Canal Commission, whose responsibilities extended to the whole of the United Kingdom.[82] To that end he did also indicate that he would be willing to consider offering state loans to Irish railway companies which came forward with plans for amalgamation.[83] But the one thing the Irish really wanted, the great reform which had been associated ever since the Act of 1844 with his name, he was no longer in a position to entertain. Nor, perhaps, in the 1880s, as he watched the German state taking over the German railways, managing them for profit, and using the proceeds to by-pass 'Parliament' and equip an 'unconstitutional' army, was he altogether sorry.

12

Gladstone, Rhetoric and Politics

H.C.G. Matthew

Here are four quotations about rhetoric:

Rhetoric is the counterpart of logic . . . a kind of off-shoot of logic, and of that department of moral philosophy which it is fair to call the science of social life . . . Rhetoric is useful, because truth and justice are in their nature stronger than their opposites. Aristotle, *Rhetoric*

Rhetoric is that Faculty, by which we understand what will serve our turn, concerning any Subject to win belief in the hearer . . . The end of Rhetoric is Victory, which consists in having gotten belief.
Hobbes', *Digest of Aristotle's Rhetoric*

The Journalists are now the true Kings and Clergy: henceforth Historians, unless they are fools, must write not of Bourbon Dynasties, and Tudors and Hapsburgs; but of stamped Broad-Sheet Dynasties . . . according as this or the other Able Editor . . . gains the world's Ear.
Carlyle, *Sartor Resartus*

It was pouring with rain, the wind was howling through the most ghastly hall and everyone knew that the Welsh vote had already been lost. Mr Foot sat huddled in his overcoat until it was his turn to speak. He then delivered the most sparkling piece of rhetoric I have ever heard, though the content was negligible and he had never probably believed in devolution in the first place. The party loved him for it.
M. Rutherford, 'Man of the Week', *Financial Times*, 15 November 1980

Rhetoric – the presentation of argument – is an essential concomitant of representative politics, and its free exercise is the distinguishing feature of a liberal political community. The first of these epigraphs illustrates the liberal objective in argument, the second the conservative, 'realist' view of what that liberal objective actually amounts to, the third the factor in nineteenth-century rhetoric which distinguishes it from earlier eras and which made possible its general dissemination in a large and complex industrial society, the fourth its twentieth-century decline. The use of the word 'rhetoric' in the *Financial Times* well illustrates its common British twentieth-century use – contentless, windy, overblown, insincere and ineffective – a usage also commonly employed by historians. But this definition is misleading as to the historical meaning of the word, the means by which argument was publicly presented, summed up by Richard Whately, as 'Persuasions . . . Style, Arrangement, and Delivery'.[1] Until the mid nineteenth century, the study of Aristotle's *Rhetoric* was a necessary and central part of a liberal education; Chairs of Rhetoric were common, and, as Sir Robert Peel observed when discussing Cicero in 1837, classical rhetoric was of 'immense importance to all who aspire to conspicuous stations in any department of public or learned professional life'. Peel added perspicaciously that steam was fertilising the intellectual as well as the material waste [and] supplying you, in the mere faculty of locomotion, with a new motive for classical study'.[2]

The subject of rhetoric has been little studied by historians. A few bearings can be taken from English Literature scholars, who tend to use 'rhetoric' very generally to mean any form of communication, from studies of Nazi rhetoric; and from American works, largely on Burke and the eighteenth century and largely non-historical.[3] The aim of this essay is first to describe the phenomenon of late Victorian extra-parliamentary rhetoric; secondly to argue that its existence depended on a set of technical developments in the media; thirdly to argue that the liberal political culture within which this phenomenon flourished was closely related to and largely conditioned by those developments; fourthly, I shall argue that when further developments occurred in the franchise and in the media, both the rhetorical phenomenon and the political culture to which it was related declined together.

Some discussion of the nature and extent of the electorate – the politician's raw material – is a necessary preliminary. The political community as it existed between 1867 and 1918 differed markedly in scale and tone both from its predecessor and its successor. The 1867 and 1884 Reform Acts, enfranchising about 55 per cent of adult males in the boroughs and rather more in the counties, had as their aims the enfranchisement of what Gladstone called the 'capable citizen', that is, an employed adult male, with a regular domicile, of some substance, the head of a household with the initiative to get himself registered.[4] Those who applied for public assistance (though not, after

1885, mere medical relief) under the Poor Law were automatically disfranchised: there was, therefore, a deliberate, explicit relationship between economic and civic competence, reinforced by the excluding power of the astonishing complexities of the registration system.

This electorate was a halfway house between the very limited electorate of the 1832 Reform Act and the achievement of what was effectively (though not completely) universal suffrage for men in 1918. The changes of 1867 introduced new problems for politicians: a change in numbers, and a change in system in the form of the accompanying secret ballot of 1872. Taken together, these changes posed problems of party organisation in the constituencies: there were more electors to manage and to bribe, and less was known about them. The ending of poll-books disadvantaged election agents and historians alike. The larger electorate was much less easy to know as individual electors, and thus not only more expensive but more difficult to bribe. The 1883 Corrupt Practices Act offered a way out acceptable to both parties.

How did politicians cope with the post-1867 electorate? One solution was a more complex party organisation (already developing in some constituencies before 1867) to replace the solicitor with his 'face-to-face' knowledge of the propertied electorate, many of whom were his clients. Both Liberals and Tories developed their national and local organisations in the 1870s. At a local level, there was a marked development of political clubs, small versions of the House of Commons, flourishing in many towns and villages. Whereas before 1867 their function had been to demand entry into Parliament, now they imitated it, thus representing the successful incorporation into political life (defined in Westminster terms) of elements of the population which during the early part of the century had seemed in danger of being alienated. In these local parliaments, a high level of organisation and effort was involved. Members were allocated a parliamentary constituency, and some formed the government, issuing printed Queen's speeches, moving motions and answering opposition criticisms. The movement was considerable and widespread. Blanchard Jerrold estimated in 1883 that there were over a hundred Houses of Commons (including four each in Glasgow and Manchester) with about 35,000 members overall; they constituted, he thought, 'an educational machine of national proportions, for constructing politically thoughtful members of the community'. Jerrold found a fairly even political balance: of fifty-nine Houses in 1882, twenty-six (with 11,051 members) were Conservative and thirty-three (with 10,854 members) Liberal. Some of the parliaments were large – Glasgow, Lambeth and

Hackney each having 1000 members.[5] The National Association of Local Parliaments, with offices at 14 Langham Place, London, coordinated from 1892 this remarkable experiment, which seems to have lasted from the 1860s (the first known local parliament was in Liverpool from 1860) until the First World War. A feature of these local parliaments was that men (those so far discovered had an entirely male membership) of both parties took part, suggesting a considerable homogeneity of the political community.[6] As the printed rules for the Croydon House of Commons said: 'It is earnestly hoped that members will bear in mind that the Croydon House of Commons is in the first place a debating society; and will assist the Council in every way in making it a success as such, and not endeavour to secure triumphs for their party at the expense of the Society'.[7]

The local parliaments show that the drive towards oratory was self-generated, and not merely an imposition from above. They were an important training ground and means of political and oratorical upward mobility, their most successful *alumnus* being Bonar Law (Member for North Staffordshire for a decade in one of the Glasgow parliaments). Their success partly depended on the expanding provincial press which reported their proceedings – for example, in 1867 in Yorkshire sixty-six out of eighty local papers (77 per cent) had been founded since 1853, and in Lancashire forty-six out of seventy-four (62 per cent).[8] The form these local parliaments took was a product of a mixture of the rules and conventions of the Oxford University Union and of the House of Commons, whose debates were widely reported. Guides to public speaking, such as the many editions of G.J. Holyoake's *Public Speaking and Debate*, directed the electorate into appropriate canons of behaviour. *The Times* observed on the jubilee of the Oxford Union (23 October 1873):

> In the course of these fifty years we have become a nation of public speakers. Everyone speaks now, and tolerably well too. Any country gentleman, or respectable tradesman taking a part in local affairs, might well compound for a speech a day, and be glad of that relief for the speeches of his neighbours. Even the clergy are throwing away their cork jackets, and interpolating with free speech, even if they must still ride at anchor ... Eloquence is but a facility, or instrument, or weapon, or accomplishment, or, in academic terms, an art ... We are now more than ever a debating, that is, a Parliamentary people.

But from the viewpoint of national political leaders, these societies, and the general enthusiasm for political action in the localities, had their difficulties: they had to be given a lead. Moreover, the enthusiasm for the newspaper reporting of Parliament was wearing off: the clogged timetable of the Commons was becoming more and more specialised – the old days of the 1840s and 1850s, when leisured debates on the 'condition of the people' took up to ten days, gave way to Parliaments dominated by the details of committee work. Government majorities, except at certain times such as 1885–86, became after 1867 more predictable: the role of rhetoric in the Commons in immediately influencing the survival of the ministry as in the 1850s and 1860s became less important, and consequently less exciting for newspaper readers. The press developed a resistance to anticipating *Hansard* (in turn diminishing the extent and accuracy of the latter, which was partly compiled from press reports). Alex Ritchie of the *Leeds Mercury* told the Press Association in 1870: 'It would, as a rule, be a great inconvenience to me to give more than two columns of a [parliamentary] debate. Gentlemen like to peruse their newspaper at breakfast time, and they will not always care to wade through four or five columns of parliamentary matter'.[9]

Summing up a debate on 20 April 1877 on the appointment of a committee on making *Hansard* official and verbatim, Hartington remarked, 'it is universally admitted that the reports in the newspapers ... are not as full and as correct as they were a few years ago, and that what passes in Parliament is not known as fully by the public as it was formerly considered desirable it should be known'. When Lady Monkswell noted in her diary in January 1878 that 'The great men's speeches in this exciting time are the most interesting reading in the world', she referred not to parliamentary speeches, but to the torrent of public speaking generated by the Eastern Question.[10]

What is sometimes regarded as a golden age of parliamentary oratory – the gladiatorial clash of Gladstone and Disraeli, Randolph Churchill and Parnell, Chamberlain, Asquith, Balfour and Lloyd George – was in fact the era which saw the ascendancy of a new medium of communication long in genesis: this was the growth of regular extra-parliamentary speechmaking by leading politicians and by ordinary MPs. From 1872, the famous speeches – famous in their day and in the history books – are, on balance, extra-parliamentary speeches. Parliamentary speeches of general political significance are few compared with those of the Manchester Free Trade Hall, the Crystal Palace, 'Peace with Honour', the Midlothian campaigns, the tariff reform campaign.

Fundamental to the successful use of political oratory of the type practised by the late Victorians – long, serious, detailed, well-informed; rarely demagogic, with few concessions to the audience in simplification of matter, style or language – was the notion of an integrated political community, using roughly the same vocabulary, interested in similar issues, willing to sustain a press which exploited the newly available telegraph to bring the words of the politicians to every educated household the morning after they were spoken. This integrated electorate the extended but still limited franchise supplied. The extension of the franchise made extra-parliamentary speechmaking necessary; the continuing limits on the electorate made it effective.

In 1863, when the platform system was in early development, Salisbury (then Cecil) presciently identified both the phenomenon of the two audiences and the difficulty it posed:

> The speechmaking usually takes place after dinner. The farmers or townspeople to whom the speeches are addressed are mainly drunk; and the speakers themselves are not wholly exempt, perhaps, from the moment's genial influence. The public . . . who read these speeches in the *Times* two or three days afterwards, usually get through their newspapers in the morning, when they are not only sober, but cross and critical. Is it possible for human ingenuity to construct a speech that shall suit both audiences – that shall be warm and slipshod enough to elicit the cheers of farmers who have dined, and yet calm and polished enough to extort the admiration of readers who have not breakfasted?

Later, the difficulty was equally often the other way round: could a complex speech given to an earnest meeting be understood by the electors reading the more popular newspapers? But the extent of extra-parliamentary speechmaking in the second half of the century, and the thoroughness of its reporting, suggests that 'human ingenuity' did indeed succeed in suiting 'both audiences', aided perhaps by a swing in the balance of the audience from drunk farmers to earnest Nonconformists.[11]

Only two media were open to the Victorian politician: speech and the printed word (or cartoon). Regular speechmaking by all politicians in their constituencies each autumn came to reach a high proportion of the electorate. The thoroughness and regularity of the stump 'season' was new. In the mid century, politicians as a rule visited their constituencies, and rarely any other than their own constituencies, at election times or for some special occasion. Thus Cobden found it necessary in 1849 to excuse his presence in his constituency, telling his constituents: 'There is peculiar advantage in Members of the House of Commons coming, from time to time, in contact with the people, and especially with their own constituencies'.[12] As in many aspects of Victorian politics,

Palmerston, following his mentor Canning, was an unsung pioneer, with a series of public speeches in the 1850s, but he was not at first followed up. Gladstone's speeches between 1864 and 1868 in Lancashire were the most prominent examples of a growing tendency of Cabinet Ministers to talk on a wide range of political subjects directly to the people. Salisbury indicated in 1864 the extent to which the process had developed; his metaphor, though used with characteristic distaste, caught the theatrical spectacular quality of the speechmaking season; 'the stage manager ... who arranges the appearance of Ministerial actors in the autumn performances evidently goes upon the principle of putting his best leg foremost. He begins the season with the stars, and leaves the sticks to the fag end'.[13] Care must be taken not to give Gladstone too prominent or original a role in the development of this process. The *Biograph's* comment of 1879 gives a fair assessment:

> Provincial journalism entered upon a new phase with the repeal of the paper duties and the extension of the telegraph system. Daily newspapers soon became a necessity for all large centres ... and with their establishment a change has followed, which Mr Gladstone was, perhaps, the first public man to recognise, if by no means to first to discern.[14]

Disraeli made the first extra-parliamentary speeches by a former Prime Minister which had a really major impact – his speech in Manchester in 1872, which lasted three and a half hours (during which he drank two bottles of white brandy, believed by the audience to be water) and at the Crystal Palace in London, also in 1872: both of these speeches, were, significantly to assemblies of Tory Party workers rather than to open audiences. Speech series directly to the electors on a big scale began with Gladstone's orations on Bulgaria in 1876–77, and his Midlothian campaigns of 1879–80. By the 1890s regular tours of autumn speeches – mini Midlothians – had become the rule for most MPs, and for any MP who expected any sort of national prominence; a requirement which dismayed politicians who did not take naturally to the activity. There was, then, a codification and regularising of the stump oratory which had been developing haphazardly through the century.

At some of these meetings, politicians addressed vast audiences without any form of mechanical aid. These great occasions – for example, Gladstone's address to his constituents at Blackheath in September 1876 on Bulgaria – had in fact two audiences: first the audience actually present; and secondly, the audience to be reached through the press. The latter was clearly the more important.

For the audience present, a speech by a party leader was often

Fig. 23. Gladstone addressing the electors of Greenwich at Blackheath (1871). His speech is being taken down by representatives of the press.

Fig. 24. The rear of the hustings at Blackheath.

Fig. 25. Incident during Gladstone's speech at Blackheath: a dispute amongst the sandwich-men.

as much an occasion – 'a happening' – as a detailed examination
of the issues. At the Blackheath open-air meeting, between ten and
fifteen thousand people were present, but little could be heard of
the speech for the rain on the umbrellas. At the Bingley Hall
meeting in May 1877, when Gladstone spoke to the National Liberal
Federation, he noted in his diary: 'A most intelligent and duly
appreciative audience – but they were 25,000 and the building I
think of no acoustic merit'; in fact the speech was inaudible to
about half of the audience. When Rosebery made a famous speech
at Chesterfield in 1901, a special train brought MPs and the press
from London, and miners and railway workers assembled from all
over Derbyshire to see his lordship. The fact that the speech, given
in a vast, echoing railway repair shed, was completely inaudible to
all but the big-wigs sitting on the platform (it was even inaudible to
the stenographer) in no way diminished the success of the occasion.
although the speech lasted nearly two hours. *The Daily Telegraph* (8
September 1876) commented generally about the phenomenon:

> In the open air, it is questionable whether more than 1000 to 1500 persons,
> in a gathering which may possibly exceed 30,000, will catch all that is said;
> but the mere assemblage is in itself an eloquent utterance of popular fee-
> ling; and, as all present will be assured, the next morning's papers are
> certain to contain full reports.

It would be misleading to suggest that huge meetings were characteristic of late-Victorian speechmaking. The routine speeches were
given to rather specifically controlled audiences with three areas.
First, tickets for the male party faithful were distributed and sometimes sold. Secondly, there was a women's enclosure, usually in the
gallery, following what was still quite a common division in churches;
the presence of politicians' wives on the platform, a custom made
prominent by Catherine Gladstone in 1879, reflected the growing
importance of women in politics as public encouragers and organisers
and even, on the rare occasion, speakers; as well as reflecting, not
always justifiably, the assumed orderliness of such meetings. Thirdly,
there was usually an open area at the back of the hall for all-comers;
it was from this area that the 'heckling', a venerated and sometimes
rather formalised part of the proceedings much welcomed by adroit
speakers such as Gladstone and Lloyd George, was directed. Not surprisingly, electors had first call on the accommodation. When Gladstone spoke in 1880 in a church near Edinburgh, the *Scotsman* (20
March 1880) reported that 'admission was, in the first instance, lim-

ited to electors . . . of Cramond, of whom there are about 120, and to each of them was allowed the privilege of bringing a lady to the meeting', the doors being opened to non-electors half an hour before the meeting. A big speech was sometimes a two-tier affair: a solemn full-scale address to a restricted audience, followed by a short homily to a general audience (often predominantly working-class) afterwards in a separate hall or in the open air.

These political occasions, and especially the opportunity to see a national figure in the flesh, often generated considerable local excitement; they can be related to the general growth of organised team spectator sports characteristic of the period. The association of Cabinet Ministers with this sort of occasion caused alarm in high circles: what was in fact a remarkable exercise in political integration was seen as vulgarising politics and politicians, as in the Queen's objection to the Midlothian Campaign as 'democratic'.

But important though the occasion was in generating local interest and encouraging the party activists, the speech was not simply or even mainly declaimed to those present. Politicians' early appreciation of the nature of the vital audience is seen in this account by James Picton of a meeting in St George's Hall, Liverpool, in 1868: Gladstone was shouted down by the Tories in the hall: 'He proceeded, however, speaking to the reporters who were just below him.'[15]

Systematic extra-parliamentary oratory on the scale of late Victorian Britain, in which a great national debate was carried on over periods of weeks, was made possible by, indeed was the consequence of, technical developments in the press. The reporting of the speeches was largely done by the Press Association, the Central News Agency and the Exchange Telegraph. The Press Association was set up in London in 1868 to act as a central news agency for the expanding, largely Liberal, provincial press.[16] Under the Telegraph Act of 1868 agencies such as the Press Association and Exchange Telegraph, which mainly acted for the London papers from its establishment in 1872, received very favourable rates of transmission, the Tories thereby making amends for their bitter opposition to the repeal of the duty on paper, which the Lords delayed in 1860. These agencies reduced the reporting to a fine art: in the 1860s over seventy reporters had been needed for Bright's reform speeches, now only a few teams were needed, one team for each agency. These teams were highly skilled – by Lloyd George's time a speech begun at 2.45 p.m. was included in four and a half columns in the *Daily Leader* on the streets by 4.30, just after he had finished delivering it. The Press Association had a special team for covering Gladstone's speeches headed by the twenty-stone Walter Hepburn – it was through Hepburn that Gladstone in 1880 started a custom, new to Britain, though already common in the USA, of dictating a speech *after* the train had left the station – there having been no time to address it to the assembled crowds: the immediate audience could become superfluous.

Hepburn could not, in the manner of today, simply have been given the 'hand-out', for speeches usually followed the parliamentary convention of being delivered only from brief notes. Gladstone believed that such delivery, made after careful preparation, most accurately revealed the speaker's quality of character to the audience. Disraeli as a young man was said to have rehearsed his invective with friends. According to T.H.S. Escott's information from Montagu Corry, Disraeli's secretary, Disraeli changed this habit in later life: 'Lord Beaconsfield, to the best of my knowledge, deeply reflected on his forthcoming speeches long beforehand, and only put them mentally into verbal shape during a seclusion of two or three hours which he obtained before delivering an address of much importance.' Joseph Chamberlain was characteristically well prepared. He told John Morley in November 1877 (before the platform arrangements had reached their most sophisticated form): 'For the first time in my life I have at the urgent request of the reporters (who say they fear a breakdown in telegraphic arrangements as Lord Hartington is speaking the same night) prepared an abstract of what I am going to say for the country and possibly for the London papers.'[17]

For some, such speechmaking came easily. Cobden told Delane: 'it is known that I am not in the habit of writing a word beforehand of what I speak in public. Like other speakers, practice had given me as perfect self-possession in the presence of an audience, as if I were writing in my closet.' But for others, however experienced, meetings remained a strain. Randolph Churchill, like his son (who wrote out his speeches in advance), found speechmaking a great burden:

> I find . . . that addressing these large meetings is such anxious and exciting work that for a day or two afterwards I am quite useless and demoralised . . . I have made up my mind to give up almost entirely attendance at these public meetings. It is simply killing and the constant necessity of trying to say something new makes one a drivelling idiot.[18]

As there was free trade in newspapers, so was there free trade in speeches. The agencies were profit-making and so, after a fashion, were the papers: they were certainly competitive. As Alfred Kinnear wrote: 'the market in great men's oratory is worked on sound commercial lines. It is a whole-sale market. There is no retail business. Speeches are offered in bulk.' The financing of speech reporting worked in this way: the Post Office was paid £1 per column (reckoned at 2000 words) for the first report that the agency sold, and 3s. 4d. per column for each subsequent report sold. The agency sold to all newspapers at 10 shillings per column; there was therefore a balance of 6s. 8d. per column on each report sold beyond the first for the agency to cover reporting costs and make a profit. If there were insufficient orders, the profit margin would diminish or disappear, and it would not be worthwhile for the agency to send reporters to the meeting. As Kinnear observed, 'Newspapers regulated the trade by fixing the demand. They fix the demand on their part by testing the sale of the papers . . .'[19]

The demand for speeches was therefore of central importance to the culture of extra-parliamentary speechmaking. A sophisticated system developed for assessing it. On Saturdays each week each paper got a list of 'fixtures' – the Whips arranged between themselves that there should not be clashes such as Gladstone and Salisbury speaking and the same evening – and on Monday the papers sent in orders for the coming week. There were three kinds of report: first, a 'verbatim' (sometimes as much as five columns); secondly, 'full' (first person report but judiciously trimmed and shortened to about one and a half columns from the verbatim); and thirdly, third-person 'summary', usually half a column. On the basis of the papers' orders, the agency decided which of these sorts of report to arrange: if the number of orders did not justify a 'verbatim' report, the agency would switch to 'full' or 'summary'. The elite of verbatim speakers was always very small: in 1885 the *Pall Mall Gazette* noted that only Gladstone, Salisbury, Chamberlain and Randolph Churchill were reported verbatim; and in 1897 only Salisbury, Rosebery, Balfour and Chamberlain created enough demand for the agencies to supply verbatim reports. Harcourt, much to his chagrin, was not on the verbatim list until he resigned the Liberal leadership, when renewed interest in his career, or lack of career, got him briefly promoted from 'full' to 'verbatim'.

The reporting of speeches was thus conditioned by the law of supply and demand. Newspapers had to sell and the notion that they printed speeches out of a sense of duty, knowing that they would not be read, is quite false; news agencies exist to make profits. When Gladstone retired from public speaking, the Press Association reported a loss: its chairman explained:

Last year [1895] was the dullest we have had for many years ... the most
serious loss we had was, no doubt, the withdrawal of Mr Gladstone ...
Probably two thirds of the falling off in the revenue was due to that cause,
but not only did Mr Gladstone make a large number of speeches himself,
which almost every newspaper in the country reported, but he also pro-
voked a large number of replies, which were also reported.[20]

Clearly an MP's position in this league table of speech reporting was
of great importance for his reputation: if, at a time when promotion
in both parties was rather slow, he could get from the summary into
the 'full' report category, he could substantially improve his political
position. In this area, the Commons was of great significance. The cut
and thrust of debate – especially unorthodox *ad hominem* debate – could
quickly promote a politician. Randolph Churchill in the 1880s, Lloyd
George in the Boer War with his attacks on Chamberlain, are
examples of politicians who, having promoted themselves into the
'full' report category on a single issue or personal attack, used their
ability to widen their oratorical base to keep in the 'full' report category, or even reach the 'verbatim' level, once the original topic was
forgotten.

The selection of substantial reporting of extra-parliamentary
speeches depended therefore very much on intra-parliamentary man-
oeuvring between politicians. After the 1886 split the British press
became predominantly Unionist, having been overwhelmingly Liberal.
In 1884 there were 518 Liberal newspapers to 293 Tory; by 1901 the
figures were 403 Liberal, 456 Unionist.[21] This excludes the 'independent' papers; before 1886 these were predominantly Liberal – 'enemies
in disguise', as Hartington called them, of the Tory Party. After about
1888 independent papers had on the whole become definitely Unionist
in tone. Thus 1886–90 is the period in which the British press became
predominantly a Unionist, Conservative press, a tendency reinforced
by the growth of *Daily Mail* type newspapers after 1896 (the *Mail*
started as a Liberal Imperialist paper, but was Unionist by the end of
the Boer War). In Scotland, for example, both the main dailies, the
Glasgow Herald and the *Scotsman*, went Unionist in 1886.

Important beyond the extent of their circulation were the London
papers. Whereas in the mid-century the brash self-confidence of the
new press in the provinces had allowed the development of a regional
tone which owed little to London, by the 1870s and 1880s the London
press was more dominant. The best known paper was *The Times*,
although its circulation was steadily falling (60,000 in 1879; 40,000 in

1890). The most widely-read was the *Daily Telegraph*, the flagship of the Liberals in the 1860s; it turned Conservative over the Liberals' Bulgarian atrocities campaign in the 1870s, but retained its circulation (250,000 in 1880). By 1912 the Unionists had thirteen London morning and evening papers to the Liberals' three *(Daily News, Daily Chronicle* and the evening *Westminster Gazette)*.

Getting on the 'verbatim' or 'full' reporting level was thus of particular importance to Liberals, since this was an effective way of achieving publicity in the enemy camp – whose voters had to be won over – for Liberal and Unionist papers tended to report the same people; that is, the market value of verbatim speeches did not vary much from party to party or paper to paper at a national or regional level. A four-column Liberal speech in a Unionist paper by a good Liberal speaker was effectively a four-column advertisement. As advertisements, these space-consuming speeches were effective, for they were placed in newspapers which had as yet virtually no illustrations, and whose format was, between the 1860s and the 1900s, almost unchanged.

In the sense of advertisement, therefore, the Boer War, despite its short-term disadvantages to the Liberals, was of long-term help: it promoted to the 'full' level several unknown Liberal politicians, and ensured that, when the Tariff Reform campaign began shortly afterwards, there was a much larger body of Liberals well known to readers of both parties than was the case in the late 1890s. Considering that the party had been out of power for twenty years, and out of office for ten, the Liberal government of 1905 was very familiar to the public, and this was largely an oratorical familiarity.

Thus far, I have shown that the need and the conditions for extra-parliamentary speaking, developed with particular enthusiasm by the Liberals but energetically participated in by both parties, were a product of the political structure of the second half of the nineteenth century and of the technical means at the disposal of politicians and journalists. The two together had produced a national debating society inconceivable in the pre-telegraphic days. The nationally integrated reporting system offered the means for a nationally integrated political rhetoric: the same speech reaching the breakfast tables of Wick, Penzance, London and Liverpool on the same morning; the same reply reaching those same breakfast tables the next morning. Linked to this was the local reporting of politicians significant only at a local or regional level – these men offered a code to the national politicians.

When we come to the content of these speeches we find ourselves faced by two of the quotations with which this essay began: Aristotle's view that rhetoric is a discipline with its own purpose, rules and methodology; and Hobbes's denial of this, and his view that rhetoric is merely part of propaganda – that there are no rules or limitations, but simply the desire to win. A number of recent historians, particularly on the right, but with the cheerful concurrence of certain labour historians for whom progressivism is deviationalism, have seen oratory of this sort as merely an aspect of a struggle for ascendency within the ruling elite, one weapon among several in a game whose rules are only known to the players at Westminster. The verbatim reporting of speeches poses problems for this view: it is one thing to give a speech in the manner of the 1990s, whose contents are revealed only to those who receive the handouts, and whose significance is confined to the use of certain code words; it is another regularly to produce four columns subject to national public scrutiny. On the other hand, it is certainly true that speeches were weapons against colleagues as well as opponents. What is misleading is to see this as a game with secret or closed rules: the extent of open argument created a national rather than an elitist game. Public oratorical accountability was the link between Westminster and a politically fascinated national constituency.

If we look at the two main protagonists in the national debate, we shall see two rather different approaches to content. It is no accident that the first well-remembered Tory speeches were Disraeli's Manchester and Crystal Palace speeches of 1872, given, significantly, to constituency association workers, for it was essentially on organisation rather than speechmaking that the Tories relied. At the Crystal Palace Disraeli made the following claim:

> If you look to the history of this country since the advent of Liberalism – forty years ago – you will find that there has been no effort so continuous, so subtle, supported by so much energy, and carried on with so much ability and acumen, as the attempts of Liberalism to effect the disintegration of the Empire of England.[22]

With these remarks, Disraeli dramatically seized the wand of patriotism from the dead Palmerston's hand, captured the initiative from the Liberal Party on the dominant theme of late Victorian Britain – Imperialism – and effectively wrote the election address of every Tory MP until the 1950s. This extract from the Tory manifesto of 1951 is merely Disraeli without the style:

> Six years ago Britain stood high in fame and greatness. Under Socialism, we have fallen far from those heights of achievement and expectation: to

retain and develop the great and unique brotherhood of the British Empire is a first task of British statesmanship. The Conservative party, by long tradition and settled belief, is the Party of the Empire ... the socialists should have set country before party, and shown that they were Britons first, and socialists only second.[23]

What Disraeli realised was that, in the age of extended electorates, rhetoric may be only loosely connected with the realities of policy, that is, that the presentation of politics is distinct, or can be made distinct, from their content. Of course Disraeli did not think the Liberal Cabinet wanted the disintegration of the Empire. Nor was Disraeli himself particularly imperialistic in his *policy* when in office. It was under Gladstone, not Disraeli, that the crucial decisions of the founding of the third British Empire took place. But it was Disraeli, at Victoria's prompting, who made the Queen Empress of India, the greatest symbolic and propagandist act of the nineteenth century. In vain might Liberals protest that Gladstone's interest in the Empire, and in its extension, went back to the days when Disraeli had called colonies 'millstones around our necks'; in vain might Liberals point to the reality of their imperial achievements in the empire of settlement, and in expanding that of the tropics. The Queen, the Church of England and the Empire: these were the three simple, telling cries of Tory rhetoric, with the odd nod to social reform when convenient.

It would be quite misleading to argue that all Tory speeches were non-rational or intended to be so, but it would be fair to say that Tories in general distrusted the concept of politics based on rationality; that they perceived the growing significance of symbol in politics; that they had, especially in the heritage of Disraeli, a clear and early understanding that, as Graham Wallas observed, 'the empirical art of politics consists largely in the creation of opinion by the deliberate exploitation of sub-conscious, non-rational inference'.[24] The themes of monarchy, religion, race and imperialism fell conveniently into this category. Linked to these was the well-known Tory capacity for efficient organisation, by which the potency of slogans could be turned into votes. On the other hand, the reporting verbatim of speeches was a stimulus to rational presentation; to fill four columns required more than mere repetition of stereotypes. But the context of political speechmaking was of Liberal emphasis, and it imposed Liberal restrictions. Thus in the Tariff Reform campaign Joseph Chamberlain was encouraged to present his programme rationalistically and publicly – Liberal exposition of its deficiencies and self-contradictions was therefore possible and prominent as well as the sloganeering of the 'big loaf and the little loaf'. It would be interesting to compare the rationalistic public presentation of the Tariff Reform campaign and its failure with the behind-the-scenes manipulations which were essential to the success of the Common Market initiative.

If Tory politics thus centred around organisational politics and a growing awareness of the potency of images, the position for the Liberals was more complex. Of course the Liberals had their organisations; they had their interest groups, the Celts, the Nonconformists, and so on; and they had their slogans. But they also had the need, even the craving, for public discussion of issues, actions and programmes; for Liberals, politics without public discussion and argument lacked essential ingredients. Liberalism at its most successful involved the combining of various types and levels of political activity. But for Liberal Party workers the rhetorical appeal was not merely the centrepiece but the distinctive characteristic of liberal politics. Liberals persistently gave speeches on the nature of liberalism: the Tories avoided rationalistic articulation of the underpinning of their appeal. That is, the Tories did not depend on rhetoric for the maintenance of party unity, though they used it. The Liberals to some extent did – or thought they did. Gladstone developed the rhetorical idea of the overarching issue: Bulgarian atrocities; Home Rule; the House of Lords – issues which served as a focus for Liberal rhetoric and which would enable the very different aims of the various Liberal interest groups to unite.

The Liberals were also the party of progress, and thus, at least on paper, the party of action. Certainly in the 1886–1914 period, when the Tories were in office about sixteen years and the Liberals about eleven, the Liberal legislative proposals – not necessarily achievements – were far more numerous. The Liberals, therefore, while they had their fair share of Tory baiting, also used their speeches for the ventilation of ideas and for the struggle within the party for legislative priority. Liberals were always ready to spend money on the publication of speeches: the best-financed and most carefully organised branch of the National Liberal Federation was the *Liberal Magazine*, most of which was made up of speeches. When the Liberal Imperialists set up the Liberal League in 1902, they spent almost all their income on the distribution of speeches: their publication department was run by Sidney Webb. The Liberals – or at any rate those Liberals who made the sort of speeches which were widely reported – believed that reasonable men, presented with the full case, would naturally vote Liberal;

they believed, in other words, that the presentation and quality of political ideas and policies were central to vote-winning. They believed, in fact, that class or personal interest was not the determining factor in voting behaviour. Speechmaking and good coverage by the press were thus absolutely essential to their strategy.

It may be objected that this is a caricature of the Liberal Party in any constituency in which it had a chance of winning. Many examples of efficient Liberal organisations can be cited. Moreover, the reception of these speeches – their incidence in terms of votes – is hard to estimate. There are many interesting questions, of popular assumptions about newspapers, of the general intelligibility of the language used by politicians in their speeches, of the relationship of the newspapers' leaders to the speeches, which unfortunately there is not space to discuss here. That it is hard to estimate and impossible to quantify this incidence should not, however, be a reason for explaining away the phenomenon, especially by reference to the very different political culture of late twentieth-century Britain. The existence of the phenomenon in itself asserts the distinctiveness of the age in which it flourished.

The sort of rhetoric discussed in this essay was that exercised by a political elite which found itself increasingly otherwise isolated from its rank and file. The decline of Whiggery and the loss of Chamberlain meant that the upper levels of the Liberal Party increasingly depended on rhetoric as their link with the party as well as the electorate. Men such as Gladstone, Morley and Asquith had no base for power within their party save their own rhetoric and their legislative achievements. They controlled no machine, they spent no money on politics, they had no base in the localities, no real patronage except when in office. Their standing in the party depended on their success as rhetoricians and legislators, and Liberal governments after 1884 until 1906 could point to few legislative achievements. The absence of a formal party structure allowed them and the policies developed in their rhetoric to become the national focal point, the unifying and determining element in what made up the Liberal Party in the late nineteenth century. Max Weber pointed out the extent to which Gladstone's speeches, belief in 'the ethical substance of his policy' and 'belief in the ethical character of his personality' became fused together: this can be expanded to suggest not the 'Caesaristic plebiscitical element' dominated by one man which Weber saw as characteristic of this period,[25] but rather as the means by which a university educated, non-industrial, intellectual elite succeeded in coordinating the working of a great political movement in a predominantly industrial and commercial state. They did so by expressing the rationalistic values which the Liberal 'hundreds' regarded as the stuff of national politics.

Changes in the structure of politics and in the structure and techniques of the media drastically altered the forum in which this approach had been effective. The *Daily Mail* (1896) introduced something of a new style of political reporting, taking up the techniques introduced in the 1880s by W.T. Stead, who was himself mainly inspired by his observation of the American press. The *Mail*'s importance was its size (a circulation of over one million by 1900), its national distribution, which undercut the provincial morning press, and its relative simplicity of presentation and reporting. Appealing to the rapidly expanding service sector of the economy, it was the newspaper of the retailing revolution: the advertisements were much more visual, more punchy and less wordy, and its political reporting mirrored this. We should not exaggerate: the *Mail* maintained a high political content, but it packaged politics in a way that verbatim speech reporting could not do. On the whole, the provincial press did not respond: its techniques began to atrophy. It reflected its Liberal tendency in its reluctance to abandon the importance it gave to what was coming to be seen as 'high-minded' rather than 'normative' political reporting. By 1914 the provincial press and the old metropolitan press was under strong pressure from the *Mail* and its imitators.

The 1918 Representation of the People Act, doubling the male electorate and enfranchising many women, opened a new phase for politicians. The scale of political appeal necessarily had to be much wider: the concept of 'capable citizenship' virtually ceased to exercise any limitation of the electorate. The Tory and Labour Parties both stood to capitalise on these developments; they were both parties whose appeal was essentially to the 'deliberate exploitation of subconscious, non-rational inference', whether, respectively, of imperialistic nationalism and property or of class, although they both used rationalistic methods when it suited them and speechmaking continued to be of importance in both cases in intra-party debate.

The vast new electorate and the changing structure of the press meant that the complex structure of extra-parliamentary national debate, which had, of course, been largely suspended during the First World War, never recovered its rude late Victorian health. Although certain speeches continued to be reported quite fully, gone for good was the notion that at certain times of the year newspapers should report over a period of weeks the verbatim reports of the national debate and the reaction of local politicians to it. Ironically, as the cultural significance of the speeches declined, their cost rose, politicians beginning to hire speechwriters or to allow civil servants to draft their public statements as well as their letters. The age of the 'handout' had begun. Political figures continued to speak as if on the platform in Midlothian. Sometimes, as with Ramsay MacDonald's speeches in 1923, something of a similar effect was achieved, at least with the audience actually present. But increasingly politicians' words – or their speech-writers' words – reached only the 'professional' audience: media men, the party faithful and their political opponents. The electorate had not turned to other interests (apart from the freak conditions of 1918, turnout under the universal franchise stayed above 70 per cent), but it no longer met its representatives, except occasionally, through verbatim reporting.

How then was the integration of the new electorate to be achieved? As new techniques of advertising spread, linked to the development of a new popular press, so politics began to be more packaged for consumption by the readership of the newspaper. When speeches had been reported either verbatim or in full, the journalist's views had not come between the politician and the reader in the way we today take for granted, except in the instance of the interview which was used, but not very extensively from the 1870s: 'It is perhaps this abuse of the interview in many American journals which has retarded its adoption in leading English newspapers ... The interview is, however, slowly but surely obtaining respectful recognition in this country.'[26]

Kennedy Jones remarked of the *Daily Mail*: 'our influence did more ... than anything else [to reduce] the speeches of politicians to their right proportions'.[27] This clearly exaggerates the importance of the *Mail*, which was a function of change as much as a cause of it, but it highlights the new role of journalists as political interpreters in addition to their role as leader writers. Although the number of papers with a declared political allegiance fell spectacularly, the partisanship of reporting increased markedly: *Exchange Telegraph* told the Royal Commission on the press of 1947–48, 'Subscribers to whom the opinions expressed [in a speech] are sympathetic and in line with their own convictions will require perhaps 800 words. Organs with a different frame of mind will require 200 words only.' E.W. Davies of the Press Association told the commission: 'I may pick up a speech and say "that is what I want to be given" ... Sir Stafford Cripps ... sends me his speeches and I mark them myself and my staff knows exactly what I want to go out.'[28] Thus during the interwar years the chief means of political communication of the late Victorians had become the whim of an agency editor.

This process was speeded on its way by the development of radio, which even in its early days reached huge audiences: George V's broadcast opening the British Empire Exhibition in 1924 was estimated to have been heard by at least ten million. By 1939, about 75 per cent of households had radio sets. Political broadcasting was from the start a sensitive matter and, partly for this reason, Sir John Reith of the BBC always tried to keep the political broadcasts short, though he encouraged their use in moderation: in the 1924 election all the Party Leaders made political broadcasts. Broadcasting was vital, Lloyd George said, 'to enable the vast mass of the electorate to know what the issues were . . . he did not know of any other way by which [politicians] could get at them'.

There were other ways, but not for Liberals. Nor were the short snaps permitted by the BBC conducive to the exposition of Liberal rationalism, and still less were the image-based media of film and television. The provincial press, the extensive reporting of extra-parliamentary speeches, the culture of a self-improving, capable citizenship, and a liberal ethos which pervaded one party and to some extent penetrated the other – all rose and fell together. 'A true Democracy is only possible when Society . . . becomes conscious in its intelligence and will', wrote J.A. Hobson in 1909.[29] Hobson's statement was intended as an exhortation for the future, but today it reads elegiacally. The peculiar technical and structural conditions of the second half of the nineteenth century had offered one solution, but necessarily one limited to a particular phase, to the problem of 'democracy' in industrial Britain.

13

Gladstone and his Library

Peter J. Jagger

The foundation of St Deiniol's Residential Library was Gladstone's final legacy. What follows is an account of his unique vision of a residential library to house his own outstanding collection, gifted to the nation; the building of a temporary library; his appointing of a body of trustees to ensure the embodiment of this vision; and, finally, the building of the permanent library enshrining all aspects of Gladstone's vision and purpose.

An examination of Gladstone's diaries leaves us in no doubt that he was a lifelong student and scholar and as such a voracious reader; and that the reading and collecting of books played a very important part in his life. For Gladstone books were both a consuming interest and a cause for concern and hard work in identifying, purchasing, shelving and repairing them. His study in Hawarden Castle was named the 'Temple of Peace'. The thousands of books he collected and read were fundamental to his life in politics and to his life in the church. Theology in all its branches was his greatest love, but he also read widely in other areas including classical studies, history, literature, philosophy and political affairs.

Gladstone's political greatness is an undeniable fact of modern British history. He was a man of great vision and action but his achievements were inspired, nurtured and undergirded by what he believed and what he read. The inscription on the foundation stone of St Deiniol's Library sums up the man and the history and purpose of St Deiniol's:

> In this building, erected to his memory by a grateful nation, is preserved the Library of William Ewart Gladstone who, eminent no less as a theologian than as a statesman, established this foundation for the advancement of Divine Learning.

The library which Gladstone was to give to the nation was entirely of his creating. The collection housed at St Deiniol's includes books, with his notes and annotations, from his Eton and Oxford days. While theology in all its branches was his first love, this could not be separated from history. Homer, Dante, Shakespeare, Bishop Butler, as well as Aristotle and Augustine, were among the areas of great interest, as seen in his collection. Eventually his library grew to well over 30,000 volumes. For him it was always seen as a working library. It may be said that a man's library is his best portrait, but this is only true if the collector is also a reader and student of the books collected. His collection shows the breadth of his reading and his interests.

In the latter years of his life Gladstone began to consider how he could share his great personal library with others. Letters, memos for his own consideration and sometimes to others, notes on scraps of paper, diary entries also record the evolution of his thought on the matter. He gradually reached the conclusion that somehow others ought to have access to his library. His wide-ranging collection in theology would, he believed, be of great value to clergy and laity of all denominations, but especially to those of the Anglican Communion, of which he was a member, for the study of what he called 'Divine learning'. He also wrote that his collection would be of value to all students of the Humanities, including those with no religious affiliation. Potential users needed access to the collection, so his books required a new home.

His diaries and correspondence record the evolution of his unique vision: a residential library, a place where his books could be rehoused and where users could retreat from the demands and pressures of everyday life to read, to think, to reflect and to be part of a community of others seeking the same opportunity. The first mention of what was to be St Deiniol's Library is recorded in his diary on 12 July 1886, following a conversation on the same day with his son, the Rev. Stephen Gladstone. By September the following year he was considering possible sites for the library. On 12 November 1888 he wrote a memo headed 'St Deiniol's Library', where among other things he stated his aim as: 'To raise only temporary buildings and have the Library placed and arranged in them so as to allow of later transmigration'. A separate, undated sheet mentions giving 'much power over the new foundation to my family', while a later, but undated holograph, begins: 'The first and main purpose of this foundation, and the Trust [half of the first trustees were related to Gladstone] which has charge of it is to promote: 1. Devotion, 2. Divine Learning [and] the promotion of learning at large, especially historical learning'.

In 1889 he decided on the site for the building and bought three acres of land close to the ancient parish church of Hawarden. In August 1889 he recorded his decision that the foundation was to be 'a temporary scheme'. Before the end of the month J. C. Humphreys, of Hyde Park, London, makers of corrugated iron buildings, had produced plans for a 'temporary library'. On 2 September he recorded a meeting with 'Mr Humphreys with whom I arranged for the new structure at Hawarden: the nucleus I trust if it please God of something considerable'. The name of the institution had already been decided: it was to be named after the sixth-century Welsh missionary bishop, Deiniol. Within days the actual site was determined and pegged out. On 8 November he settled on the new building with Humphreys and the next day he 'worked much on measuring books and planning bookcases'.

The following year, 1890, the temporary building was complete. In that same year he wrote what was to prove an important and historic article in the periodical *The Nineteenth Century* entitled 'On Books and the Housing of Them'. It was a subject to which he had given much thought for some time and approached 'professionally'. What he wrote there was to receive practical application in the foundation and the arrangement of St Deiniol's Library. The design and layout of the shelves in the new library were of Gladstone's creation and based upon those he had erected in the Temple of Peace. The catalogue card cabinets and other items of library furniture also bore his mark. Personal items of furniture, pictures and Gladstonian memorabilia were also eventually to adorn the new library.

Gladstone began his careful selection of 32,000 books from the castle library; those left there were regarded as temporarily housed in 'the annex at the Castle', awaiting transfer to their new location. Transfer of the collection began in 1890 and continued until the end of 1893. Gladstone packed and unpacked the books, and placed them personally, although sometimes assisted by his daughters and other members of the family, one by one in the bookcases specially prepared for them. 'What man', he would say, 'who really loves his books delegates to any other human being . . . the office of introducing them into their new home?'

A manuscript written by Gladstone in September 1894 has the title 'The Library of St Deiniol: Retrospect'. Here he writes of his bookcases and his placing of his books upon them and of the use of low-level shelving for large books. On an undated sheet he enlarges on the advantages of shelving octavo books together, 'while quartos and folios are shelved separately but near to the main body of the quarto subject collections'. He also writes of the introduction of a simple alphabetical catalogue and of a system of classification. An added pencil note on cataloguing and classification states that the notes were written for the further guidance of his son-in-law, the Rev. Harry Drew, whom he appointed as acting warden in August that year taking up office in September. Thus Gladstone was responsible for the classification and the arrangement of the books.

Another manuscript by Gladstone, dated September 1894 and entitled 'The Library of St Deiniol's', contains further observations and developments: 'The Library of St Deiniol's is the core of the institution . . . it is to be regarded as at present only in its . . . embryo'. Initially he placed about 25,000 books in the temporary building, 'but I retain at the Castle, mainly for my own use a smaller portion [which he indicates as in the thousands] the two should be regarded as eventually in substance one'. These were later transferred to St Deiniol's.

He wrote that there should be a budget of £300 per annum for the purchase of books. In connection with the arrangement of the books he felt that a foundation had been laid with his own hands. 'Most serious of all is the formation of a Catalogue, of course with much care and accuracy, and with a view to the expansion already mentioned.' He recognised the need to weed out duplicates and to have books properly bound, upon which he made his recommendations. Books, his treasured library, were at the heart of his vision, but this was only a part of the planned bequest to the nation.

On 25 January 1894 the seventeenth-century Grammar School and Master House, situated near to the new library, and which Gladstone had bought and converted to a hostel, welcomed the first residents. Gladstone's temporary residential library was born.

On 23 November 1894 a Supplement to *The Westminster Budget* was published devoted to 'Mr Gladstone's Gift: The Hawarden Library and Hostel'. The following precedes the article: 'Mr Gladstone having read and approved of the article wrote: "I think the article has been drawn with much ability and care . . . describing an institution still in its embryo, or at any rate not advanced beyond its cradle!"' This article, with its various pictures, provides an early, interesting and detailed record of St Deiniol's Library. Here we read of the iron building, the object of the institution, its idyllic location, the shelving, the books, the catalogue, the painting of Dr Döllinger, the German theologian, the small terracotta medallion of Cardinal Manning, a large carved-oak armchair given to Gladstone by his Liberal constituents of Greenwich. Details of the hostel are provided with the observation: 'It is not Mr Gladstone's idea that luxurious living is conducive to the well being or the increased intellectual activity of those whom the institution is intended to benefit.' An important observation is made about the future location of the institution:

> It is Mr Gladstone's idea that a retreat such as St Deiniol's should be situated, not in a large town, but in the country, where, during their stay, those who avail themselves of the advantages of hostel and library will have pure, strengthening air, pleasant country surroundings, and none of the distractions of town life. Meanwhile Liverpool is coming nearer . . . the time may not be very far off when the great town shall come too near not to disturb, in some degree, the rural life of Hawarden. In such a case, Mr Gladstone thinks it will be comparatively easy to remove an iron building, whereas the removal of a large brick-and-mortar structure would not be so easily effected.

The article ends by referring to the many hours Gladstone spent with his son Stephen at the Rectory, situated near to the library. As Stephen was the one with whom he first shared his vision of a residential library in 1886, there can be little doubt Gladstone discussed with him his vision of a more permanent institution. He had, after all, written to Stephen at some length on 8 April 1893:

> While the Library is in some sense the foundation, I want to build upon it an institution . . . Could you not become the first head of my Trust? We should have much Counsel and I think sweet Counsel upon it. You see my position is this, that while I continue in this life of contention I have not brain freedom to prosecute the subject unaided, or to take the 'labouring over'. But in association I think we could get on, and you would have a full share of influence.

Early in 1895 Gladstone was involved in the setting up of a trust with a body of trustees. He wrote to George Russell MP, an ardent admirer of his, inviting him to become a trustee. Russell accepted the invitation and wrote of the permanent location at Hawarden: 'I attach great value to the Hawarden site . . . It would be specially associated with the life and work of the Founder; and a moral and sentimental bond of this kind is not to be lightly esteemed'. It had been suggested that the library could be moved to some centre of learning such as Oxford or that 'Pusey House could take over the books ... for the promotion of Divine Learning'. But, stressed Russell, 'the distinctiveness, individuality and characteristic features of the foundation would be lost'. He rejected the idea that a religious community could run the institution founded by Gladstone and fulfil his vision for the same.

Gladstone was increasingly concerned about the permanence of St Deiniol's and, in correspondence with the Society of St John the Evangelist, suggested they could oversee the foundation. On 29 August 1895 Russell wrote: 'I think that permanence could be much more safely and reasonably anticipated from a nominated body of Trustees, animated by the same beliefs and designs and empowered to fill vacancies in the body by cooptation'. Russell felt that, if a religious superior or community took over St Deiniol's, 'the Founder's hand would cease to operate; and the distinctiveness and individuality of the institution would disappear as completely as if the Library were bodily removed to Oxford'. Russell concluded that he was in favour of the permanent site at Hawarden under the direction of an independent warden.

It was felt that a body of trustees would ensure the permanence of the foundation on the site of the temporary building (which Gladstone had come to accept as the ideal), and that the founder's vision for such an institution would be effectively fulfilled by a body of trustees committed to the same. Eleven trustees were eventually appointed by the foundation deed of December 1895. They were all either relatives of Gladstone or very close friends, all entirely committed to the founder's intention of a future permanent residential library. Replies accepting the invitation to become a trustee clearly indicate a commitment to the founder and his vision.

Sir Walter Phillimore QC, a close friend of Gladstone, wrote that as a trustee he was fully prepared to carry out Gladstone's wishes and work with the other trustees in this respect. In a later letter he wrote: 'Your trustees must be persons who have the legal estate in the land and who are trusted to use it as you direct'. Lady Sibell Grosvenor wrote: 'As long as I live I will do my best to carry out your wishes for St Deiniol's ... You could not have given me greater joy than in letting me thus share in all that is connected with its welfare'. George Russell wrote on 18 October 1895: 'I welcome the duty which you now entrust to me, as linking me, in sentiment and ideal as well as in practical effort, with that which is the glory of your great career in

your public and unswerving loyalty to our Divine Lord'. Similar sentiments and commitments were expressed in other replies accepting
the office of a trustee.

The continuity of the founder's long-term intention for St Deiniol's
and the establishment of a permanent building to house his library, to
accommodate readers and to fulfil his vision for the foundation, were
fully accepted by all the trustees. In future, correspondence and meetings the outworking of the vision and the permanent nature of the
foundation were to be discussed in detail. In carefully choosing trustees
who shared his vision and would work to accomplish the same, Gladstone produced a document, to which some of those who were to be
trustees contributed in the drafting stage. It was printed on 9 October
1895 with the title *St Deiniol's Trust and its Purpose: Preliminary Paper.*

This document, which became the basis of the later 'Foundation
Deed', clearly outlined Gladstone's thoughts and objectives at this
stage. Here he declared the purpose of the institution to be 'the effective
promotion of Divine learning'. Defining 'Divine learning', he states:

> Divine learning, in order to reach its fullest efficiency, has been and ought
> to be associated with the various branches of human knowledge, especially
> with History and Philosophy; and it is upon *the widest* basis that the Library
> is being formed . . . The religious *intuitus* of the Institution will be conform-
> ity to the living spirit of the Church of England.

But this was not restrictive in any way, for he goes on to state 'that
the hospitality of the Institution and its conveniences and advantages,
should as far as possible be made available for persons beyond the
pale of the Anglican Church or even of the Christian Religion'. The
aim of welcoming those of all Christian traditions and more especially
those of other world religions was indeed a 'prophetic vision' in 1895.
Gladstone's intention was that its community of resident readers
would form an extended international family with no restriction on
the grounds of race or creed.

Turning to the type of trustees to be appointed to work with him
in his few remaining years of life and continuing his intentions after
his death, he wrote:

> I seek to compose the Trust of persons in sympathy with the main objects
> of the Institution . . . able as well as willing to give them the necessary
> attention; and it will be my aim to place the trustees, subject to the condi-
> tions of Foundation, in the position which I hold myself. They will therefore
> be invested with all the powers I possess; to be used always for the further-
> ance of the main design . . . They will have full authority to develop the

Institution, and even to alter its form or change its site in whole or in part should any of such changes be deliberately judged by them to be required for the better fulfillment of the main Design of the Institution.

By the following year the founder and the trustees had come to agree that the three acre site, on which the small temporary library and hostel stood, should indeed be the site for the permanent building – a residential library – which they now saw as the ultimate objective.

In this document Gladstone made it clear that his own involvement would continue through his family: 'It is my purpose that the Institution should continue to be in relations both with my family and the parish of Hawarden, but always in subordination to the main design'. The head of the institution is to be called the 'Warden and Principal Librarian'.

Even while this paper was being drafted and printed Gladstone was working with Sir Walter Phillimore, who had offered to produce a draft indenture for the 'Foundation Deed'. The Foundation Deed, of 23 December 1895, included all major points set out in Gladstone's *St Deiniol's Trust and its Purpose*. It listed all the trustees and stated it 'is desirous of founding a permanent Institution'. All the land, the buildings, the books and the furniture, the stocks, funds and securities are assigned to the trustees 'upon trust to form and preserve a Library and Institution to be called St Deiniol's Library . . . for the promotion of Divine learning . . . declared and defined to be the main design of the founder'.

The continuity of the founder's designs for St Deiniol's were covered in correspondence and conversation with others, especially Sir Walter Phillimore. The Foundation Deed, therefore, requires that 'a person being tenant of the freehold of Hawarden Castle . . . and descended from the founder . . .' should, after Gladstone's death, be appointed a trustee. The Rector of Hawarden should always be invited to be a trustee and 'if a trustee, shall be chairman of the trustees'. After the death of Gladstone, his son the Rev. Stephen Gladstone, the then Rector of Hawarden, became chairman of the trustees.

In an undated manuscript, which appears by its contents to have been produced before the foundation deed, Gladstone outlined his intended use of the £30,000 endowment for the foundation. It was to cover the warden's salary and the purchase of books, but 'a considerable portion of the Income is given with a view to accumulation: and this accumulation will be required to form a fund for the creation of permanent buildings, which after a term of years will become necessary'. An attached document outlines many of the points which were later included in *St Deiniol's Trust and its Purpose*.

The author of the article on St Deiniol's Library, published in the *Westminster Budget* in November 1894 published a book in January 1896 entitled *In The Evening of his Days: A Study of Mr Gladstone in Retirement, with Some Account of St Deiniol's Library and Hostel*. A note in the preface states that Gladstone had read the chapter on St Deiniol's and agreed with. Here there is clear evidence of a fundamental change regarding one aspect of St Deiniol's. In the author's previous account Gladstone accepted the possibility that, at some future date, a permanent building might be on another site. Here the writer states: 'It is Mr Gladstone's wish that the permanent building should be in the same place where, in the present iron structure, the scheme came first into operation . . . the trustees of the fund are all personal friends of "the Settler", and fully in sympathy with his views'.

From 1893 the Rev. Harry Drew, who was married to Gladstone's daughter Mary, was acting warden, and under Gladstone's direction spent much time cataloguing the collection. On 27 March 1896 Gladstone sent out a printed letter to a number of personal friends briefly outlining the objectives of the foundation and requesting their help in identifying a suitable warden. He told them that, while the present buildings were temporary, 'the erection of permanent buildings for all purposes is contemplated, but this must depend on the gradual accumulation means'. One of the tasks of the warden would be 'the gradual extension and development of the Library which embraces, as its two main departments, Divinity and Humanity . . .'

By October 1896 Gladstone had found his man and wrote to the Rev. Gilbert Joyce, then Sub-Warden of St Michael's Theological College, offering him the appointment of Warden of St Deiniol's Library 'for a term . . . to be a minimum of six months'. He remained in office from 1897 to 1916, nineteen years. During his short remaining life Gladstone spent many hours with the warden sharing with him his vision for the future. Because of this close contact with the founder, and with Stephen his son, Joyce was acutely aware of the need to ensure the 'living embodiment' of the founder and the continuity of his influence and his vision in the transfer from the temporary iron library and the hostel to the permanent building to be eventually founded on the same site.

On 7 May 1898, while Gladstone was on his deathbed (he died 19 May 1898), the Duke of Westminster wrote to Stephen Gladstone, the chairman of the trustees:

There will be a number of proposals 'in memoriam'. Might not a good *local* one take the shape of a permanent and handsome building for the books, if as I suppose, they will remain at Hawarden? Do you know what the family would think and feel as to this? It would be wise, if they approve of the idea, to be early in the field after any announcement in that direction. . . . This hardly requires an answer! I write, of course, in complete ignorance of your Father's wishes in respect of the Library.

Was this letter encouraged or inspired by his daughter-in-law, Lady Sibell Grosvenor, a devoted and informed trustee of St Deiniol's? Unfortunately, no reply to the duke's letter has been preserved at St Deiniol's Library.

The Duke of Westminster was to suggest to the trustees both an architect and a builder. A letter from Henry Neville Gladstone to his brother Stephen suggests that John Douglas had been recommended. Henry suggested to Stephen that no approach should be made to Douglas until the matter had been discussed at a meeting of the trustees. The duke, a well-known patron of John Douglas, may have been simply confirming the Gladstone family's own decision that John Douglas, an outstanding local provincial architect, ought to be the one to design the nation's memorial to their father which, it had been agreed, should be sited in Hawarden.

Gladstone recorded his first thoughts about St Deiniol's in his diary in July 1886. By September 1887 and for the next two years he was looking at possible sites on which to build the temporary structure; and the later permanent library which was uppermost in his mind until 1898, the year of his death. The same diary records that from the early days of his life he had had a keen interest in architecture, especially Gothic. His own library housed at St Deiniol's contains more than one hundred books on architecture, many of them annotated. In the later years of his life the books he read on architecture include James Dallaway, *Observations on English Architecture*, and William H. White, *Architecture and Public Buildings: Their Relation to School, Academy and State in Paris and London*.

During this period of concentrated thought on St Deiniol's Library and his continued reading on architecture his diaries recorded what he described as a 'Conclave', i.e. a private meeting with Douglas: such meetings took place between 1887 and 1896 when Gladstone gave Douglas various commissions. In 1887–88 the strong room (the Octagon), was built at Hawarden Castle, for Gladstone a very important and personal commission. In the year 1889 plans were produced for the porch to the castle involving more discussions and meetings with Douglas, with further plans and discussion in 1890, during the same period that Gladstone's iron library was being built. Thus Gladstone was looking at sites and considering the design of his temporary library and also reading on architecture. While discussing with Douglas his strong room and the new porch, he may well have talked about his other and greater project. Did not his family and especially his sons meet with Douglas and come to know him? The diaries reveal that Gladstone had also met and corresponded with many of the leading architects of his time: Barry, Pugin, Scott and others.

Designs for a memorial tablet for his son W.H. Gladstone were carried out between 1891–93. In 1896, a period when Gladstone was actively considering the possibility of a future permanent library, he and his son, the rector of that church and soon to be chairman of the library trustees, were meeting John Douglas in connection with the chancel porch (and the canopied niche of the south porch) at St Deiniol's Church, Hawarden, to be built by the Gladstone family. Stephen Gladstone, who knew of his father's contact with John Douglas over many years, not to mention his knowledge of the extensive work which Douglas had done for the Duke of Westminster, may also have been prompted, as chairman of the trustees, to think of John Douglas as a most suitable architect for the new building.

John Douglas may not have been on the same level as some of his contemporaries of national and international renown but, to the people of the area in which he worked, he was regarded as an outstanding provincial architect. Edward Hubbard, in *Clwyd (Denbighshire and Flintshire): The Buildings of Wales*, acclaims John Douglas (1830–1911) as highly talented and as the most important and active local architect of his period, who 'received national and a degree of international recognition'. In his book *The Work of John Douglas*, Hubbard describes St Deiniol's Library as 'not only the most important secular building . . . but in view of the nature of the commission is something of a crowning achievement in Douglas's professional career'.

The letter of 7 May 1898 to Stephen Gladstone from the Duke of Westminster, Chairman of the National Memorial Executive Committee, established an immediate link with Gladstone's trustees. From 7 May, twelve days before Gladstone's death, a permanent residential library, built 'in the image of Mr Gladstone', became a reality for the near future. The whole project began to move forward with remarkable speed. By 21 July the executive committee reported to the general committee of the memorial fund its recommendation that £10,000 be set aside to build a permanent library, at Hawarden, as the national memorial to Gladstone.

The trustees were fortunate that from the outset the duke was committed to building a library to house Gladstone's great collection, he also believed that such should be built in Hawarden. Lady Sibell Grosvenor provided a close link with the duke, while George Russell MP served as both a trustee and as a member of the National Memorial Committee.

On 12 August the Warden of St Deiniol's Library, Gilbert Joyce, met Stephen Gladstone as chairman of the trustees and representative of the Gladstone family to discuss the new building. Regarding the future use of the present iron building, the warden rejected the Duke of Westminster's suggestion that it be used as a storage room for books. He pointed out that, unless carefully maintained, it would become too damp for books. The warden produced a 'Memorandum of a consultation with the Rector with regard to proposed requirements in a new building for St Deiniol's Library', in which he stated:

1. That one room should be so built as to accommodate a portion of the library according to the plan devised and adopted by Mr Gladstone himself. (Such a room would perhaps form a convenient 'Reading Room' attached to the main library and might be fitted up with some of the present bookcases in which Gladstone arranged the books with his own hands.)
2. That there should be a certain number of small studies such as are now in use at the library, and which experience has shown to contribute greatly to the convenience of students.
3. That there should be storage rooms allowing for the future expansion of the library.
4. That the design for the library should take into account the intention of the trustees at some future date to construct an adjoining hostel.

The aim to preserve the original bookcases as a living continuity with the founder is stated at the outset. Gladstone had insisted on the provision of some small studies in the original building. He had always stressed the need to provide additional accommodation for the future expansion of the collection, while the future hostel was essential to the whole Gladstonian vision.

Stephen wrote to his brother Henry Neville Gladstone, who was an active trustee and entirely devoted to his father's vision for St Deiniol's. Living in London, Henry kept in close contact with the memorial committee. In his letter Stephen raised the question of contacting John Douglas, but Henry, in a letter of 13 August, advised that this be delayed until they had had a meeting of the trustees, who knew nothing of the proposals beyond what they had read in the papers.

Henry wrote that Lord Rendel, a member of the executive committee, 'holds the strong opinion that the proper course would be for the Memorial Committee to hand over a cheque to the trustees and that they should not interfere with detail in any way at all'. The trustees, wrote Henry, 'were bound by the exact terms of the Deed and would not want a large body of men involved'. Henry felt it would be reasonable for the memorial committee to want to see 'the design before finally deciding upon it'. But Lord Rendel was not even in favour of this requirement. In a postscript he expressed the opinion that even before getting to a first drawing there were 'a great number of difficult points as regards position, interior design, etc, to consider'.

On 15 August Henry informed Stephen that Sir Walter Phillimore was to be elected a member of the Memorial Committee and would be able to advise them on appropriate offers. Henry had recently met the executive committee but it had nothing to report to the trustees at present. He therefore advised a further delay before seeing Douglas, if they had 'nothing to give him'. Stephen had reminded his brother that the duke was a friend, neighbour, benefactor and patron as well as president (chairman) of the memorial committee and that without him nothing would have been done for St Deiniol's.

A 'Strictly Private' Memo written by Henry Gladstone, dated 6 September 1898, lists five important points:

1. Lord Rosebery, a member of the General Committee, urged that 'the interior of the Library, all placed and arranged by Father himself, should not be touched, and that merely an outside shell should be added'. Is this practicable or desirable?
2. If not, and a completely new building is to be erected, ought it to be placed on the present site, or if not where?
3. If the present building occupies all or part of the best site for the new building should it be removed?
4. The grant to be received is to be devoted strictly to a building to hold the Library only. 'Should such a building form part only of a larger scheme? ... Should it be complete in itself or be capable of expansion?'

5. 'Will not Mr Douglas wish to have the general basis of the Scheme settled before he can prepare plans?' He suggests it would be useful to have Douglas's observations on all these points 'with a view to reporting by the trustees'.

All of Henry's points were submitted to Douglas who, in a letter dated 18 September, rejected the idea of an outside shell. The proposed buildings would be entirely new buildings leaving the present ones in use while the new ones were built. The library would be complete in itself but capable of extension. The hostel could be added afterwards. Douglas had inspected the site and proposed a new site only thirty feet away from the existing building.

He gave estimates for the Library at £6500, the Hostel £4200, the Chapel £1000, a total of £11,700 for Sketch Plan 'A'; Sketch Plan 'B' shows a simpler arrangement at £10,000. Thus even at this stage the exact plans were not fixed and cost-cutting alternatives were being considered by both the national committee and the trustees. These estimates were to prove far too low. Throughout this and future correspondence runs the conviction that meaningful and 'living links' with the founder needed to be maintained at all cost. Ways of doing this were to evolve as the scheme progressed, but throughout it remained central to the scheme, not least to the trustees who sought to ensure that the new building enshrined the vision of the founder and wherever possible tangible links with him should be implemented.

Correspondence continued between the trustees through its chairman, as did meetings of trustees, of the trustees sub-committee, and of representatives of the National Memorial Committee, and of trustees with such representatives. By March 1899 only ten months after the founder's death, the project was well in hand. It was acknowledged by the committee that the trustees must have the final decision on all major issues but should consider suggestions made by the national committee, especially on the plans and points of design.

On 23 March 1899, the duke received Douglas's plans and wrote to Stephen Gladstone: 'The plans seem to be good and to meet . . . difficult requirements as to the bookshelves etc'. Elevations were criticised as too commonplace and not sufficiently 'monumental'. Douglas agreed and submitted an alternative design; the trustees were offered another £1000 if they agreed to the improved design. They accepted.

Stephen Gladstone, as chairman of the trustees, replied to the duke on 24 March. The trustees had considered the question of 'more dignity' in connection with the design of the building. He informed the duke that they had expressed concern regarding 'more and permanent costs in upkeep' and that it would necessitate a more costly hostel at a future date. He went on to state: 'The trustees have to keep steadily in view my Father's one great aim: the establishment of this Foundation (to which he devoted £40,000) for the promotion of Divine learning. The trustees never would have built a mean building . . .' Both parties reached agreement on the new plans and the memorial committee agreed to offer the additional funding.

Stephen Gladstone had hoped that the laying of the foundation stone would take place on Ascension Day 1898 which, he felt, would have been timely, being the anniversary of Gladstone's death, but acknowledged that this was now quite impossible. Consultation continued between John Douglas, Stephen Gladstone, the trustees, the duke and the memorial committee. By 13 May 1899 mutual agreement was reached between the trustees and the memorial committee on all aspects of the building.

Unfortunately, the architect's original estimates were found to be too low. In a letter to Henry Gladstone, Douglas wrote, on 20 July 1899, that two of the seven contractors had declined tendering 'due to having so much work in hand'. Douglas added that this was 'an indication of the exceptional activity in the building trade which together with the advance in prices of material and labour in a great measure accounts for the tenders coming out as much and which we regret exceeds the anticipated amount'. He pointed out that the new estimates included the use of oak throughout the library and added: 'While the character of the work is necessarily expensive there is nothing that can be considered extravagant but only what is suitable and substantial of the several kinds'.

Two days after that letter, on 22 July, the trustees sub-committee with the architect met the memorial committee in London where it was agreed that the new and improved design and plans, and the extensive use of stone and oak, should not be compromised. The memorial committee, therefore, confirmed the final grant to cover the entire cost of the library. The committee stated its complete satisfaction and agreed that everything should now be left entirely in the hands of the library trustees.

On 29 July 1899 the builder's tender was received and accepted after slight revision. Work began almost immediately. A ceremony marking the 'Laying of the Foundation Stone' by the Duke of Westminster took place on 5 October 1899.

The trustees, in seeking to fulfill the 'great aim', had worked with the memorial committee and John Douglas the architect, with whom Gladstone had no doubt shared his vision and his own ideas regarding the architectural style, design and layout of the building, with its two large rooms devoted to Divinity and Humanity. The temporary iron library, in connection with every aspect of which Gladstone had spent the remaining years of his life, was a 'template' regarding many details of the permanent building and 'kept steadily in view' to ensure that it was indeed 'the visible embodiment of a continuity with Gladstone and his unique Vision for Mankind'.

This deliberate attempt to link Gladstone, his vision and the first, temporary St Deiniol's with the new building, as the national memorial to Gladstone, was achieved in many ways. The first, and most important link, was Gladstone's own library as the core of all that was to follow, and his classification of the collection, illustrating his understanding of the development of human knowledge. As with the first library, so in the new, a number of small studies were provided to give a setting of complete silence. The shelves Gladstone designed in the iron building, onto which he had personally placed each book belonging to his treasured collection, were relocated in the two galleries of the new building. These and the new oak shelves on the ground floor were set out according to Gladstone's own plan, based upon the layout in the Temple of Peace. Special shelves made for larger books were relocated from the original library and placed in such a way as to keep them near to their smaller counterparts. The card catalogue cabinets made for Gladstone were installed in their new home and are still used in the library today. Other items, such as tables, chairs and memorabilia given by Gladstone, were all moved to the new building. The impressive carved chair given to him by his constituents at Greenwich, the terracotta plaque of his old friend Cardinal Manning, which had hung near the Roman Catholic collection in the iron library, and his treasured painting of Döllinger were all given their place; to these were added busts, statues and pictures of Gladstone himself. This was all part of the deliberate attempt to establish meaningful links between the founder and the permanent buildings established as the national memorial to him.

In the less ornate design of the hostel there is an attempt to continue Gladstone's philosophy for the first hostel (the old Grammar School), that simple residential accommodation is all that is required for the serious student, for Gladstone believed 'that luxurious living is not conducive to the well being or the increased intellectual activity of those whom the institution is intended to benefit'. The four statues of Gladstone's greater mentors and masters which were to adorn the outer walls, embellishments to which some had objected, were to be the final touch. Aristotle, Augustine, Dante and Bishop Butler all had made their contribution to the formation of Gladstone, the churchman, statesman and lifelong student.

The official opening of St Deiniol's took place on 14 October 1902, just three years after the laying of the foundation stone. Earl Spencer, presiding over the gathering, moved two resolutions. The first was: 'That this meeting records its veneration for Mr Gladstone's life and character in memory of whom the nation has erected this Building'. The second resolution stated: 'That this meeting recalls with gratitude and admiration Mr Gladstone's lifelong devotion to the cause of those higher interests of mankind, which also he desired to promote by the foundation of St Deiniol's Library'.

A little after this great event James Bryce wrote to Stephen Gladstone in answer to an invitation to become an 'honorary associate' of St Deiniol's that he would 'feel highly honoured by being connected in any way with the admirable foundation which your Father's noble love of learning and desire to help all who seek to prosecute theological and historical studies led him to establish. It is a memorial equally of his piety and the amplitude of his thoughts and purposes'.

A letter from the King to Lord Spencer, as Chairman of the National Gladstone Memorial Fund, was sent to the trustees. It states: 'His Majesty trusts it will be possible before long to raise a sum sufficient for the proper keeping up of the Library and likewise for the erection of a new hostel'. The King, wrote Lord Spencer, 'has always taken much interest in the Gladstone Memorial'.

The hostel, which was recognised by the library trustees as an essential part of Gladstone's vision, had prompted Stephen Gladstone to write to the secretary of the memorial committee: 'The present Hostel must be replaced before very long, if possible, with the Dwelling Portion which would make it [the Library] complete'.

Work on the hostel eventually began in 1904, the cost of it being met entirely by Gladstone's children. It was to provide suitable but simple accommodation for residential guests, including a number of study bedrooms, communal facilities and all the required domestic accommodation and a small chapel. Its design was in keeping with the library but a little simpler both externally and internally. It was not meant to be of quite the same dignity in design as that part which constituted the National Memorial to Mr Gladstone, nor was it to compete with that memorial, for this was the family memorial to their much loved father.

By September 1906 the residence was complete and was officially opened on 3 January 1907. King Edward VII visited the completed St Deiniol's Residential Library on 15 May 1908. So Gladstone's vision in its permanent form, the only residential library of its kind in the world, was established in Hawarden.

Gladstone had made it clear to the trustees he appointed to fulfil his vision that they and, through the provisions in the foundation deed their successors, in fulfilling their trusteeship must 'move with the times'. In fulfilling the purpose for which St Deiniol's was created they must be ready to adapt and grow and so it has been for a hundred years.

Growth in all aspects of the library's work illustrates the development of a living institution firmly linked with its founder and rooted in his vision and in history but continuing to grow to meet new and changing needs in the three essential areas of its existence: the facilities, the book collection, the residential guests. Over the years numerous extensions and improvements have been carried out in connection with the residential facilities and the housing of the library. An unexpected addition to the National Memorial to Mr Gladstone at Hawarden was a further gift from the Gladstone Memorial Fund of the monument designed by John Hughes, consisting of a statue of Gladstone, with supporting figures of Erin and Classical Learning: and the Genius of Finance and Eloquence on a pedestal with carved decorative work. Hughes worked in Paris on the five figures cast in bronze but the First World War interrupted the work which was eventually completed in 1923. Dublin was the intended site for this great work but the political situation there made this impossible. In 1924 it was offered to the trustees of St Deiniol's Library, in the belief that the site of the National Memorial to Gladstone, St Deiniol's Library, was the ideal location for this great work. It was erected in 1925 in the library grounds abutting the main road through Hawarden and directly in line with the front entrance of the library.

Gladstone's library, his own books, are still at the very centre of the library's existence and purpose. The collection continues to grow around the 'core collection': it now contains in the region of 200,000 books and 50,000 pamphlets. Gladstone's own books remain the foundation of the accessions policy in the areas which make up his collection.

Residential guests are inseparable from Gladstone's vision and his stipulation that anyone, without regard to denominational affiliation is welcome to stay and study. That international family continues to grow: in recent years St Deiniol's Residential Library has welcomed, as guests, people from over forty nations of the world.

Notes

Chapter 1: Gladstone, Oratory and the Theatre

1. *Gladstone Diaries*, i, p. xlviii.
2. Ibid., p. 595.
3. *Max's Nineties*, ed. Osbert Lancaster (1958), plates 35–45.
4. Arthur Godley, *Reminiscences of Lord Kilbracken* (1931), p. 142.
5. *Gladstone Diaries*, i, pp. xlvii–xlix.
6. Special commemorative edition of the *Graphic*, 18 May 1898, p. 4.
7. The full title of this book is *The Academic Speaker: or A Selection of Parliamentary Debates, Orations, Odes, Scenes and Speeches from the Best Writers Proper to be Read and Recited by Youth at School. To Which is Prefixed Elements of Gesture; or Plain and Easy Directions for Keeping the Body in a Graceful Position and Acquiring a Simple and Unaffected Style of Action, Explained and Illustrated by Plates*. All quotations are here taken from the 4th edn (London, 1801).
8. In the USA they were reprinted in Philadelphia as late as 1857 and became a standard text in the emergent Departments of Speech and Rhetoric in American Universities. Thus James Bryce, Liberal MP for Tower Hamlets and then for South Aberdeen between 1880 and 1906, could rely upon a knowledge of these *Lectures* when, as Viscount Bryce and British Ambassador to Washington, he was called upon to address staff and students of the State University of Iowa in April 1910, on 'The Values of Speech'. This address is printed in full in *International University Reading Course: A Distinctive and Independent Library of Reference* (7 vols, London and Glasgow, n.d.), i, pp. 110–18.
9. *Gladstone Diaries*, i, p. 37.
10. Ibid., i, p. 57. From the diary we also learn that he had already struck out on his own in the Debating Society, unaided by text books. within two months of his arrival at Eton and had found it a more agreeable experience than he had expected. 'Sept. 29th, 1825: After 4 made my 1st or maiden Speech at the Society on education of the poor: funced [sic] less than I thought I should – by much.' *Gladstone Diaries* i, p. 15; see also Morley, *Gladstone* i, pp. 35–36.
11. Ibid., i, pp. 151–52.
12. Ibid., i, pp. 385–86.
13. Godley, *Reminiscences*, p. 147.

14. In his diary, under 23 February 1827, he says that he not only acquired this set-book, but that armed with it he was tutored in its application to recitation before an audience for three successive nights by Mr Keate in preparation for his first appearance in front of the sixth form. This recitation was delivered on 27 February. He records this as follows: 'went into school with Selwyn: found myself not at all in a fume; and went through my performance with tolerable comfort . . . Horrors of speaking chiefly in the name'. *Gladstone Diaries*, i, p. 103.
15. Walker, *Elements of Gesture*, p. vi.
16. Ibid., p. x.
17. *Gladstone Diaries*, i, p. 32.
18. On 12 November 1833, his diary records tersely, 'wrote a Paper on Racine'. This survives as BL, Gladstone Papers, Add. MS 44722, fos 274–75.
19. By 1879, when Gladstone embarked upon his first Midlothian campaign – travelling by train and speaking to mass-meeting after mass-meeting wherever it stopped – even the new 'melodramatic' rhetorical style of the 1850s and 1860s was nearing its limits, as both press reporters and theatre critics began to remark in the 1880s when complaining about inaudibility. Gladstone himself was rebuked on this account by the critic of the *New York Times* when describing his performance at the stupendous banquet given to celebrate the founding of the National Liberal Club.

> Mr Gladstone's Speech was a strong one, but it was also one of the most ineffective I ever heard him deliver. A discourse on finance is hardly the most appropriate means of stirring a body of men who have just dined, and to finance Mr Gladstone devoted a large part of the hour he occupied. For the first time I heard him speak twenty minutes without eliciting a general cheer. Finance was, perhaps, not altogether responsible for this. Mr Gladstone had, in fact, attempted an impossible task. He undertook to speak for an hour to an audience spread over a vast space which no human voice could for such a length of time completely fill. The Aquarium was never meant to be used for oratorical purposes. Its large size would make it unfit and every arrangement is perfectly adapted to add to the difficulty of hearing, including the flags which drooped from the roof almost to the tables. Mr Gladstone was aware that he had to make an unusual demand on his voice. He began in a tone that reached the outermost range of his hearers. The grand notes rolled out and spread through the space and filled it. But at the end of ten minutes they grew perceptibly weaker, and during the remainder of the hour not more than half the people heard every sentence. (*New York Times*, 20 May 1883.)

20. Since Edmund Kean's son, Charles, was born in 1811 and arrived at Eton when Gladstone had already been there for two years, it is unlikely that they ever became closely acquainted there. Rather does it seem that the first time Kean's prowess in his chosen profession made any serious impression upon him was in 1857 when he records this in his diary under 22 April, 'We went to the Princess's [Theatre] to see *Richard II*; some good acting and wonderful spectacle'. This is followed three days later by, 'Wrote to Mr C. Kean'. *Gladstone Diaries*, v, pp. 216–17. (See also n. 32 below.) In the course of his testimonial address to the Keans on behalf of the Old Etonians in 1862, Gladstone saw fit to apologise for having so rarely visited their performances, while excusing this on the grounds that in the evenings he had had so often 'to appear . . . in another place'.
21. See George Rowell, *Queen Victoria Goes to the Theatre* (London, 1978), especially pp. 47–65.

22. Irving produced Tennyson's *Queen Mary* in 1876; *The Cup* in 1881; and *Beckett* in 1893. His many essays, lectures (including the first ever to be given by an actor at Harvard and Oxford Universities) and public addresses have recently been collected, edited and printed by Jeffrey Richards under the title of *Sir Henry Irving: Theatre, Culture and Society* (Keele, 1994).

23. He went twice to the Théâtre Français: on 17 October to see Sarah Bernhardt in Victor Hugo's *Hernani* and on 25 October to see Cocquelin in Molière's *Les fourberies de Scapin*. The engraving of the auditorium at the Lyceum Theatre, on 12 December 1878, was made from a drawing by Alfred Bryan published in *The World* under the title of 'At the Play'. Gladstone is here shown seated between the Marquis of Hartington and the Duchesses of Sutherland and Manchester. Above them sat the Prince and Princess of Wales. The adjacent boxes at the upper level were occupied by Disraeli, Cardinal Manning and Oscar Wilde. Among the many distinguished people seated in the stalls were Lord Rosebery, the Marquis of Queensbury, the Duke of Beaufort, W.S. Gilbert, James Whistler, J.E. Millais, Anthony Trollope and Wilkie Collins. A key to the names and placement of everyone depicted in this drawing is provided by A.E. Wilson in *The Lyceum* (London, 1952), p. 201.

24. Bram Stoker, *Personal Reminiscences of Henry Irving* (2 vols, London, 1906). *The Life of Henry Irving*, by his stage manager, Austin Brereton, was published in 1908.

25. Writing in *The Theatre: A Monthly Review and Magazine*, on 1 May 1879, Clement Scott began his editorial ('Echoes from the Green Room') as follows: 'The allegation that cultured persons have ceased to go to the play continues to be at variance with the facts. Last month Mr Gladstone went twice to the Lyceum to see *Hamlet*, and Mr Tennyson was observed to applaud Mr Irving's performance with particular warmth.' (New series, 2, p. 267.)

26. Stoker, *Personal Reminiscences of Henry Irving*, i, pp. 167–68.

27. Ibid., ii, p. 27.

28. His Downing Street 'Breakfast Book' has survived and is presently in the library at Hawarden Castle in Sir William Gladstone's care. The page headed '29th June 1882' contains nine signatures including that of Henry Irving. His fellow guests were R.W. Church, George Curzon, H. d'Orleans, J.A. Godley, Lord Grenville, Henry Parkes, Alberta Ponsonby, Mary G. Ponsonby.

29. See Stoker, *Personal Reminiscences of Henry Irving*, ii, p. 24.

30. Esme Wingfield-Stratford, *Before the Lamps Went Out* (London, 1945), p. 212.

31. Stoker, *Personal Reminiscences of Henry Irving*, ii, p. 37.

32. Stoker printed a facsimile of the postcard from Gladstone containing this request on 18 November 1890. In it, he cites as a precedent – 'a post which C. Kean once gave me', and then adds 'and which alone would make me sure to hear.' (Ibid., ii, facing p. 28.) Was this the subject of Gladstone's letter to Charles Kean written on 24 April 1857 and recorded in his diary? See note 20 above. If so, deafness could not have prompted it then.

33. Stoker, *Personal Reminiscences of Henry Irving*, ii, pp. 29–32.

Chapter 3: Gladstone and Disraeli

1. For a fuller account see Robert Blake, *Disraeli* (1966).

Chapter 4: Gladstone and the Working Man

1.   Flora Thompson, *Lark Rise to Candleford* (Oxford, 1945), p. 55.
2.   Working man has more self-reliant overtones than the modern 'worker'. The change in usage is not unimportant.
3.   *The Times*, 7 September 1891, 7 f.
4.   Samuel Smiles, *Self-Help* (1859).
5.   For Ruskin's visit to Hawarden, see *Some Hawarden Letters, 1878–1913*, ed. L. March-Phillipps and B. Christian (1917), pp. 5–38.
6.   See Georgina Battiscombe, *Mrs Gladstone: The Portrait of a Marriage* (1956), pp. 129–32.
7.   For thirty years he was a regular visitor at Millbank Prison; and when his local crossing sweeper, the lowest of the low, fell sick, he was visited by the Chancellor of the Exchequer, Herbert, Viscount Gladstone, *After Thirty Years* (1928), p. 66.
8.   At a parliamentary level, Gladstone made plain that his support for allotments was of long standing. At village level, he eschewed the subject, except to draw attention to the practical inferiority or inconvenience of allotments.
9.   Machine labour, he held, impoverishes the mind, whereas hand labour helps develop the mind.
10. It was not the poverty of the urban working man which weighed on Gladstone's mind, but rather, as he wrote at the time of the Plug Plot (semi-Chartist) disturbances of 1845, their alienation: 'This is the time when we may reflect on the thorough rottenness, socially speaking, of the system which gathers together huge masses of population having no other tie to the classes above them than that of employment, of high money payments constituting a great moral temptation in times of prosperity, and then reductions in adversity which seem like robberies, and which the people have no discipline or training to endure', Gladstone to Catherine Gladstone, 18 August 1842; *Gladstone to His Wife*, ed. A. Tilney Bassett (1936), p. 44.
11. One party of 1500 came to a fête at Hawarden from Cornwall and Torquay, *The Times*, 17 August 1894, p. 6e. The working men of Derby appeared with a dessert service of Derby china, specially manufactured for the occasion.
12. He did not disapprove of Sunday cycling, and opened Hawarden Park to cyclists on Sunday, though closing it to ordinary tourists, J. Ewing Ritchie, *The Real Gladstone: An Anecdotal Biography* (1898), p. 200.
13. From Victor Percy Graham of 1 White Friars, Chester, 10 February 1886. Victor said he had seen Mr Gladstone at Chester Station, adding: 'Papa says you are the greatest man in the world': Glynne-Gladstone MSS, General Correspondence, Anonymous Collection, Clwyd County Record Office, Hawarden. See Simon Peaple 'Dear Mr Gladstone' (unpublished Ph.D. thesis), for Gladstone's fan mail.
14. The 'sale of chips and wood' from a 'tree felled by Mr Gladstone' was 'put on a business footing in the Estate Office', the proceeds going to Mrs Gladstone's orphanage, Herbert, Viscount Gladstone, *After Thirty Years*, p. 63.

15. Letter of 3 October 1877, Glynne-Gladstone MSS, Anonymous Collection, Clwyd County Record Office. We are much indebted to the County Archivists for their generous guidance.

16. Letter, probably 1886, the thirty-third in the bundle dated January 1885-March 1896, Glynne-Gladstone MSS.

17. Letter of 27 December 1884, in bundle dated 1870–1884, Glynne-Gladstone MSS.

18. Present from R.C. Rosenberg, marked in Gladstone's hand 'thanked, Dec. 30th, 1882' (29 December was Gladstone's birthday, so the flowers were a birthday present), Glynne-Gladstone MSS.

19. Probably summer 1886: from the 27th letter in the bundle marked January 1885-March 1896, Glynne-Gladstone MSS.

20. Ripples from the cult spread far outside Gladstone's immediate circle. Lord Derby, Disraeli's Foreign Secretary till 1878, and not a member of Gladstone's government until 1882, noted in his diary (4 May 1881): 'Many letters & notes – some very odd. One man, a perfect stranger, not even from Lancashire, writes to me to express his wish that I would obtain for him an autograph of Mr Gladstone!'

21. Including a semi-feudal generosity on family occasions. On the marriage of his eldest son, he feasted 550 of his cottage tenants on the first day, and upwards of 400 on the second, Ritchie, *The Real Gladstone*, p. 207. In 1887, he gave a Jubilee treat to all Hawarden parishioners of the same age or more as the Queen, providing dinner and tea in a tent in front of the castle for about 250 *The Times*, 31 August 1887, p. 10a.

Chapter 5: Gladstone and America

1. On the international repercussions of the Civil War, David P. Crook, *The North, the South and the Powers, 1861–1865* (New York, 1974) is a sound brief account. Peter J. Parish, *The American Civil War* (London and New York, 1975), ch. 13, analyses the cross-currents of international opinion on the war, while Belle B. Sideman and Lillian Friedman, eds, *Europe Looks at the Civil War* (New York, 1960), offers a wide range of contemporary views. On British attitudes and policy, see Brian Jenkins, *Britain and the War for the Union* (2 vols, Montreal, 1974–80).

2. Abraham Lincoln, Message to Congress, 4 July 1861, Roy P. Basler, ed., *The Collected Works of Abraham Lincoln* (8 vols, New Jersey, 1953), iv, p. 439.

3. Parish, *American Civil War*, p. 386.

4. See, for example, the Crittenden-Johnson Resolutions passed by large majorities in both Houses of Congress in July 1861, *Congressional Globe*, 37th Congress, 1st session, pp. 222–23.

5. Sarah A. Wallace and Frances E. Gillespie, eds, *The Journal of Benjamin Moran, 1857–1865* (2 vols, Chicago, 1948–1949), ii, p. 1220; Carlyle, quoted in Donaldson Jordan and Edwin J. Pratt, *Europe and the American Civil War* (London, 1931), p. 73.

6. Worthington C. Ford, ed., *A Cycle of Adams Letters, 1861–1865* (2 vols, Boston, 1920), i, p. 192.

7. Sarah F. Hughes, ed., *Letters and Recollections of John Murray Forbes* (2 vols, Boston, 1899), ii, pp. 17–18.

8. John Morley, *Life of William Ewart Gladstone* (3 vols, London, 1903), ii, p. 71. Among the numerous Gladstone biographies, I have found Morley's classic work and Richard Shannon, *Gladstone, 1809–1865* (London, 1982) the most illuminating on his attitude to the American Civil War. I have also relied heavily on the important essay by Cedric Collyer, 'Gladstone and the American Civil War', *Proceedings of the Leeds Philosophical and Literary Society* (1944–52), pp. 583–94.

9. Parish, *American Civil War*, p. 388.

10. *Gladstone Diaries*, vi, pp. 138–39.

11. Letters to Duchess of Sutherland and Cyrus Field are quoted in Collyer, 'Gladstone and the American Civil War', p. 586; the Manchester speech is quoted ibid., p. 585.

12. Ibid., p. 585.

13. Letter to the Duke of Argyll, quoted ibid., p. 588; letter to Speaker of the House of Commons, quoted in Shannon, *Gladstone*, p. 476.

14. Morley, *Gladstone*, ii, p. 84 n. 1.

15. Collyer, 'Gladstone and the American Civil War', pp. 585–88.

16. Morley, *Gladstone*, ii, p. 77 n. 1.

17. Ibid., p. 71; Collyer, 'Gladstone and the American Civil War', pp. 584–85.

18. Shannon, *Gladstone*, pp. 440, 466–67, 514–15; Morley, *Gladstone*, ii, pp. 72–73.

19. Lincoln, Second Inaugural, 4 March 1865, *Collected Works*, viii, pp. 332–33.

20. Keith Robbins, *John Bright* (London, 1979), p. 164.

21. Collyer, 'Gladstone and the American Civil War', pp. 593–94. For a thoughtful discussion of Gladstone's inclination to treat the Civil War as simply a political contest, and to neglect its importance as a social revolution, see Morley, *Gladstone*, ii, p. 70.

22. The most thorough modern account of the 'intervention crisis' of 1862 is Howard Jones, *Union in Peril: The Crisis over British Intervention in the Civil War* (North Carolina, 1992). A good brief account and evaluation may be found in Jenkins, *Britain and the War for the Union*, ii, pp. 167–82.

23. There are good accounts of the background and circumstances of the Newcastle speech in Morley, *Gladstone*, ii, pp. 76–80; and Shannon, *Gladstone*, pp. 464–70.

24. Morley, *Gladstone*, ii, pp. 75–77; Shannon, *Gladstone*, pp. 462, 466.

25. Collyer, 'Gladstone and the American Civil War', pp. 588–90.

26. Jenkins, *Britain and the War for the Union*, ii, pp. 172–73; *Journal of Benjamin Moran*, ii, p. 1078.

27. Henry Adams, *Education of Henry Adams* (New York, 1931), pp. 152–66. Adams' scintillating narrative of the intervention crisis is scathing in its criticism of the main British participants, but scarcely to be treated as an altogether fair or reliable account.

28. Morley, *Gladstone*, ii, pp. 85–86.

29. Gladstone to Charles Sumner, 5 November 1863, quoted in Shannon, *Gladstone*, p. 494; *The Times*, 3 May 1864.

30. Morley, *Gladstone*, ii, pp. 81–82. See also Henry Adams, *Education*, pp. 155–57, and especially pp. 164–66, for a characteristically scornful and highly coloured account.

31. Morley, *Gladstone*, ii, pp. 70, 79.

32. Gladstone to Charles Sumner, 25 August 1865, quoted in Shannon, *Gladstone*, p. 553.

33. Collyer, 'Gladstone and the American Civil War', pp. 592–93.
34. Morley, *Gladstone*, ii, p. 124.
35. Hugh Tulloch, *James Bryce's American Commonwealth: The Anglo-American Background* (Woodbridge, Suffolk, 1988), pp. 70–71.
36. Francis H. Herrick, 'Gladstone and the Concept of the "English-Speaking Peoples"', *Journal of British Studies*, 12 (1972), pp. 150–56; Tulloch, *Bryce's American Commonwealth*, p. 69.
37. W.E. Gladstone, 'Kin Beyond the Sea', *North American Review*, 127 (1878), pp. 179–212. The comparison between the British and American constitutions is on pp. 185–86.
38. Ibid., pp. 186–89.

Chapter 6: Gladstone and Ireland

1. J.C. Beckett, *The Making of Modern Ireland, 1603–1923* (London, 1966), pp. 397–98.
2. For example A.B Cooke and John Vincent (eds), *The Governing Passion: Cabinet Government and Party Politics in Britain, 1885–6* (Brighton, 1974).
3. A.J.P. Taylor, *English History, 1914–1945* (London, 1985), p. 213.
4. Lord Eversley, *Gladstone and Ireland* (London, 1912); J. L. Hammond, *Gladstone and the Irish Nation* (London, 1938; reissued London, 1964).
5. Eversley, *Gladstone and Ireland*, p. 383.
6. Hammond, *Gladstone and the Irish Nation*, preface, pp. 721, 726.
7. Ibid., p. 67.
8. Ibid., pp. 68–69.
9. H.G.C. Matthew, *Gladstone*, i, *1809–1874* (Oxford, 1986), p. 144.
10. D.G. Boyce, *Nineteenth-Century Ireland: The Search for Stability* (Dublin 1990), p. 147.
11. Brian Walker, *Ulster Politics: The Formative Years, 1868–1886* (Belfast, 1989), p. 48.
12. Ibid., pp. 71–73.
13. Eversley, *Gladstone and Ireland*, pp. 23, 45.
14. Hammond, *Gladstone and the Irish Nation*, p. 67.
15. Walker, *Ulster Politics*, pp. 89–90.
16. Ibid., pp. 113–16.
17. Hammond, *Gladstone and the Irish Nation*, p. 85.
18. Ibid., p. 68.
19. *Dublin Daily Express*, 8 November 1877.
20. Ibid.
21. Hammond, *Gladstone and the Irish Nation*, p. 162.
22. Ibid., p. 248.
23. Ibid., pp. 254–56.
24. This, and most of what follows on Gladstone and the land question, is based on two excellent articles by Allen Warren, 'Gladstone, Land and Social Reconstruction in Ireland, 1881–1887', *Parliamentary History*, 2 (1983), pp. 153–73; and 'Forster, the Liberals and New Directions in Irish Policy, 1880–1882', ibid., 6 (1987), pp. 95–126.
25. Warren, 'Forster, the Liberals and New Directions', pp. 110–11.
26. Ibid., pp. 113–14.

27. Warren, 'Gladstone, Land and Social Reconstruction', p. 162.
28. Hammond, *Gladstone and the Irish Nation*, p. 115.
29. H.C.G. Matthew (ed.), *The Gladstone Diaries*, xi, *June 1883-December 1886* (Oxford, 1990), p. 658.
30. *Gladstone Diaries*, x, *January 1881–June 1883* (Oxford, 1990), p. cxxiii; xi, pp. 87, 192.
31. *Gladstone Diaries*, x, pp. 451, 455.
32. Warren, 'Gladstone, Land and Social Reconstruction', 166–67.
33. Alan O'Day, *Parnell and the First Home Rule Episode, 1884–87* (Dublin, 1986), pp. 90–91.
34. Ibid., pp. 113–14.
35. Quoted in D. George Boyce, 'Parnell and Bagehot', in D. George Boyce and Alan O'Day (eds), *Parnell in Perspective* (London, 1991), p. 120.
36. O'Day, *Parnell and the First Home Rule Episode*, p. 128.
37. Warren, 'Gladstone, Land and Social Reconstruction', pp. 167–69.
38. D. George Boyce, *The Irish Question and British Politics, 1868–1996* (London, 1996), p. 33.
39. R.V. Comerford, 'The Parnell Era, 1883–91', in W.E. Vaughan (ed.), *A New History of Ireland*, vi, *Ireland under the Union*, pt 2, *1870–1921* (Oxford, 1996), pp. 63–64.
40. D. George Boyce, 'Parnell and Bagehot', p. 121.
41. Ibid., p. 122.
42. D. George Boyce, *Nineteenth-Century Ireland*, pp. 179–80.
43. Pauric Travers, 'Parnell and the Ulster Question', in Donal McCartney (ed.), *Parnell: The Politics of Power* (Dublin, 1991), ch. 4.
44. See the speeches in the publication *Ulster Unionist Convention, June 1892* (Belfast, 1892), passim.
45. H.C.G. Matthew, *Gladstone Diaries*, x, p. cxlvi.
46. A.W. Hutton and H.J. Cohen (eds), *The Speeches of the Right Hon. W.E. Gladstone on Home Rule, Criminal Law, Welsh and Irish Nationality, National Debt and the Queen's Reign, 1888–89* (London, 1902), pp. 67–97.
47. D. George Boyce, *Ireland, 1828–1923: From Ascendancy to Democracy* (Oxford, 1992), p. 59.
48. Speech at Hastings, 17 March 1891, 'The Finance of the Government, the Irish Party, and Mr Parnell', in Hutton and Cohen, *Speeches of W.E. Gladstone*, pp. 351–63.
49. H.C.G. Matthew (ed.), *The Gladstone Diaries*, xii, *1887–1891* (Oxford, 1994), p. 354.
50. Hammond, *Gladstone and the Irish Nation*, pp. 309–10.
51. Ibid., p. 544.

Chapter 7: Gladstone, Wales and the New Radicalism

1. *Ardrossan and Saltcoats Herald*, 27 May 1887 (written by Hardie under the pseudonym of 'Trapper').
2. *Labour Leader*, 28 May 1898.
3. See Roy Hattersley, *Choose Freedom* (London, 1987).
4. *The Times*, 6 June 1887; ibid., 14 September 1892.

5. William George, *My Brother and I* (London, 1958), p. 176; A.S.T. Griffith-Boscawen, *Fourteen Years in Parliament* (London, 1907), p. 47.

6. See especially D.A. Hamer, *Liberal Politics in the Age of Gladstone and Rosebery* (1972), on this theme.

7. Ibid., pp. 173ff.

8. Henry Richard, *Letters on the Social and Political Condition of Wales* (London, 1867), p. 80. This was a published version of articles that appeared in the *Morning and Evening Star* in 1866.

9. See C.S. Miall, *Henry Richard MP* (London, 1889), p. 143.

10. *The Times*, 20 August 1873. On these themes, see Kenneth O. Morgan, *Wales in British Politics, 1868–1922* (3rd edn, Cardiff, 1980), especially chapter 2 and 3.

11. See Kenneth O. Morgan, 'The Member for Wales: Stuart Rendel, 1834–1913', Hartwell Jones lecture for 1984, *Transactions of the Honourable Society of Cymmrodorion* (1984), pp. 149–71.

12. *Parliamentary Debates*, 3rd series, 201, pp. 1295ff.

13. *Gladstone Diaries,* introduction, pp. xxxiv–xxxvi; R.T. Shannon, *Gladstone* (London 1982), i, p. 317. Gladstone added that 'It would be an error to recognise a knowledge of the Welsh tongue as dispensing with any of the still more essential qualifications for the Episcopal office'.

14. Gladstone to the Archbishop of York, 12 January 1870, BL, Gladstone Papers, Add. MS 44424, fol. 90.

15. Gladstone to the Bishop of Durham, 28 December 1882, BL, Gladstone Papers, Add. MS 44478, fos 271–72.

16. Gladstone to H.A. Bruce, 18 January 1870, BL, Gladstone Papers, Add. MS 44086, fol. 123.

17. Joshua Hughes to Gladstone, 20 March 1870, BL, Gladstone Papers, Add. MS 44425, fol. 29.

18. Lord Aberdare to Gladstone, 31 December 1882, BL, Gladstone Papers, Add. MS 44087, fos 165–70.

19. See Kenneth O. Morgan, 'Gladstone and Wales', *Welsh History Review*, 1 (1960), pp. 72–73.

20. *Parliamentary Debates*, 3rd series, 260, p. 1772 (4 May 1881).

21. Ibid., 247, p. 1160 (1 July 1879).

22. Morgan, *Wales in British Politics*, pp. 48–49.

23. Ibid., pp. 52–53. Aberystwyth was at first granted only £2500, in contrast to £4000 each for Bangor and Cardiff, but the new Conservative government under Salisbury provided the balance of £15,000 in August 1885. This followed a great fire which burned down much of the old college at Aberystwyth.

24. See Kenneth O. Morgan, 'The Liberal Unionists in Wales', *National Library Wales Journal*, 16 (1969), pp. 163–71.

25. A.C. Humphreys-Owen to Rendel, 20 June 1886, National Library of Wales, Rendel Papers, 14, fol. 293.

26. The outstanding work on this theme is Michael Freeden, *The New Liberalism* (Oxford, 1976).

27. *Parliamentary Debates*, 3rd series, 336, p. 135 (15 May 1889).

28. *Eisteddfod Genedlaethol y Cymry: Cofnodion*, edited by E. Vincent Evans, National Eisteddfod Association (Liverpool, 1889), pp. xxiv–xxx, for the text.

29. Cf. Lord to Lady Aberdare, 3 June 1887, *Letters of Lord Aberdare* (Oxford, 1902), ii, p. 224.

30. *Parliamentary Debates*, 3rd series, 250, pp. 1264ff (20 February 1891).
31. See Morgan, *Wales in British Politics*, pp. 124–26.
32. *Parliamentary Debates*, 4th series, 9, p. 277 (23 February 1893).
33. Gladstone to Asquith, 10 November 1893, BL, Gladstone Papers, Add. MS 44459, fol. 154; draft Welsh Disestablishment Bill, 1893, Bodleian Library, Asquith Papers, box 14.
34. *The Times*, 19 June 1895; Morgan, *Wales in British Politics*, pp. 154, 268–69.
35. T.A. Jenkins, *Gladstone, Whiggery and the Liberal Party, 1874–1886* (Oxford, 1987), especially pp. 141ff.
36. On this, see H.C.G. Matthew, *The Liberal Imperialists* (Oxford, 1973).
37. See Morgan, 'Gladstone and Wales', p. 65.
38. Hamer, *Liberal Politics*, pp. 195ff, is excellent on this.
39. Gladstone to Rendel, 12 November 1892, BL, Gladstone Papers, Add. MS 44549, fol. 39.
40. W.E. Gladstone, 'Kin Beyond the Sea', *North American Review*, 127 (September–October 1878).
41. J. Morley, *Gladstone* (London, 1903), iii, p. 491. Also see the valuable thesis by my former pupil, M.M. Gerlach, 'British Liberal Leaders and the United States, 1874–1898' (unpublished D.Phil. thesis, University of Oxford, 1982), especially pp. 223–76.
42. For an interesting analysis of Liberalism in 1914, see Michael Bentley, *The Climax of Liberal Politics* (London, 1987), especially the final chapter, 'Arguments' which begins with a treatment of Gladstone.

Chapter 8: Gladstone and Garibaldi

1. J. Morley, *The Life of William Ewart Gladstone* (3 vols, London, 1903), ii, pp. 109, 114. Rather more than half of this essay derives from an essay entitled 'Garibaldi in England: The Politics of Italian Enthusiasm', published in *Studies in Italian History in Honour of Denis Mack Smith*, ed. J.A. Davis and P.A. Ginsborg (Cambridge, 1991), pp. 184–216. There will be found acknowledgment of the help I received in working on this subject, a fuller account of Garibaldi's visit of 1864 and additional references.
2. The theme of the revolutionary saint is developed in A. Soboul, 'Religious Feeling and Popular Cults during the French Revolution: "Patriot Saints" and Martyrs for Liberty', in S. Wilson (ed.), *Saints and Their Cults* (Cambridge, 1983), pp. 217–32.
3. G. Sacerdote, *Le vita di Giuseppe Garibaldi* (Milan, 1933), p. 22 and passim, for the whole paragraph; pictures on pp. 23, 830, 843, 848, 945.
4. G. Garibaldi, *Autobiography* (trans. A. Werner, 3 vols, London 1889), iii, p. 455 (J.W. Mario's Supplement).
5. The fundamental account is in G. Guerzoni, *Garibaldi* (2 vols, Florence, 1882), ii, pp. 338–93. In English, as well as Denis Mack Smith's *Garibaldi* (London, 1957), ch. 13, the most important treatments are C. Hibbert's in his *Garibaldi and his Enemies* (London, 1965), pp. 339–51, and J. Ridley's in his *Garibaldi* (London, 1974), ch. 36. See the extensive bibliography by A.P. Campanella, *Giuseppe Garibaldi e la tradizione garibaldina: una bibliografia dal 1807 al 1970* (2 vols, Geneva, 1971), ii, pp. 678–92.
6. Shaftesbury's diary, 12 June 1860, E. Hodder, *The Life and Work of the Seventh Earl*

of Shaftesbury, KG (popular edition, London, 1892), p. 563; *The Times*, 22 April 1864; G.B.A.M. Finlayson, *The Seventh Earl of Shaftesbury, 1801–1885* (London, 1981), p. 458.

7. *The Times*, 19 April 1864; Hodder, *Shaftesbury*, p. 596; *Bedford Times and Bedfordshire Independent*, 19 April 1864.

8. *The Times*, 9 April 1864.

9. *Bedford Times*, special edition, 19 April 1864.

10. From a circular requesting donations for the 'Excursionists' of 1860 (Bishopsgate Institute, George Howell Library, no. 3956 collection of newspaper cuttings). The reluctance to stress the Protestant element in this story has been partly due to the secularism of most modern historiography, especially in Italy, and partly to the rise of the ecumenical spirit and of Christian Democracy. Recent English writing has somewhat redressed the balance for other periods of the nineteenth century: see esp. J.P. Parry, *Democracy and Religion: Gladstone and the Liberal Party, 1867–1875* (Cambridge, 1986). For English attitudes to Italy see my brief early manifesto, 'Il Risorgimento protestante', *Rassegna storica del Risorgimento*, 43 (1956), pp. 231–33; my *England and Italy, 1859–60* (London, 1961), especially. pp. 22–25; and, more extensively, C.T. McIntire, *England against the Papacy, 1858–1861* (Cambridge, 1983).

11. Cavour to E. D'Azeglio, 1 August 1860: *Cavour e l'Inghilterra: carteggio con V.E. D'Azeglio* (2 vols, Bologna, 1933), ii, p. 119.

12. *Scotsman*, 19 April 1864.

13. For this and the quotation later in the paragraph: Granville to the Queen, 21 April 1864, ed. G.E. Buckle, *The Letters of Queen Victoria . . . between . . . 1862 and 1878* (2 vols, London, 1926), i, pp. 175–76.

14. H. Cunningham, *The Volunteer Force* (London, 1975), p. 108, and many references in the Bishopsgate Institute material (see n. 10 above).

15. E.g. references in J. Fyfe (ed.), *Autobiography of John McAdam, 1806–1883: With Selected Letters*, Scottish History Society (Edinburgh, 1980), pp. 69, 70, 73; *Scotsman*, 19 April 1864, describing a masonic deputation being received at Stafford House.

16. *Beehive* 9 April 1864. Cf. the large collection of press cuttings about Italian aspects of working-class political activity in the Bishopsgate Institute (see n. 10 above).

17. G.M. Trevelyan, *Garibaldi's Defence of the Roman Republic* (London 1912), p. 110 and n.; *Punch*, 23 April, 1864.

18. E.g., *Bedford Times*, 19 April 1864; *Scotsman*, 4 April 1864.

19. *Reynolds's Newspaper*, 1 May 1864. Generally on Garibaldi's appeal, C. Seton-Watson, 'Garibaldi's British Image', *Atti del LI congresso di storia del Risorgimento italiano* (Genoa, 10–13 November 1982), pp. 247–58.

20. Unfortunately I do not know exactly when these fashions began.

21. H.W. Rudman, *Italian Nationalism and English Letters* (London, 1940), p. 327 (citing W.W. Vernon's *Recollections of Seventy-Two Years*).

22. See A. Oliver, *The Victorian Staffordshire Figure: A Guide for Collectors* (London, 1971), especially p. 162.

23. This information comes from observation, and from working through current directories and yellow pages, and is certainly incomplete. I have not pursued the question systematically back into nineteenth-century sources. See E.R. Delderfield, *British Inn Signs and Their Stories* (Dawlish, 1965).

24. The obvious source is *The Times* of 12 April 1864, but I have used also the *Illustrated London News*, the *Beehive*, *Reynolds's Newspaper*, the *Scotsman* and *Punch*.
25. Munby's diary for 11 April 1864, Trinity College Library, Cambridge. See D. Hudson, *Munby, Man of Two Worlds: The Life and Diaries of Arthur J. Munby, 1828–1910* (London, 1972), pp. 186–87.
26. See e.g. D.A. Jánossy, *Great Britain and Kossuth* (Budapest, 1937), especially pp. 83–112.
27. Hudson, *Munby*, p. 187. The comparison is also found, e.g., in *The Times* and *Reynolds's*.
28. Palmerston's diary, 11 April 1864, Broadlands papers, consulted in the National Register of Archives.
29. Morley, *Gladstone*, ii, p. 109.
30. Palmerston to Russell, 6 April 1864, Public Record Office, Russell Papers, 30/22/15.
31. For this paragraph chiefly *The Times*. On the Queen and the Prince of Wales, E. Longford, *Queen Victoria* (London, 1964), pp. 363–64; P. Magnus, *King Edward the Seventh* (London, 1964), p. 84.
32. Palmerston to Queen Victoria, 18 April 1864, *Letters of Queen Victoria, 1862–1878*, i, p. 173.
33. *Punch*, 23 April 1864.
34. J. Cartwright (ed.), *The Journals of Lady Knightley of Fawsley, 1856–1884* (London, 1915), pp. 75, 275, reveals the Commons episode, thereby explaining Granville's cryptic remark to the Queen: 'It is much for the dignity of Parliament, that some demonstrations in Garibaldi's favour, which were threatened, did not take place'. *Letters of Queen Victoria, 1862–1878*, i, p. 176. Cf. Malmesbury, *Memoirs of an ex-Minister*, p. 595, on similar disputes in the Lords.
35. H.E. Manning, *The Visit of Garibaldi to England: A Letter to the Right Hon. Edward Cardwell, MP* (London, 1864), republished in Manning's *Miscellanies* (3 vols, 1887–88), i, pp. 123–48, quotation below from p. 141; Malmesbury, *Memoirs*, p. 594; F.M.L. Thompson, *English Landed Society in the Nineteenth Century* (London, 1963), pp. 272–73.
36. G.E. Buckle, *The Life of Benjamin Disraeli, Earl of Beaconsfield*, iv (London, 1916), p. 327. Cf. J. Vincent, *The Formation of the Liberal Party, 1857–1868* (London, 1966), pp. 261–67; and K.T. Hoppen, 'Tories, Catholics and the General Election of 1859', *Historical Journal*, 13 (1970), pp. 48–67.
37. Marx to Engels, 19 April 1864, *Karl Marx-Frederick Engels: Collected Works*, xli, (1985), pp. 516–17.
38. Guerzoni, *Garibaldi*, ii, pp. 339–40 and 340n.; Finlayson, *Shaftesbury*, p. 458; Munby diary, 18 April 1864; Bishopsgate Institute material (see n. 10 above) and Cowen MSS (see below, n. 40).
39. Guerzoni, *Garibaldi*, ii, pp. 341, 343–46; Palmerston to Russell, 21 January 1861; Hudson to Russell, 2 February 1861, Public Record Office, Russell Papers, 30/22/21 and 30/22/68.
40. The Queen to Granville, 21 April 1864, echoing if not exactly quoting Palmerston's letter to her of 4 April 1864: Granville to the Queen, 21 April 1864, *Letters of Queen Victoria, 1862–1878*, i, pp. 175, 169, 176. I have dealt fully with the differences among Garibaldi's sympathisers in the essay cited in n. 1 above. The principal primary source for them is the Cowen MSS, now in the

Tyne and Wear Record Office, Newcastle-upon-Tyne. I am grateful to the archivists there for their help.

41. Taylor to Joseph Cowen, 25 April 1864, Cowen MSS, A 810.

42. R.A.J. Walling (ed.), *The Diaries of John Bright* (London, 1930), p. 277 (19 April 1864).

43. The Queen to Russell, 13 April 1864, *Letters of Queen Victoria, 1862–1878*, i, p. 169.

44. *The Times*, 14 April 1864. In my essay referred to in n. 1, I have expanded on the serious and embarrassing international situation in which the government found itself. For further information: W.E. Mosse, *The European Powers and the German Question, 1848–71* (Cambridge, 1958), especially. ch. 7; idem, 'Queen Victoria and her Ministers in the Schleswig-Holstein Crisis, 1863–1864', *English Historical Review*, 78 (1963), pp. 263–83; and K.A.P. Sandiford, 'The British Cabinet and the Schleswig-Holstein Crisis, 1863–1864', *History*, 58 (1973), pp. 360–83.

45. See, e.g., many letters in the Cowen MSS and in the correspondence of Mazzini, *Scritti editi ed inediti di Giuseppe Mazzini* (106 vols, Imola, 1906–73), vol. lxxviii.

46. Of the first-hand accounts, Guerzoni, *Garibaldi*, ii, pp. 373–81, has the chronology hopelessly muddled, but he was involved in the Italian side of the story and he also quoted in his footnotes the main English versions. For the English side, see Gladstone (*The Times*, 22 April, 11 May 1864), Seely (*The Times*, 21 April 1864), Shaen (*The Times*, 9 May, 1864) and Stansfeld in *The Review of Reviews*, 11 (1895), pp. 512–13. Ridley, *Garibaldi*, pp. 553–54, has made the only convincing reconstruction of the earliest stages of the intrigue, but I think there is more to be said of Seely's part.

47. J.R. Vincent, *Disraeli, Derby and the Conservative Party: Journals and Memoirs of Edward Henry, Lord Stanley, 1849–1869* (Hassocks, 1978), p. 372n.; R.T. Shannon, *Gladstone* (London, 1982), p. 503. Both practitioners have entries in the *Dictionary of National Biography*.

48. The *Scotsman*, 21 April 1864, gives the figure sixty; G.H.L. Le May, 'Mr Gladstone and Italy, to 1874', Gladstone Prize Essay, Bodleian Library, Oxford, p. 43n., cites thirty-two.

49. Gladstone's in *The Times*, 22 April, 11 May 1864, and other newspapers; Guerzoni, *Garibaldi*, ii, pp. 376–78 and nn.

50. Mazzini to Bagnasco, 3 May 1864, *Scritti di Giuseppe Mazzini*, lxxviii, p. 143.

51. *The Times*, 23 April 1864 (my italics).

52. Not only Guerzoni's account but Garibaldi's statements to radical sympathisers reveal his suspicions (e.g. Tyne and Wear Record Office, Cowen MSS, A 809, 810). But, having insisted in the early days that he was '*obbligato*' to leave England, he later wrote to *Il Movimento* denying that he had been put under pressure, Ridley, *Garibaldi*, p. 563.

53. *The Times*, 20, 22 April, 11 May 1864.

54. Cf. Gladstone's letter to Clarendon, 23 April 1864, BL, Gladstone Papers, Add. MS 44534, fol. 72, partly quoted in Morley, *Gladstone*, pp. 112–13. I cannot see how H.C.G. Matthew, in his introduction to vols v and vi of *The Gladstone Diaries* (Oxford, 1978), v, p. xxviii n., can write that this letter 'shows the extent of Gladstone's involvement in persuading Garibaldi of *the cabinet's* embarrassment at his presence in Britain' (my italics). It is certainly additional evidence of Gladstone's *involvement*. But Gladstone expresses in this letter his feeling of

grievance that Garibaldi has taken him for the spokesman of the Cabinet. To justify describing Gladstone's conduct in this affair as 'shuffling', ibid., p. xxviii, Matthew does not need this letter. At the least, Gladstone certainly found himself in an equivocal position. However, I have myself come to feel less critical of his role since I wrote my article 'Il governo inglese e la visita di Garibaldi in Inghilterra nel 1864', in V. Frosini (ed.), *Il Risorgimento e l'Europa: studi in onore di Alberto Maria Ghisalberti* (Catania, 1969), pp. 27–40. There (p. 38) I suggested that Gladstone misled his critics when he told them he knew nothing of any meeting at Stafford House on 17 April before 9 p.m., whereas his diary for that day (vi, p. 269) records: 'At Stafford House $5\frac{1}{4}$ – $6\frac{1}{2}$ & $9\frac{1}{4}$ – $12\frac{1}{2}$ on Garibaldi's movements'. However, having looked at the evidence again, it seems to me that the entry is reconcilable with his public statements, because what he was denying was first-hand knowledge of negotiations and of any meeting at Stafford House before 'the evening'.

55. Palmerston to the Queen, 18 April 1864, Granville to the Queen, 21 April 1864, *Letters of Queen Victoria*, 1862–1878, i, pp. 172–73, 176.

56. *The Times*, 20 April 1864 (Palmerston's statement, and also Clarendon's in the Lords), 21 April 1864 (Seely's), 22 April and 11 May 1864 (Gladstone's), 23 April 1864 (Shaftesbury's).

57. Mrs Chambers to Cowen, 4 May 1864, Tyne and Wear Record Office, Cowen MS A 823, a very important letter. This is exactly what Seely said publicly, *The Times*, 21 April 1864.

58. John Lang to Cowen, 19 April 1864, I. McFarlane to Cowen, 7 May 1864, Cowen MS A 796, A 826. The latter wrote, 'it is all over for the present heaven be praised'.

59. For Palmerston's letter see n. 55 above.

60. *Review of Reviews* (1895), p. 513. The old biography by J.L. LeB. and L.B. Hammond, *James Stansfeld: A Victorian Champion of Sex Equality* (London, 1932), ch. vi, is useful on the whole episode. See also B. Porter, *The Refugee Question in Mid-Victorian Politics* (Cambridge, 1979), pp. 203–5, 212. On the riots see S. Gilley, 'The Garibaldi Riots of 1862', *Historical Journal*, 16 (1973), pp. 697–732; F. Neal, The Birkenhead Garibaldi Riots of 1862', *Transactions of the Historic Society of Lancashire and Cheshire*, 131 (1981), pp. 87–111.

61. Seely in his explanations talked about six or eight towns, Gladstone of only three. But it would have been hard to choose even three major towns without a substantial Irish minority.

62. D.M. Schreuder, 'Gladstone and Italian Unification, 1848–70: The Making of a Liberal?', *English Historical Review*, 85 (1970), pp. 475–501, quotations from pp. 492–93. Schreuder also speaks, in reference to 1864, of Gladstone's 'extreme dislike for . . . Garibaldi'. This article seems to me a lamentable example of perverse and ill-informed revisionism. On p. 492, for example, Schreuder's argument depends on his belief that Cavour died in 1860.

63. Shannon, *Gladstone*, p. 502.

64. Gladstone to Manning, 2 July 1864, BL, Gladstone Papers, Add. MS 44534, fol. 97, quoted by Morley, *Gladstone*, ii, pp. 110–11; Shannon, *Gladstone*, p. 504.

65. I have been much helped here by the conversation of Dr E.F. Biagini, and his book *Liberty, Retrenchment and Reform: Popular Liberalism in the Age of Gladstone, 1850–1880* (Cambridge, 1992). Contrariwise, a member of Garibaldi's family told me that they thought his origins rather less humble than has been supposed.

66. Statement of Gladstone's to Ruskin, 1878, Morley, *Gladstone*, ii, p. 582; G. Cingari (ed.), *Garibaldi e il socialismo* (Bari, 1984), especially G. Giarrizzo's essay 'Il "Popolo" di Garibaldi', pp. 13–29; A. Briggs, *Victorian People* (London, 1954), p. 127.

67. See Matthew's introductions to *The Gladstone Diaries*, vols iii, v, vii, ix, x; idem, *Gladstone, 1809–1874* (Oxford, 1988); and Parry, *Democracy and Religion*.

68. Gladstone, 'Farini's *Stato Romano*', *Edinburgh Review*, 95 (1852), p. 382.

69. See n. 64 above. This sting in the tail of Gladstone's letter, which turns it into a sharp defence of Garibaldi, is *not* quoted by Schreuder in 'Gladstone and Italian Unification', p. 493.

70. *Gladstone Diaries*, iv, pp. 138–39; Trevelyan, *Garibaldi's Defence of the Roman Republic*, p. 229.

71. Beales, *England and Italy*, p. 27.

72. Rudman, *Italian Nationalism and English Letters*, p. 323, quoting the 9th Duke of Argyll, *Passages from the Past* (2 vols, London, 1907), i, p. 118.

73. *Gladstone Diaries*, iv, pp. 278 and n., 292, 309.

74. Ibid., p. 371 and passim; letters between Gladstone and Panizzi in BL, Gladstone Papers, Add. MSS 36716 and 44274.

75. On Mrs Bennett and Gladstone, Matthew, *Gladstone*, p. 246.

76. L.C. Farini, *The Roman State from 1815 to 1850* (4 vols, London, 1851–54), iv, pp. 97, 208, 235; Trevelyan, *Garibaldi's Defence of the Roman Republic*, p. 105n.

77. See n. 68. Morley, *Gladstone* i, pp. 403–4, is characteristically economical and informative about this translation.

78. BL, Gladstone Papers, Add. MS 36716, fos 242–44.

79. Ridley, *Garibaldi*, pp. 390–93; G.B. Henderson, 'Lord Palmerston and the Secret Service Fund', *English Historical Review*, 53 (1938), pp. 485–87; E. Miller, *Prince of Librarians: The Life and Times of Antonio Panizzi of the British Museum* (London, 1967), pp. 252–56. Schreuder, 'Gladstone and Italian Unification', does not mention this.

80. Schreuder, 'Gladstone and Italian Unification', p. 492.

81. Russell Papers PRO, 30/22/19; BL, Gladstone Papers, Add. MSS 44394 and 44291. Schreuder quotes only the third of these letters, and only one and a half sentences from it in two separate passages, see 'Gladstone and Italian Unification', pp. 488, 491. According to him, Gladstone here 'stressed the conservative aspect again'.

   The long and important letter to Massari contains also the following hypothesis, which sounds almost like a wish and is certainly not rejected out of hand: 'If Italy must be won [?one], & if Rome is its only possible centre, then even the liberal doctrines of "le Pape et le Congrès" will not suffice, & the people of Rome instead of dedication to art and prayer, must be the inhabitants of the Italian metropolis, in order to which consummation, a delicate though not I suppose hopeless question, must be settled with France.'

82. Morley, *Gladstone*, ii, p. 111; *Gladstone Diaries*, vi, p. 269; Schreuder, 'Gladstone and Italian Unification', p. 493.

83. E.g. Shannon, *Gladstone*, p. 277.

84. J.H. Whyte, *The Independent Irish Party, 1850–9* (Oxford, 1958); K.T. Hoppen, *Elections Politics and Society in Ireland, 1832–1885* (Oxford, 1984), p. 263; J.R. Vincent, *The Formation of the Liberal Party, 1857–1868* (London, 1966), p. 262.

85. Tyne and Wear Record Office, Cowen MS A 783. This early manifestation of the caucus spirit seems unknown to biographers of Chamberlain and historians of Birmingham and the Liberal Party.

86. *The Times*, 2 April 1864; *Beehive*, 2 April 1864; *Reynolds's Newspaper*, 10 April 1864; *Scotsman*, 21 April 1864.

87. F.E. Gillespie, *Labor and Politics in England, 1850–67* (Durham, North Carolina, 1927), pp. 219, 250–51.

88. Ibid., chs 8 and 9; R. Harrison, *Before the Socialists* (London, 1965), chs 3 and 4.

89. Beales, *England and Italy*, pp. 27, 86–91. But see the full text of Gladstone's huge letter to Acton of 6 January 1864, BL, Gladstone Papers, Add. MS 44093, fos 32–40.

90. The main authority on Gladstone's general progression to liberalism (and therefore for this whole paragraph) and particularly on his connections with trade unions is H.C.G. Matthew, most conveniently in his *Gladstone*, ch. 5. See also Vincent, *The Formation of the Liberal Party*, and W.E. Williams, *The Rise of Gladstone to the Leadership of the Liberal Party, 1859 to 1868* (Cambridge, 1934).

91. G.I.T. Machin, 'Gladstone and Nonconformity in the 1860s: The Formation of an Alliance', *Historical Journal*, 17 (1974), pp. 347–64.

92. Disraeli to Derby, 13 May 1864, Buckle, *Disraeli*, iv, p. 404.

93. *The Times*, 12 May 1864. Letters between Palmerston and Gladstone, 11–23 May 1864, P. Guedalla, *Gladstone and Palmerston* (London, 1928), pp. 279–87. The popular newspapers are full of the significance of the speech.

94. *Reynolds's Newspaper*, 27 March 1864.

95. *Gladstone Diaries*, vi, p. 274.

96. Walling, *Diaries of John Bright*, p. 276 (13 April). This meeting is not mentioned in J.R. Vincent's stimulating 'Gladstone and Ireland', *Proceedings of the British Academy*, 63 (1977), pp. 193–23; it bridges a gap in his chronology of Gladstone's concern with Ireland.

97. Matthew, *Gladstone*, pp. 44, 144–45 and 145n.; P.M.H. Bell, *Disestablishment in Ireland and Wales* (London, 1969), p. 79; Parry, *Democracy and Religion*, pp. 38–39.

98. G.M. Trevelyan, *The Life of John Bright* (London, 1913), p. 331.

99. E.R. Norman, *The Catholic Church and Ireland in the Age of Rebellion, 1859–1873* (London, 1965), pp. 84–85 and ch. 4.

100. Parry, *Democracy and Religion*, pp. 177–78.

101. Matthew, *Gladstone*, pp. 245–48.

Chapter 9: Gladstone and Grote

1. E.A. Freeman, *Historical Essays*, 2nd series (1873), p. 150, quoted by J.W. Burrow, *A Liberal Descent: Victorian Historians and the English Past* (Cambridge, 1981), p. 174n.

2. Frank M. Turner, *The Greek Heritage in Victorian Britain* (New Haven, 1981), p. 95.

3. Arnaldo Momigliano, 'George Grote and the Study of Greek History', *Studies in Historiography* (London, 1966), p. 65.

4. John Morley, *The Life of William Ewart Gladstone* (3 vols, London, 1903), i, p. 200; ii, pp. 366–67, 370, 430.

5. Hugh Lloyd-Jones, 'Gladstone on Homer', in the *Times Literary Supplement*, 3 January 1975, p. 15.

6. Turner, *Greek Heritage*, pp. 234–44.
7. Ibid., p. 161.
8. *The Gladstone Diaries*, iii, 19 March 1847.
9. W.E. Gladstone, 'On the Place of Homer in Classical Education and in Historical Inquiry', in *Oxford Essays* (London, 1857), p. 49.
10. Harriet Grote, *The Personal Life of George Grote* (London, 1873), pp. 1, 9–10, 61–62, 143.
11. Ibid., p. 71.
12. Ian Newbould, *Whiggery and Reform, 1830–41* (London, 1990), pp. 167, 191.
13. Grote, *Grote*, p. 118.
14. Alexander Bain, ed., *The Minor Works of George Grote* (London, 1873), pp. [53], [49], [51], [43].
15. *Gladstone Diaries*, ii, 22 December 1837.
16. Bain, ed., *Minor Works*, pp. [54–56].
17. Ibid., pp. [1–3].
18. Grote, *Grote*, p. 71.
19. Bain, ed., *Minor Works*, pp. [19–22].
20. Morley, *Gladstone*, ii, p. 367; i, p. 99.
21. BL, Gladstone Papers, Add. MS 44728, fol. 26. *Gladstone Diaries*, ii, 10–13 February 1838. The pamphlet was S.C. Denison, *Is the Secret Ballot a Mistake?* (1838).
22. William Thomas, *The Philosophic Radicals: Nine Studies in Theory and Practice, 1817–1841* (Oxford, 1979), p. 425.
23. T.H. Lewin, ed., *The Lewin Letters: A Selection from the Correspondence and Diaries of an English Family, 1756–1884* (2 vols, London, 1909), i, p. 148; Lady Eastlake, *Mrs Grote: A Sketch* (London, 1880), p. 6.
24. Lewin, ed., *Lewin Letters*, ii, p. 345.
25. Sydney Smith, 'Ballot', *The Works of the Rev. Sydney Smith* (3 vols, London, 1839), iii, p. 18.
26. Grote, *Grote*, p. 109.
27. Ibid., pp. 49, 44.
28. Eastlake, *Mrs Grote*, p. 41.
29. Grote, *Grote*, p. 70.
30. Lewin, ed., *Lewin Letters*, i, p. 150.
31. Harriet Grote to Mme Frances Eliza von Koch, 23 August 1833, in Lewin, ed., *Lewin Letters*, i, p. 303.
32. Grote, *Grote*, pp. 42, 60, 24.
33. James Mill, 'The Ballot', in Terence Ball, ed., *James Mill: Political Writings* (Cambridge, 1992), pp. 225–67.
34. Bain, ed., *Minor Works*, pp. 119, 159.
35. Grote, *Grote*, p. 117.
36. Grote to Frances E. Lewin, 8 April 1823, in Lewin, ed., *Lewin Letters*, i, p. 202.
37. Bain, ed., *Minor Works*, pp. [2], [100], [116].
38. Grote to Frances E. Lewin, 8 April. 1823, in Lewin, ed., *Lewin Letters*, i, pp. 201–2.
39. 'Essentials of Parliamentary Reform', in Bain, ed., *Minor Works*, pp. 27–33.
40. BL, Gladstone Papers, Add. MS 44721, fol. 24.
41. BL, Gladstone Papers, Add. MS 44726, fol. 244.
42. BL, Gladstone Papers, Add. MSS 44722, fol. 301; 44725, fol. 291; 44724, fol. 70; 44725, fol. 283.

43. BL, Gladstone Papers, Add. MS 44725, fol. 172.
44. BL, Gladstone Papers, Add. MS 44725, fol. 162.
45. BL, Gladstone Papers, Add. MS 44721, fol. 17.
46. BL, Gladstone Papers, Add, MS 44721, fol. 31.
47. George Grote, 'Institutions of Ancient Greece', *Westminster Review*, 5 (1826), p. 331.
48. Ibid., p. 281.
49. George Grote, *A History of Greece* (12 vols, London 1846–56), ii, p. 125.
50. Ibid., iii, p. 23.
51. Bain, ed., *Minor Works*, pp. [46], [54].
52. BL, Gladstone Papers, Add. MS 44793, fol. 314.
53. Freda Harcourt, 'Gladstone, Monarchism and the "New" Imperialism, 1868–74', *Journal of Imperial and Commonwealth History*, 14 (1985).
54. BL, Gladstone Papers, Add. MS 44727, fos 52–52v.
55. BL, Gladstone Papers, Add. MS 44725, fol. 186v.
56. BL, Gladstone Papers, Add. MS 44729, fol. 17.
57. Grote, *History*, i, p. v.
58. William Mitford, *The History of Greece* (2nd edn), i, p. 181, quoted by M.L. Clarke, *Greek Studies in England, 1700–1830* (Cambridge, 1945), p. 108.
59. Grote, 'Institutions', p. 282.
60. George Grote Papers, BL, Add. MS 29520, fol. 170.
61. Grote, *History*, ii, pp. 89–90.
62. W.E. Gladstone, *Studies on Homer and the Homeric Age* (3 vols Oxford, 1858), iii, pp. 28, 67, 47.
63. Ibid., iii, p. 143.
64. W.E. Gladstone, *Landmarks of Homeric Study* (London, 1890), pp. 102–3.
65. Gladstone, *Studies*, iii, p. 116.
66. Ibid., iii, pp. 119–20, 127–28, 139, 102–11, 207.
67. Ibid., iii, p. 138.
68. Bain, ed., *Minor Works*, p. [78].
69. Grote, *Grote*, p. 22.
70. Ibid., pp. 43, 132.
71. 'Parliamentary Reform', in Bain, ed., *Minor Works*, p. 5.
72. Grote, *Grote*, p. 31.
73. 'Parliamentary Reform', in Bain, ed., *Minor Works*, p. 23.
74. Grote, 'Institutions', pp. 293, 280.
75. BL, Gladstone Papers, Add. MS 44722, fos 194–200v; *Gladstone Diaries*, ii, 11 April 1833. The acquaintance was S.C. Denison, who was to write the pamphlet on the ballot that Gladstone read in 1838.
76. BL, Gladstone Papers, Add. MS 44721, fol. 13.
77. BL, Gladstone Papers, Add. MS 44722, fol. 50v.
78. BL, Gladstone Papers, Add. MS 44725, fol. 33v.
79. M.L. Clarke, *George Grote: A Biography* (London, 1962), pp. 115, 126.
80. Grote, *History*, ii, p. 91.
81. Gladstone, *Studies*, iii, p. 98.
82. W.E. Gladstone, *Juventus Mundi: The Gods and Men of the Heroic Age* (London, 1869), pp. 70–71.
83. Ibid., p. 390.

84. H.C.G. Matthew, *Gladstone, 1809–1874* (Oxford, 1986), pp. 149–50.
85. Grote, *Grote*, pp. 6, 12, 18, 32, 48, 22.
86. Clarke, *Grote*, p. 30.
87. Grote to G.C. Lewis, 10 June 1861, in Grote, *Grote*, p. 251.
88. Grote, *Grote*, p. 71; Bain, ed., *Minor Works*, p. [41].
89. Peter J. Jagger, *Gladstone: The Making of a Christian Politician* (Allison Park, Pennsylvania, 1991).
90. BL, Gladstone Papers, Add. MS 44723, fol. 107v.
91. Momigliano, 'Grote', p. 62.
92. Grote, *History*, ii, pp. 276, 120.
93. George Grote, 'On the Origin and Nature of Ethical Sentiment', *Fragments on Ethical Subjects* (London, 1876).
94. Grote, *History*, ii, pp. 120–24.
95. Gladstone, 'Place of Homer', p. 5.
96. Gladstone, *Studies*, ii, p. 419.
97. Ibid., ii, pp. 484, 479.
98. W.E. Gladstone, 'Lachmann's *Essays on Homer*', *Quarterly Review*, 81 (1847).
99. Grote, *History*, ii, ch. 21.
100. Gladstone, *Studies*, iii, pp. 378–79.
101. Grote, *History*, i, p. xii.
102. Gladstone, *Studies*, i, pp. 94–96.
103. E.g. W.E. Gladstone, *Homeric Synchronism: An Enquiry into the Time and Place of Homer* (London, 1876), especially pp. 19–20.
104. Gladstone, 'Place of Homer', p. 23.
105. Grote, *Grote*, p. 248; Harriet Grote to Lieutenant W.C.J. Lewin, 27 January 1845, in Lewin, ed., *Lewin Letters*, ii, p. 34; BL, Gladstone Papers, Add. MS 44793, fol. 317.
106. Morley, *Gladstone*, ii, p. 430.
107. Grote to Gladstone, 9 November 1869, in Grote, *Grote*, p. 307.
108. Harriet Grote to A. Hayward, 14 March 1874, in Eastlake, *Mrs Grote*, p. 149.
109. Harriet Grote to Gladstone, 29 November 1873, 1 March 1874, 28 April 1874; Gladstone to Harriet Grote, 29 April 1874, copy, BL, Gladstone Papers, Add. MSS 44441, fol. 143; 44443, fos 54, 178, 182–82v.
110. Gladstone, *Studies*, iii, p. 316; ii, p. 17.
111. Bain, ed., *Minor Works*, p. [78].
112. Turner, *Greek Heritage*; E.F. Biagini, 'Liberalism and Direct Democracy: John Stuart Mill and the Model of Ancient Athens', in E.F. Biagini, ed., *Citizenship and Community: Liberals, Radicals and Collective Identities in the British Isles 1865–1931* (Cambridge, 1996).

Chapter 10: Gladstone and Ruskin

1. See the *Daily Telegraph*, 6 June 1991, p. 20, and 7 June 1991, p. 18.
2. Tim Hilton, *John Ruskin: The Early Years, 1819–1859* (New Haven and London, 1985), pp. 19–22.
3. *The Works of John Ruskin*, Library Edition, 39 vols, edited by E.T. Cook and Alexander Wedderburn (London and New York, 1903–12), xxxv, p. 13; xxvii, p. 116.
4. David Newsome, *Two Classes of Men: Platonism and English Romantic Thought*

(London, 1974), p. 52. Newsome contrasts Gladstone's Oxford Aristotelianism, ibid., pp. 63–64, 73–74.

5. *The Works of Ruskin*, xxxiv, p. 549.
6. Richard Shannon, *Gladstone*, i, *1809–1865* (London, 1982), p. 21.
7. *The Works of Ruskin*, xxxv, p. 311.
8. Ibid., xxxv, p. 205.
9. V. Alan McClelland, 'Gladstone and Manning: A Question of Authority', in *Gladstone, Politics and Religion: A Collection of Founder's Day Lectures Delivered at St Deiniol's Library, Hawarden, 1967–83*, edited by Peter J. Jagger (London, 1985), p. 149.
10. McLelland, 'Gladstone and Manning'; also Michael Wheeler, 'Tennyson, Newman and the Question of Authority', in *The Interpretation of Belief: Coleridge, Schleiermacher and Romanticism*, edited by David Jasper (London, 1986), pp. 185–201.
11. Cited in McClelland, 'Gladstone and Manning', p. 151.
12. *Gladstone Diaries*, iv, p. 23.
13. *The Works of Ruskin*, viii, p. 3.
14. E.J. Feuchtwanger, *Gladstone*, British Political Biography (London, 1975), p. 65.
15. *The Works of Ruskin*, xxxv, p. 428; xxxvi, p. l; xxviii; see also John Morley, *The Life of William Ewart Gladstone*, 3 vols (London, 1904), i, p. 329.
16. Shannon, *Gladstone*, p. 211. On Gladstone's religious development, see Perry Butler, *Gladstone: Church, State, and Tractarianism. A Study of his Religious Ideas and Attitudes, 1809–1859* (Oxford, 1982).
17. *The Works of Ruskin*, xii, pp. 573–89.
18. Ibid., xxix, p. 89.
19. Ibid., xxxv, p. 496. For discussion of this crisis see Michael Wheeler, *Ruskin's God* (forthcoming), chapter 6.
20. Elisabeth Jay, *The Religion of the Heart: Anglican Evangelicalism and the Nineteenth-Century Novel* (Oxford, 1979), pp. 51–105.
21. *The Works of Ruskin*, xxxvi, p. 424.
22. Shannon, *Gladstone*, pp. 352–67.
23. *The Works of Ruskin*, xxxviii, p. 137.
24. John Ruskin, *Letters from the Continent*, 1858, edited by John Hayman (Toronto, 1982), p. 139.
25. Morley, *Gladstone*, i, p. 87.
26. Owen Chadwick, 'Young Gladstone and Italy', in Jagger, *Gladstone, Politics and Religion*, pp. 69–70.
27. *Gladstone Diaries*, vi, p. 655, 31 December 1868.
28. *Mary Gladstone (Mrs Drew): Her Diaries and Letters*, edited by Lucy Masterman (2nd edn, London, 1930), p. 128.
29. Feuchtwanger, *Gladstone*, p. 189.
30. *Gladstone Diaries*, ix, p. 279, 30 December 1877.
31. *The Works of Ruskin*, xxxvi, p. lxxix.
32. Ibid., xxii, pp. 529–38.
33. Ibid., xxiv, p. xxxviii; xxix, p. 365.
34. Ibid., xxii, p. 533.
35. [Hallam Tennyson], *Alfred Lord Tennyson: A Memoir* (London, 1899), p. 557.
36. *The Works of Ruskin*, xxxvi, p. lxxix.
37. *The Diaries of John Ruskin*, edited by Joan Evans and John Howard Whitehouse, 3 vols (Oxford, 1956–59), iii, p. 971.

38. *Letters of Lord Acton to Mary, Daughter of the Right Hon. W.E. Gladstone*, ed. Herbert Paul (London, 1904), pp. 172–73.
39. *The Works of Ruskin*, xxviii, p. 403.
40. Ibid., xxviii, p. 402.
41. John Ruskin and Joan Severn correspondence, Ruskin Foundation (Ruskin Library, Lancaster University). I am grateful to J. S. Dearden, formerly Curator of the Ruskin Galleries, Bembridge, for drawing my attention to this letter, and to subsequent letters cited below.
42. *Diaries of Ruskin*, iii, p. 974.
43. *Gladstone Diaries*, ix, p. 282, 12 January 1878.
44. Edith Lyttelton, *Alfred Lyttelton: An Account of his Life* (London, 1917), p. 70.
45. Mary Drew, *Acton, Gladstone and Others* (London, 1924), p. 57.
46. H.S. Holland, 'Gladstone and Ruskin', *The Commonwealth*, July 1898, p. 211.
47. Mary Gladstone, *Diaries*, p. 128.
48. Extracts from Edward Bickersteth Ottley's journal are reprinted in *John Ruskin: Letters to M.G. and H.G*, preface by G. Wyndham (privately printed, 1903), pp. 3–27. Holland's narrative is also reprinted here.
49. Holland, 'Gladstone and Ruskin', p. 211.
50. Wyndham, *John Ruskin: Letters to M.G.*, p. 13.
51. *Diaries of Ruskin*, iii, p. 974.
52. In Hawarden Castle Visitors' Book the following entries are bracketed together: 'John Ruskin Jan. 12 1878', 'Henry. Scott. Holland. Jan. 15 1878'; 'Acton'; 'Alfred Lyttelton Jan. 17 1878'. (Cited by kind permission of Sir William Gladstone.)
53. Mary Gladstone, *Diaries*, p. 129.
54. *The Works of Ruskin*, xxxvi, p. 425.
55. *The Correspondence of John Ruskin and Charles Eliot Norton*, edited by John Lewis Bradley and Ian Ousby (Cambridge, 1987), p. 348.
56. *The Works of Ruskin*, xxviii, pp. 244–45.
57. Ibid., xiv, p. 285n.
58. Morley, *Gladstone*, ii, p. 168.
59. Ibid., ii, p. 313.
60. *Gladstone Diaries*, viii, p. 315, 11 April 1873; p. 489, 3 May 1874.
61. *The Works of Ruskin*, xxii, p. 536.
62. Mary Gladstone, *Diaries*, p. 129.
63. *Gladstone Diaries*, ix, pp. 282–83, 13 January, 1878.
64. The MS reads 'as he was so nervous', Mary Gladstone's Diary, BL, Add. MS 46258, fol, 24r. Lucy Masterman transcribes the MS passage as 'and he was so nervous', Mary Gladstone, *Diaries*, p. 129. See also *The Diary of Lady Frederick Cavendish*, ed. John Bailey, 2 vols (London, 1927), ii, p. 208.
65. Wyndham, *John Ruskin, Letters to M.G.*, pp. 127–28.
66. Anon, *Edward Bickersteth Ottley, Canon of Rochester: An Impression* (n.d.), p. 22. Clwyd County Record Office holds Helen Gladstone's copy of this privately printed memorial volume.
67. *Gladstone Diaries*, ix, pp. 220–21, 20 May 1877.
68. Mary Gladstone, *Diaries*, p. 129.
69. Drew, *Acton*, pp. 1–2; cf. Butler, *Gladstone*, pp. 234–35.
70. *The Works of Ruskin*, xxix, p. 92.
71. *Diaries of Ruskin*, iii, pp. 974–75.

72. *The Works of Ruskin*, xxii, p. 530.
73. Mary Gladstone, *Diaries*, p. 129.
74. Mary Drew, *Catherine Gladstone* (London, 1919), pp. 161–63.
75. Mary Gladstone, *Diaries*, p. 129.
76. *Gladstone Diaries*, ix, pp. 282–83, 13 January 1878.
77. *Diaries of Ruskin*, iii, p. 975.
78. Mary Gladstone, *Diaries*, p. 129.
79. Lyttelton, *Alfred Lyttelton*, pp. 71–72.
80. Mary Gladstone, *Diaries*, p. 130.
81. Wyndham, *John Ruskin: Letters to M.G.*, pp. 14–15.
82. Mary Gladstone, *Diaries*, p. 130.
83. Drew, *Acton*, pp. 105, 108.
84. Lyttelton, *Alfred Lyttelton*, p. 71.
85. Wyndham, *John Ruskin: Letters to M.G.*, p. 18.
86. *Gladstone Diaries*, xi, p. 283, 14 January 1878.
87. Mary Gladstone, *Diaries*, p. 130.
88. *Diaries of Ruskin*, iii, p. 975.
89. Mary Gladstone, *Diaries*, p. 130.
90. Holland, 'Gladstone and Ruskin', p. 212.
91. *The Works of Ruskin*, xxviii, p. 403.
92. Ibid., xxix, p. 364.
93. Ibid., xxix, p. 368.
94. *Gladstone Diaries*, ix, p. 283, 15 January 1878.
95. *The Works of Ruskin*, xviii, pp. 459–93.
96. J.B. Mozley, *Sermons Preached before the University of Oxford and on Various Occasions* (London, 1876), pp. 110–37.
97. Wyndham, *John Ruskin: Letters to M.G.*, pp. 25–27.
98. Feuchtwanger, *Gladstone*, p. 257.
99. *The Works of Ruskin*, xxxvi, p. lxxxv.
100. W.E. Gladstone, *Studies Subsidiary to the Works of Bishop Butler* (Oxford, 1896), p. 206; see Michael Wheeler, *Death and the Future Life in Victorian Literature and Theology* (Cambridge, 1990), pp. 77, 78, 178, 185–88.
101. *The Works of Ruskin*, i, p. xi.
102. Ibid., xxxv, p. xl.
103. Ibid., xxxiv, pp. 548–49.

Chapter 11: Gladstone and the Railways

1. The topic I have chosen is one that scholars have looked at before. See especially E.E. Barry, *Nationalisation in British Politics: The Historical Background* (1965), and H. Parris, *Government and the Railways in Nineteenth-Century Britain* (1965).
2. *Parliamentary Papers*, 38 (1867), p. viii.
3. *Parliamentary Debates*, 76, p. 501, 8 July 1844.
4. BL, Gladstone Papers, Add. MS 44734, fos 34–35, memo by Gladstone, 18 May 1844.
5. 7 and 8 Victoria, c. 85.
6. *Parliamentary Debates*, 76, p. 484, 8 July 1844.
7. Ibid., p. 487.

8. *Parliamentary Papers*, 38 (1867), question 7348.
9. BL, Gladstone Papers, Add. MS 44734, fos 34–35.
10. Galt's view is summarised in *Parliamentary Papers*, 38 (1867), questions 7351, 7365.
11. E. Chadwick, 'Results of Different Principles of Legislation and Administration in Europe: of Competition for the Field, as Compared with Competition within the Field, of Service', in *Journal of the Statistical Society* (1859), pp. 381–420.
12. E. Chadwick, *Address on Railway Reform*, presented to the National Association for the Promotion of Social Science (1865), p. 12.
13. *Gladstone Diaries*, vi, 8 September 1864, 13 January 1865; BL, Gladstone Papers, Add. MS 44753, fol. 188.
14. BL, Gladstone Papers, Add. MS 44753, fol. 197.
15. BL, Gladstone Papers, Add. MS 44753, fol. 189.
16. Chadwick, *Address on Railway Reform*, p. 48.
17. BL, Gladstone Papers, Add. MS 44753, fol. 197.
18. BL, Gladstone Papers, Add. MS 44753, fol. 188.
19. P. Guedalla (ed.), *Gladstone and Palmerston* (London, 1928), pp. 291–92.
20. Ibid., p. 308.
21. Ibid., p. 309.
22. *The Times*, 10 December 1864, 7a.
23. *The Economist*, 10 December 1864.
24. Guedalla, *Gladstone and Palmerston*, p. 318.
25. Ibid., pp. 318–19.
26. Ibid., pp. 319–20.
27. BL, Gladstone Papers, Add. MS 44753, fos 146–53, proposition 29.
28. Recall 7 and 8 Victoria, c. 85, section vi, 'And whereas it is expedient to secure to the poorer class of Travellers the Means of travelling by Railway at moderate Fares, and in Carriages in which they may be protected from the Weather' &c.
29. BL, Gladstone Papers, Add. MS 44753, fos 146–53, propositions 20, 32.
30. Guedalla, *Gladstone and Palmerston*, pp. 319–20.
31. *Parliamentary Debates*, 215, p. 1161, 29 April 1873.
32. *Parliamentary Papers*, 38 (1867), p. vi.
33. Ibid., question 6735, evidence of Mr Meldon, 27 June 1865.
34. *Parliamentary Debates*, 178, p. 912, evidence of Mr Scully, 7 April 1865.
35. Ibid., p. 917.
36. Ibid., pp. 896–98.
37. Ibid., 174, p. 1175, 20 July 1866.
38. Ibid., 178, p. 919.
39. Ibid., 178, p. 922.
40. *Parliamentary Papers*, 63 (1866), pp. 279 ff.
41. *Parliamentary Debates*, 184, p. 1186.
42. J.C. Conroy, *A History of Railways in Ireland* (1928), p. 62.
43. A good summary of these points comes in William Galt, 'On the Purchase of Railways by the State', in the *Practical Magazine* (1873), p. 54.
44. *Parliamentary Papers*, 38 (1867), p. lxxxvii, para 174.
45. Ibid., p. xxxvii, para 73.
46. Ibid., p. xxxviii, para 76.
47. For Monsell's report, dealing with Ireland, ibid., pp. xciii–cv.

48. *Parliamentary Debates*, 189, p. 614, Lord Naas, 1 August 1867.
49. *Parliamentary Papers*, 32 (1867–68), pp. 469ff.
50. Ibid., 17 (1868–69), pp. 459ff.
51. *Parliamentary Debates*, 207, p. 1769, 14 July 1871.
52. Ibid., p. 1772.
53. Ibid., pp. 1784–85.
54. Ibid., 212, pp. 1299–306, 17 July 1872.
55. Ibid., pp. 1314–15.
56. BL, Gladstone Papers, Add. MS 44144, fos 35–36, 10 February 1873.
57. BL, Gladstone Papers, Add. MS 44307, fos 153–56, 13 February 1873.
58. BL, Gladstone Papers, Add. MS 44641, fol. 25.
59. BL, Gladstone Papers, Add. MS 44144, fos 35–36, 10 February 1873.
60. BL, Gladstone Papers, Add. MS 44307, fos 153–56, 13 February 1873.
61. BL, Gladstone Papers, Add. MS 44541, 10 February 1873.
62. *Parliamentary Debates*, 215, p. 1142, 29 April 1873.
63. Ibid., pp. 1157–67.
64. Ibid., 267, pp. 652–54, 10 March 1882.
65. Conroy, *A History of Railways in Ireland*, p. 61.
66. BL, Gladstone Papers, Add. MS 44307, fos 153–56, 13 February 1873.
67. *Parliamentary Debates*, 207, p. 1770, 14 July 1871.
68. BL, Gladstone Papers, Add. MS 44143, fos 137–38, 15 January 1872.
69. *Parliamentary Debates*, 212, p. 1313, 17 July 1872.
70. BL, Gladstone Papers, Add. MS 44307, fos 153–56, 13 February 1873.
71. *Parliamentary Debates*, 229, p. 700, 30 June 1874.
72. Ibid., 220, p. 96, 27 July 1875.
73. Ibid., 215, p. 1161–62, 29 April 1873.
74. Ibid., 207, p. 1783, 14 July 1871.
75. Ibid., 215, p. 1161–62, 29 April 1873.
76. Ibid., 267, p. 653, 10 March 1882.
77. Ibid., 207, p. 1785, 14 July 1871.
78. Ibid., 215, p. 1161, 29 April 1873.
79. Ibid., 212, p. 1315, 17 July 1872.
80. Ibid., 192, p. 1331, 9 June 1868.
81. Figures in *Parliamentary Debates*, 192, pp. 1305–6, Hon. G.W. Hunt, 9 June 1868; and ibid., 197, p. 1218, Hartington, 5 July 1869. The pragmatic Conservative Chancellor of the Exchequer, Hunt, took the view that because the companies were obliged 'to regard the question in a purely commercial light', and to pay dividends, they were not able to view the service 'in the light of what might be of advantage to the public', ibid., 193, p. 1567.
82. 36 and 37 Victoria, c. 48.
83. BL, Gladstone Papers, Add. MS 44144, fos 41–42, memo by Hartington, n.d., *Parliamentary Debates*, 215, p. 1165, Gladstone, 29 April 1873.

Chapter 12: Gladstone, Rhetoric and Politics

1. R. Whately, *Rhetoric* (London, 1841), p. 3.
2. *Full and Accurate Report of Sir Robert Peel's Speeches* (London, 1837); Peel's Rectorial in Glasgow, 11 January 1837.

3. See E.K. Bramstead, *Goebbels and National Socialist Propaganda, 1925–45* (London, 1965).

4. For a discussion of this, see H.C.G. Matthew, R.I. McKibbin and J.A. Kay, 'The Franchise Factor in the Rise of the Labour Party', *English Historical Review* (1976).

5. Blanchard Jerrold, 'On the Manufacture of Public Opinion', *Nineteenth Century*, 13 (June 1883), p. 1080; see also D. Read, *England, 1868–1914* (London, 1979), pp. 158–59; and J. Newton, *W.S. Caine, MP* (London, 1907), p. 104.

6. See M. Ostrogorski, *Democracy and the Organisation of Political Parties* (London, 1902), i, pp. 419–19.

7. I am obliged to Dr Jeremy Morris for supplying me with a copy of the Croydon local parliament's printed rules.

8. *Synopsis of the Newspapers in the United Kingdom* (London, 1867).

9. G. Scott, *Reporter Anonymous: The Story of the Press Association* (London, 1968), p. 41. A further problem for parliamentary reporting was 'the midnight portcullis'. Speeches made after midnight were too late for the morning papers and were not noted by the newspaper stenographers; thus the *Hansard* report was consequently sometimes thin.

10. E.C.F. Collier, *A Victorian Diarist* (London, 1944), p. 30.

11. 'Extra-Parliamentary Utterances', *Saturday Review*, 5 December 1863, identified in J.F.A. Mason, 'The 3rd Marquess of Salisbury and the *Saturday Review*', *Bulletin of the Institute of Historical Research*, 3 (1961), p. 36.

12. *The Speeches of Richard Cobden*, ed. J. Bright and J.E.T. Rogers (London, 1870), i, p. 411.

13. 'Secondary Stars', *Saturday Review*, 10 December 1864, identified in Mason, 'The 3rd Marquess of Salisbury'.

14. *The Biograph and Review* (London, 1879), i, p. 18.

15. J.A. Picton, *Sir James A. Picton* (London, 1891), pp. 313–14.

16. For details, see G. Scott, *Reporter Anonymous*, passim; and J. Kieve, *The Electric Telegraph* (Newton Abbot, 1973), ch. 11; less useful is J.M. Scott, *Extel 100: The Centenary History of the Exchange Telegraph Company* (London, 1972).

17. H.C.G. Matthew (ed.), *The Gladstone Diaries* (Oxford 1986), ix, lxi; T.H.S. Escott, *Platform, Press, Politics and Play* (Bristol, n.d.[1895?]), pp. 337, 353; J.L. Garvin, *The Life of Joseph Chamberlain* (London, 1932), i, p. 245.

18. Cobden quoted in Holyoake, *Public Speaking and Debate*, ch. 2; R. Churchill to Dufferin, 27 October 1885, India Office, MS Eur F 130/3/77; I am obliged to Dr R. Quinault for this quotation.

19. A. Kinnear, 'The Trade in Great Men's Speeches', *Contemporary Review* (1899), pp. 439ff. The precise amount according to the Act (31 & 32 Victoria, c. 110), was one shilling per hundred words transmitted between 6 p.m. and 9 a.m. for the first report with 2d. per hundred words for subsequent reports, or one shilling per seventy-five words between 9 a.m. and 6 p.m. with 2d. per seventy-five words for further reports, these rates applying to all newspaper material.

20. Scott, *Reporter Anonymous*, p. 78.

21. Calculated from C. Mitchell, *The Newspaper Press Directory* (published annually). For the press generally, see A.J. Lee, *The Origins of the Popular Press, 1855–1914* (London, 1976); S. Koss, *The Rise and Fall of the Political Press in Britain* (London, 1981), vol. i; and A.P. Wadsworth, 'Newspaper Circulations, 1800–1954', *Manch-*

ester Statistical Society Transactions (1954–55); Lucy Brown, *Victorian News and Newspapers* (Oxford 1985).

22. W.F. Monypenny and G.F. Buckle, *Life of Disraeli* (London, 1910–20), v, p. 194.

23. Quoted in R.T. McKenzie and A. Silver, *Angels in Marble* (London, 1968).

24. G. Wallas, *Human Nature in Politics* (1908), as quoted in S. Reynolds and T. Wooley, *Seems So!* (London, 1911), p. 130. To this should be added the specific of drink: 'Tory Democracy changed the pump, not the beer', P.J. Waller, *Democracy and Sectarianism* (Liverpool, 1981), p. 46.

25. H.H. Gerth and C. Wright Mills, *From Max Weber* (London, 1948), p. 106; see also Matthew, *Gladstone Diaries*, ix, pp. lxii–lxiii.

26. *Pall Mall Magazine* (December 1898), p. 305; see also W.T. Stead's short history of the English interview in the *Idler* (December 1895), p. 495. Another means of communication, from the mid 1880s, was the lobby correspondent; his insidious influence is, by the very nature of his position, impossible to assess.

27. Kennedy Jones, *Fleet Street and Downing Street* (London, 1920), p. 139.

28. Royal Commission on the Press, *Parliamentary Papers* (1947–48), xv, p. 146. Davies was describing the editorial excision of the Christian sections of Cripps's speeches: Cripps 'for the last six years emphasised the need of a Christian bias in the post-war world . . . but no one would know that from reading the accounts of his speeches in the newspapers'. The rest of the evidence confirms the general awareness of the decline in the significance and full reporting of the platform. More recently, party bureaucracies have interposed themselves between the politician and the reporter, see J. Prior, *A Balance of Power* (London, 1986), p. 152: 'I even had some trouble in getting Central Office to publish my speeches. On one occasion I gave my speech direct to the Press Association, which attracted a lot of publicity.'

29. J.A. Hobson, *The Crisis of Liberalism* (London, 1909) p. 87.

Chapter 13: Gladstone and his Library

1. This essay is based entirely upon the contents of an uncatalogued collection of Gladstone manuscripts, relating to the foundation of St Deiniol's Library, discovered by the author in 1996. This material shows the evolution of Gladstone's thinking and subsequent action in seeking to implement his vision. This new material is enhanced by material drawn from the extensive catalogued Gladstone Manuscript Collection, including material and letters written by Gladstone, his family, trustees and contemporaries, plus contemporary and later printed works.

Contributors

Derek Beales, D.Litt., FBA, retired in 1997 from the Chair of Modern History at Cambridge. He has published *England and Italy, 1859–60* (1961), *From Castlereagh to Gladstone, 1815–85* (1969), *The Risorgimento and the Unification of Italy* (1971) and *History and Biography* (1981).

David W. Bebbington is a Reader in History at the University of Stirling. His publications include *Evangelism in Modern Britain: A History from the 1740s to the 1980s* (1989) and a biography of Gladstone, *William Ewart Gladstone: Faith and Politics in Victorian Britain* (1993). He will be an editor of the proceedings of the Gladstone Centenary International Conference at Chester in 1998.

Lord Blake (Robert Blake) Born in 1916, he was Provost of the Queen's College Oxford, 1968–87. He is a Fellow of the British Academy and has been Chariman of the Royal Historical Manuscripts Commission and a Trustee of the British Museum. He was a Student of Christ Church Oxford, 1947–68. He was made a Life Peer in 1971. His publications include *The Unknown Prime Minister: A Life of Bonar Law* (1955), *Disraeli* (1966), *The Office of Prime Minister* (1974), *The Conservative Party from Peel to Churchill* (1970), up-dated (1997) as *The Conservative Party from Peel to Major*, *A History of Rhodesia* (1977), edited with Roger Louis *Churchill* (1993).

D. George Boyce took his B.A. and Ph.D. degrees at the Queen's University, Belfast. He was appointed Graduate Assistant in the Bodleian Library Oxford in 1968 and Lecturer in the Department of Politics, University of Wales, Swansea in 1971. He is currently Professor there. He is the author and editor of various books on Irish political history and Anglo-Irish relations, including *Nationalism in Ireland* (3rd edn, 1996), *The Irish Question and British Politics, 1868–1996* (revised edn, 1996) and (edited with Alan O'Day), *Parnell in Perspective* (1991).

Asa Briggs was Professor of History and Dean of Social Sciences from 1961 to 1967, and Vice-Chancellor from 1967 to 1976, Sussex University. From 1976 to 1991 he was Provost of Worcester College, Oxford. From 1978 to 1994 he was Chancellor of the Open University. He is the author of a Victorian Trilogy (*Victorian People; Victorian Cities; Victorian Things*), reprinted and revised in a Folio Society edition in 1996.

Peter J. Jagger, Ph.D., M.Phil., M.A. He is a fellow of the Royal Historical Society. Until his retirement he was Warden and Chief Librarian of St Deiniol's Library, 1977–97. He has written and edited widely in the fields of theology, liturgiology and history. Among his historical works are *The History of the Parish and People Movement* (1978), *Clouded Witness:*

Initiation in the Church of England in the Mid-Victorian Period, 1850–1875 (1982), *Gladstone, Politics and Religion* (ed.) (1985), and *Gladstone, The Making of a Christian Politician* (1991).

H. Colin G. Matthew, D.Phil., FBA, is Professor of Modern History, University of Oxford, and the Editor of the *New Dictionary of National Biography*. He was the Editor of the *Gladstone Diaries* (1972–94). His publications include *The Liberal Imperialists* (1973), *Gladstone, 1809– 1874* (1986), *Gladstone, 1875–1898* (1985); he edited *Religion and Revival since 1700* (1993).

Kenneth O. Morgan, D.Litt. (Oxon), Hon. D.Litt (Wales), was Fellow and Praelector, the Queen's College, Oxford, 1966–89, and Vice-Chancellor of the University of Wales, Aberystwyth, 1989–95. He is a Fellow of the British Academy. He has written extensively on modern British history from Gladstone to Tony Blair. The most recent of his twenty-three books are *The People's Peace: British History, 1945–90* (1992), *Modern Wales: Politics, People and Places* (1995) and *Callaghan: A Life* (1997).

Peter J. Parish was Bonar Professor of Modern History, University of Dundee, 1976–83, and Director of the Institute of United States Studies, University of London, 1983–92. He is now Mellon Senior Research Fellow in American History at the University of Cambridge. His books include *The American Civil War* (1975) and *Slavery: History and Historians* (1989). He is the editor of the *Reader's Guide to American History* (1997).

Simon Peaple is Mayor of Tamworth, 1997–98; Head of History and Politics at Stafford College, 1998; history graduate, University of Bristol, and currently a Ph.D. student, University of Birmingham.

John Prest is an Emeritus Fellow of Balliol College, Oxford. His books include *Lord John Russell* (1972), *Politics in the Age of Cobden* (1977) and *Liberty and Locality: Parliament, Permissive Legislation and Ratepayers' Democracies in the Nineteenth Century* (1990).

John Vincent was Fellow of Peterhouse, 1962–70, and Lecturer, University of Cambridge, 1966–70; then Professor of Modern History, and subsequently of History, at the University of Bristol, from 1970. His publications include *The Formation of the Liberal Party, 1857–1868* (1966), *The Governing Passion* (with A. B. Cooke) (1974), *Disraeli, Derby and the Conservative Party* (1978), *Gladstone and Ireland* (1977), *The Crawford Papers* (1984), *Disraeli* (1990), *The Derby Diaries, 1896–1878* (1995) and *An Intelligent Person's Guide to History* (1995).

Michael Wheeler is Professor of English Literature and Director of the Ruskin Programme at Lancaster University. A literary historian of the Victorian period, with special interests in Ruskin, literature and theology, and fiction, he is a Trustee of St Deiniol's Library, and directs the Ruskin Collection Project, which has established the new Ruskin Library at Lancaster University. He is currently writing *Ruskin's God* (Cambridge University Press, 1999) and is General Editor of the Leverhulme Electronic Edition of Ruskin's *Modern Painters*.

Glynne Wickham, a great-grandson of Mr Gladstone, is Emeritus Professor of Drama and an Honorary Fellow of Bristol University. Educated at Winchester College and New College, Oxford, he has since held visiting Professorships at Yale University, the University of Queensland, Australia, and the University of the South, Sewanee, Tennessee, for which Gladstone helped to raise the funds needed to rebuild it following its near-total destruction during the American Civil War. He is a member of the Polish Academy of Arts and Sciences, President of the British Society for Theatre Research and has published many books including *Early English Stages* (4 vols), *The Medieval Theatre*, *Shakespeare's Dramatic Heritage* and *A History of the Theatre*.

Index

Illustrations are shown in bold